Grammar for Grown-Ups

Grammar for Grown-Ups

A straightforward guide to good English

Katherine Fry & Rowena Kirton

◙ SQUARE PEG

LONDON

Published by Square Peg 2012

10 9 8 9 6 5 4 3 2

Copyright © Katherine Fry & Rowena Kirton 2012

The authors have asserted their rights under the Copyright, Designs
and Patents Act 1988 to be identified as the authors of this work

First published in Great Britain in 2012 by Square Peg
Random House · 20 Vauxhall Bridge Road · London SW1V 2SA

www.vintage-books.co.uk

Addresses for companies within The Random House Group Limited can be found at:
www.randomhouse.co.uk/offices.htm

The Random House Group Limited Reg. No. 954009

A CIP catalogue record for this book is available from the British Library

ISBN 9780224087018

The Random House Group Limited supports the Forest Stewardship Council® (FSC),
the leading international forest-certification organisation. Our books carrying the FSC
label are printed on FSC®-certified paper. FSC is the only forest-certification scheme
endorsed by the leading environmental organisations, including Greenpeace. Our paper
procurement policy can be found at www.randomhouse.co.uk/environment

Designed and typeset by Christopher Wakeling
Printed and bound in Germany by GGP Media GmbH · Poeßneck

For

Minne and Lionel
Michael, Tessa, Zachary and Daisy

Enid and John
Andrew, James and William

Contents

Introduction

Grammar for Grown-Ups is an accessible, light-hearted and straightforward guide to good English in the twenty-first century, covering grammar, punctuation, spelling, common errors and not so common errors. It is for people who have forgotten the grammar they were taught at school, for those who weren't taught it in the first place and for English-language students, because, believe it or not, there is more to life and literature than a rushed-off email and textspeak.

Some of the various existing tomes on the subject often seem to be either too old-fashioned, heavy-handed, pompous and dry, or too jokey, incomplete, occasionally even incomprehensible. This book is not a bossy rant, but hopefully shows that good grammar, punctuation and spelling are more important than many people appear to think these days. In a fast-paced world, when communications jostle for attention, if your letter, email or website page is full of errors, a reader won't waste his or her time trying to work out what you're trying to say – it will just be binned, deleted or clicked off along with the annoying flashing ads.

Clearly laid out, *Grammar for Grown-Ups* comprises six chapters. Chapter 1 focuses on basic grammar; 2 on punctuation; 3 on spelling; 4 on not so basic grammar and tricky areas; 5 moves across the Atlantic to take in US English and then hops over to Australia, New Zealand, South Africa and Canada; and Chapter 6 delves into a more literary field. Dotted here and there are exercises – some very simple, some rather less so – to see if things have sunk in (and answers are at the back of the book, in case they haven't).

Language is constantly developing, and while some rules should remain hard and fast, some may be bent and once in a while even broken – when you know what you're doing . . .

KF & RK
September 2012

1 | Basic Grammar

The English language has a deceptive air of simplicity;
so have some little frocks; but they are both not the kind
of thing you can run up in half an hour with a machine.

Dorothy L. Sayers

I don't want to talk grammar, I want to talk like a lady.

Eliza Doolittle in George Bernard Shaw's *Pygmalion*

Just as Delia thought it no bad thing to go back to the basics of
cooking by showing us to how to boil water (or maybe it was an
egg), so it is no bad thing to go back to the basics of grammar.

There are nine *types* of words that make up English grammar:
nouns, **verbs**, **adjectives**, **adverbs**, **pronouns**, **articles**,
prepositions, **conjunctions** and **interjections**.

Nouns

A noun is a word used to identify people, places and things.
There are four types of nouns: **proper**, **common**, **abstract** and
collective.

Proper nouns always start with a capital, or upper-case, letter –
and so are easy to spot. Proper nouns include names of specific
people, places and things – like William Shakespeare and Katie Price,
London and Scunthorpe, the Black Sea and the Great Dismal

Swamp, the Taj Mahal and Wembley Stadium, the Houses of Parliament and Holyrood, September and Thursday.

Common nouns refer to all other types of people, places and things, and start with a small, or lower-case, letter – like 'man', 'woman', 'city', 'dead end', 'water', 'mud', 'building', 'folly', 'calendar', 'autumn', 'pedant', 'twit'.

Abstract nouns denote an idea, a feeling or a thought, rather than a physical object or thing, something that can't be seen or touched – such as 'anxiety', 'despair', 'panic', 'pride', 'relief'.

Collective nouns are groups of things – 'army', 'audience', 'choir', 'company', 'couple', 'family', 'government', 'group', 'herd', 'pair', 'panel', 'parliament', 'pride', 'team'. They can also be the name (a proper noun) of a company, a team, etc. – Square Peg, Manchester City.

Here are 20 nouns. Are they proper, common, abstract or collective?

1 bully		**11** flock	
2 telling-off		**12** tolerance	
3 York		**13** Kew Gardens	
4 gaggle		**14** crowd	
5 Rose		**15** weariness	
6 rose		**16** Stonehenge	
7 Bill Clinton		**17** litter	
8 bill		**18** teapot	
9 happiness		**19** luck	
10 apple		**20** murmuration	

Proper or common?

So those are the basic noun categories, but some, of course, encroach on each other. Why does a word like 'conservative' sometimes have a capital letter, and sometimes a small letter? The former, 'Conservative', relates to the British political party, while the latter, 'conservative', means reluctant to change, conventional. Similarly, 'Parliament/parliament' (the UK legislature/any other legislature), 'Bible/bible' (the holy book/a book considered the authority on a particular subject), 'Catholic/catholic' (relates to Roman Catholicism/broad-minded – don't get the two muddled up . . .), 'God/god' (the Almighty/all those Greeks and Romans, or a particularly idolised or adored person). Religions are always upper case, even for non-believers.

Although 'river', 'valley', 'mountain', 'desert', 'road', 'street', 'doctor', 'king', 'president', 'war', etc., are common nouns, they should be capitalised when attached to a name: River Thames, Silicon Valley, Atlas Mountains, Gobi Desert, King's Road, Oxford Street, Doctor Who, King Kong, President Bush, Iraq War, etc., etc. Similarly, when using a title as a term of address without a name attached, keep the title upper case – 'Well, General, you think this war is a good idea?' 'So you won't give me liposuction, Doctor, you just think I should go on a diet?' 'I'll do the washing-up, Mum.' On the other hand, 'sir' and 'madam' should be lower case.

With points on the compass – north, south, east and west – things get a little murkier. Those points themselves should be lower case, but when attached to continents and countries, they take a capital – North America, South Korea, East Africa, West Indies. A named geographical area also has a cap – North Yorkshire, South Dakota, East Anglia, West Sussex. For a more general hint at a direction, though, stick to lower case: north Belfast, south London, west of England (although it is the West Country – specific area, see previous sentence). Unless referring to 'the South', meaning the southern states of America, 'the South' or 'the south', etc., as a geographical area can be either upper or lower case – it's a matter of personal choice. Which looks better: 'She lives in the North' or 'She lives in the north'?

There are some common nouns that were originally proper nouns, but have become so ubiquitous – or 'common' – they are now generic terms and lower case, words such as 'aspirin', 'biro', 'escalator', 'styrofoam', 'tarmac', 'yo-yo'. However, 'Kleenex', 'Sellotape', 'Thermos', 'Tupperware', while equally generic, retain that capital letter – for the moment . . . Just to complicate things a little bit more, 'Hoover', 'Google', 'Rollerblade', 'Tipp-Ex' and 'Xerox' are nouns, but 'hoovering', 'googling', 'rollerblading', 'tippexing' and 'xeroxing' are **verbs** (see below).

Singular and plural

Singular means just one thing – 'ape', 'bird', 'cat'; **plural** means more than one thing – 'apes', 'birds', 'cats'. Plurals usually end with 's', or 'es' if the singular noun ends with 'sh', 'ch' and, sometimes, 'o' – 'thrushes', 'witches', 'potatoes'. If the singular ends with a 'y', the plural ends with 'ies' – 'bellies', 'lorries', 'tellies'. (But 'ey' endings, as in 'trolley', follow the usual plural rule and add just 's', so 'trolleys', not 'trollies'.) A singular noun ending in 'f' or 'fe' usually ends 'ves' in the plural form – 'leaf/leaves', 'scarf/scarves', 'thief/thieves' (although they are always 'roofs' and 'woofs'), 'life/lives', 'wife/wives'. However, as so often with the English language, there are exceptions, and these are called **irregular plurals**, such as 'child/children', 'foot/feet', 'person/people', 'tooth/teeth', 'woman/women'.

Making things even more irregular are those words which are the same in both singular and plural – like 'food', 'sheep', 'money', 'series', 'deer', 'offspring'.

Then there are the nouns which only have a plural form – like 'goggles', 'binoculars', 'gallows', 'pants', 'pyjamas'.

And then there are nouns which were once plural but are now taken as singular – like 'candelabra', 'confetti', 'data', 'graffiti', 'ravioli', 'spaghetti'.

Here is a helpful list of some irregular plurals (in English anyway – though a pedant might say that they are *not* irregular in their language of origin):

alumnus / alumni
analysis / analyses
antenna / antennae *or* antennas
appendix / appendices *or* appendixes
axis / axes
bacterium / bacteria
basis / bases
cactus / cacti
chateau / chateaus *or* chateaux
criterion / criteria
curriculum / curricula *or* curriculums
diagnosis / diagnoses
ellipsis / ellipses
formula / formulae *or* formulas
fungus / fungi
hoof / hoofs *or* hooves
hypothesis / hypotheses
index / indexes *or* indices (latter only in maths)
larva / larvae
louse / lice
matrix / matrices *or* matrixes
medium / media *or* mediums (though that sounds
    a bit spooky)

memorandum / memoranda
narcissus / narcissi *or* narcissuses
neurosis / neuroses
nucleus / nuclei
oasis / oases
octopus / octopuses, *not* octopi (affected)
ox / oxen
parenthesis / parentheses
phenomenon / phenomena
rostrum / rostra *or* rostrums
stadium / stadiums (sports grounds) *or* stadia (ancient
    Greek sports grounds)
stimulus / stimuli
synopsis / synopses
tableau / tableaus *or* tableaux
thesis / theses
vertebra / vertebrae

The plurals of 'aquarium', 'concerto', 'libretto' are regular ('aquariums', 'concertos', 'librettos', *not* 'aquaria', 'concerti', 'libretti' – like 'octopi', considered affected these days).

When a noun is **compound** – consisting of more than one word – most follow the regular plural pattern: 'down-and-outs', 'lay-bys', 'skipping ropes', 'stick-in-the-muds', 'voice-overs'. Some, however, attach the plural to the first word: 'hangers-on', 'holes-in-one', 'passers-by', 'rites of passage', 'sons-in-law'. With still others it's either/or: 'courts martial' *or* 'court martials', 'director generals' *or* 'directors general', 'poets laureate' *or* 'poet laureates' (though in each of these KF and RK would opt for the former example).

Here are 30 nouns in the singular. Give the plural of each one.

1	loaf	16	mouse
2	apple	17	house
3	proof	18	tomato
4	goose	19	half
5	swine	20	volcano
6	scissors	21	whisky
7	trousers	22	turkey
8	mother-in-law	23	rhinoceros
9	beach	24	sponge
10	bully	25	moose
11	copy	26	pulley
12	crisis	27	whiskey
13	calf	28	storey
14	cock-up	29	chicken
15	species	30	story

Collective nouns: singular or plural?

Are **collective nouns** – 'audience', 'government', 'herd', for example – treated as singular or plural? Either is OK, although in UK English the tendency is to make them plural. Consistency is the key (and common sense). If a noun is closely followed by a plural **pronoun**, the noun and the **verb** should be treated as plural. (See more on collective nouns in Chapter 4, p. 137.)

Verbs

A verb is a word that indicates an action or a state of being ('to sit', 'to dance', 'to be', 'to exist'). A verb is an essential part of a sentence – in fact, the only essential part. 'Bill sits' is a sentence, and 'Sit!' is also a sentence; 'Bill' all on his own, however, is not.

Verbs can be divided into two groups, **transitive** and **intransitive**, although most verbs can be in both groups.

Transitive verbs

A sentence containing a transitive verb has a subject noun and an object noun.

Adam [subject] owned [verb] a house [object].

Eve [subject] mashed [verb] a banana [object].

A transitive verb can be identified by taking away the object. If the verb is transitive, the sentence won't really make sense.

Adam owned.

Eve mashed.

They made.

For the ship to go up the Thames they raised.

Well, what did Adam own? What did Eve mash? What did they make and raise? A transitive verb needs an object, and the sentence is incomplete without one. Other verbs which are only transitive include 'buy', 'cost', 'hate', 'kick'.

Transitive verbs can also be split into two categories – **active** and **passive** – depending on how they are used.

Active verbs

'Adam owned a house' and 'Eve mashed a banana' are both active uses of transitive verbs, because Adam and Eve are the subjects actively doing the owning and mashing of the objects.

Passive verbs

The passive use of transitive verbs puts the cart before the horse (or switches the object and subject) as it were, turning the sentence round, which sometimes alters its emphasis. In 'A house was owned by Adam' and 'A banana was mashed by Eve', the subjects are being passively owned and mashed by the objects.

Intransitive verbs

A sentence containing an intransitive verb does not need an object –

> Adam looked.

– or sometimes even a subject –

> Look!

There are a few verbs which are only intransitive – such as 'lie', 'die', 'sneeze', 'snore'. They either need nothing, or they need a **preposition** or **conjunction** (see pp. 30–35) before the object.

> She sneezed. (✔)
>
> She sneezed a hanky. (✘)
>
> She sneezed into a hanky. (✔)

There are, of course, a few verbs with more than one sense – and which therefore might be transitive or intransitive depending on that sense. For example, 'jam', meaning 'squeeze', is transitive – 'Ken jammed his fingers in his ears'; but 'jam', meaning 'improvise with other musicians', is intransitive – 'Ken jammed all night'.

Here are 5 sentences. Are the verbs being used transitively or intransitively?

1 Penny threw the tedious book away.

2 Caesar came, he saw, he conquered.

3 Felicity fainted.

4 Zack ran a marathon.

5 Al beat Michael in the badminton match.

Regular and irregular verbs

A verb is regular if it ends with 'ed' (or 'd' if the verb ends in an 'e' already) in the past tense.

Harry walked to the harbour. (from the verb 'to walk')

Tanya hated table tennis. (from the verb 'to hate')

Irregular verbs are those which (believe it or not) don't end in 'ed' in the past tense.

Patsy gave a good performance. (from the verb 'to give')

Enid ate an egg. (from the verb 'to eat')

Some irregular verbs change quite clearly from their present form, as in the examples above; other irregular verbs are the same in their present and past forms, for example 'hit/hit', 'let/let', 'quit/quit'.

Look at the infinitives of the following verbs (i.e. their basic forms –
'to come', 'to see', 'to conquer') and decide whether they are regular
or irregular.

1	to feel	11	to make
2	to think	12	to lend
3	to linger	13	to be
4	to go	14	to agree
5	to swim	15	to treat
6	to levitate	16	to seek
7	to warble	17	to drink
8	to kill	18	to fish
9	to describe	19	to paint
10	to shut	20	to buy

Principal and auxiliary verbs

Principal means main; auxiliary means additional, or helping.
When the two combine they make a compound verb. In *'The
Mousetrap* has been running in the West End for three million
years', the verb is 'has been running'. The principal verb, not
surprisingly, is the one with the main meaning – 'running'. The
secondary, or auxiliary, verbs – 'has been' – help the main verb,
in this case by the use of tenses showing how long this play has
been running. If, unbelievably, *The Mousetrap* were suddenly to
close, the sentence could change to either *'The Mousetrap* had been
running in the West End for three million years' (still compound,
using principal and auxiliary verbs), or *'The Mousetrap* ran in the
West End for three million years'.

In the following sentences, indicate which are the principal verbs, and which the auxiliary.

1 British troops have been put on standby.

2 I should be told about these things.

3 Will there be cake for tea?

4 The earthquake could have triggered a tsunami.

5 There might be a heatwave this summer.

Verb tenses

There are, strictly speaking, only two tenses in the English language – the present and the past. The future tense and the numerous other tenses we use are formed from the present and the past.

I <u>want</u> two scoops of ice cream – present

I <u>wanted</u> two scoops of ice cream – past

I <u>shall want</u> two scoops of ice cream – future

However, non-strictly speaking, there are twelve verb tenses generally used in English:

present	past perfect
present continuous	past perfect continuous
present perfect	future
present perfect continuous	future continuous
past	future perfect
past continuous	future perfect continuous

	first-person singular	second-person singular and plural	third-person singular	first-person plural	third-person plural
present	I kiss	you kiss	he/she/it kisses	we kiss	they kiss
present continuous	I am kissing	you are kissing	he/she/it is kissing	we are kissing	they are kissing
present perfect	I have kissed	you have kissed	he/she/it has kissed	we have kissed	they have kissed
present perfect continuous	I have been kissing	you have been kissing	he/she/it has been kissing	we have been kissing	they have been kissing
past	I kissed	you kissed	he/she/it kissed	we kissed	they kissed
past continuous	I was kissing	you were kissing	he/she/it was kissing	we were kissing	they were kissing
past perfect	I had kissed	you had kissed	he/she/it had kissed	we had kissed	they had kissed
past perfect continuous	I had been kissing	you had been kissing	he/she/it had been kissing	we had been kissing	they had been kissing
future	I shall* kiss	you will* kiss	he/she/it will kiss	we shall kiss	they will kiss
future continuous	I shall be kissing	you will be kissing	he/she/it will be kissing	we shall be kissing	they will be kissing
future perfect	I shall have kissed	you will have kissed	he/she/it will have kissed	we shall have kissed	they will have kissed
future perfect continuous	I shall have been kissing	you will have been kissing	he/she/it will have been kissing	we shall have been kissing	they will have been kissing

*For 'shall/will', see p. 162.

Present

The present is *now*. When a verb is conjugated in the present tense, it is exactly the same as the infinitive or stem form ('to die', 'to sleep', or 'die', 'sleep'), apart from in the third-person singular (he/she/it), which has an added 's'. So, 'to write' becomes:

I write

you write

he/she/it writes

we write

they write

The main exception is the verb 'to be':

I am

you are

he/she/it is

we are

they are

Present continuous

The present is rarely just a moment in time, however, but continues – and to express this there is the present continuous tense. 'I write the book' (which would be impossible to do in a moment – trust us on this) becomes 'I am writing the book' – a construction using the present-tense auxiliary verb 'to be' and the present participle of the principal verb 'to write'. This denotes that the writing is happening now but it is taking some time.

The **present participle** is used in verb phrases and continuous tenses. It is formed by adding 'ing' to the stem of a verb – so, 'learn' becomes 'learning', 'drive' becomes 'driving', 'write' becomes 'writing'. As well as a verb, the present participle can be a noun – 'bad timing' – and an adjective – 'a sitting duck'.

The **past participle** is used in verb phrases and perfect tenses. With regular verbs, its form is the same as the past tense – 'I learned', 'I have learned' – but irregular verbs may differ in the past participle – 'I drove' *but* 'I have driven', 'I wrote' *but* 'I have written'. As well as a verb, the past participle can be an adjective – 'the heated swimming pool', 'the frozen lake' – and a noun – 'the damned', 'the unloved'.

Present perfect

The present perfect combines something that began in the past and has just finished *or* is still continuing – 'they have written the book', 'we have lived in London since 2001'. It combines the present-tense auxiliary verb 'to have' with the past participle of a principal verb, 'to write', 'to live'.

Present perfect continuous

This tense shows a continuous action from the past, which has just finished – 'I have been writing the book', 'we have been watching telly'. It combines the present-tense auxiliary verb 'to have', the present-perfect auxiliary verb 'to be' and the present participle of a principal verb, 'to write', 'to watch'.

Past

The past is *then*. It shows something that has been and gone, or something that took place regularly – 'I wrote the book', 'I wrote every night from dusk until dawn'. With regular verbs, 'ed' or 'd' (see above, p. 10) is added to the end of the stem – 'I listened' (from 'I listen), 'we danced' (from 'we dance'). Irregular verbs take various forms (again, see above, p. 10), although the idea is the same.

Past continuous

This describes something that happened in the past and took a certain amount of time, i.e. it wasn't over in a flash – 'I was writing the book', 'Michelangelo was painting the Sistine Chapel'. It is formed by using the past-tense auxiliary verb 'to be' and the present participle of a principal verb, 'to write', 'to paint'.

Past perfect

Also called the **pluperfect**, from the Latin for 'more than perfect', this describes something that has taken place prior to a point in the past (it could be called the double, or extra, past) – 'I had written the book', 'he had showered in his new bathroom'. It is formed by the past-tense auxiliary verb 'to have' and the past participle of a principal verb, 'to write', 'to shower'.

Past perfect continuous

This shows an event that continued in the past perfect for a while – 'I had been writing the book', 'they had been making plans for their holiday'. It is formed using the past-tense auxiliary verbs of 'to have' and 'to be' and the present participle of a principal verb, 'to write', 'to make'.

Future

The future is *yet to come*. It predicts something that will happen –
possibly or definitely, depending on who is doing the predicting:
'I shall write this book', 'you will do your homework'. It is formed
by using modal auxiliary verbs, 'shall', 'will', and the stem form
of a principal verb, 'write', 'do'.

> **Modal auxiliary verbs** These describe the 'mood' of a verb –
> can, could, may, might, must, shall, should, will, would.

Future continuous

This describes a future occurrence that will continue for a while –
'I shall be writing a book', 'he will be running in the marathon'.
Like the other continuous tenses, it is formed by using a modal
auxiliary verb, 'shall', 'will', the auxiliary verb stem 'be' and the
present participle of a principal verb, 'to write', 'to run'.

Future perfect

This indicates an action that will (probably) be completed at some
point in the future – 'I shall have written the book by June', 'they
will have exhausted me by lunchtime'. It is formed by using a modal
auxiliary verb, 'shall', 'will', the auxiliary verb stem 'have' and the
past participle of a principal verb, 'to write', 'to exhaust'.

Future perfect continuous

This describes something that in the future will have been
continuing for a while – 'they will have been writing this book
for ten years come June', 'she will have been teaching here for
six months'. It is formed by using a modal auxiliary verb, 'will',

the auxiliary verb stem of 'have', the auxiliary past participle of 'be' ('been') and the present participle of a principal verb, 'to write', 'to teach'.

The **subjunctive** gets a section all to itself in Chapter 4, p. 165.

Here are 20 sentences. Which tense is being used in each?

1 You will have been renovating the house for ten years come spring.

2 They are playing a dirty game.

3 She had eaten all my favourite biscuits.

4 We will be hiring a car at the weekend.

5 How tense am I?

6 Reader, I married him.

7 He will have finished his exams next week.

8 She has been churning out the same drivel for years.

9 I'll be back.

10 They had been working on the project for six months.

11 The cat was eating the goldfish.

12 We have always wondered what her name is.

13 The train had stopped yet again.

14 She will have been cooking at the same place for twenty years.

15 The goldfish will be fondly remembered.

16 She will have been in this soap for thirty years next month.

17 He lost the match yet again.

18 That's blown our cover.

19 They had been hoping for a quick sale.

20 I love you.

Adjectives

An adjective is a word that describes a noun – those places, people and things. It modifies (slightly alters) a noun, or pronoun, by identifying, qualifying and quantifying words. In its pure sense, it gives information about the noun.

Most general **descriptive adjectives** can come both before and after the noun – 'the long book', 'the bad idea', *or* 'the book is long', 'the idea is bad'. In the former examples, before the noun and with no linking verb, the adjective is called **attributive**. In the latter, after the noun and verb, the adjective is called **predicative**. The first modifies the noun; the second completes the meaning of the sentence.

There are a number of adjectives that can only be used attributively, such as 'former', 'latter', 'main', 'mere', 'sheer', 'utter', 'very' – 'the mere hint' is fine, but 'the hint is mere' is not; 'the main road', fine, but 'the road is main', not fine. Likewise, there are some adjectives that can only be used predicatively, such as 'afloat', 'afraid', 'aglow', 'alive', 'alone', 'asleep', 'awake' – 'the afloat girl'? No . . .

Then there are adjectives that can be used both attributively and predicatively, but their meaning alters according to that position:

the late Josephine Bloggs
Josephine Bloggs was late

Gordon was poor
poor Gordon

Sometimes, a **postpositive adjective** comes into the equation. This is an adjective that is placed immediately after the noun or pronoun – such as 'someone useless', 'something inspiring', 'sweets galore'.

Here are 10 examples of adjectives. Decide whether they are attributive, predicative or postpositive.

1 the cool drink

2 time immemorial

3 the evidence was inconclusive

4 a busy road

5 that meal was delicious

6 a running gag

7 a lazy boy

8 the situation is bleak

9 mission impossible

10 the milk was sour

Adjectives can also be used to *compare* things. There is an **absolute**, a **comparative** and a **superlative** form – 'the good teacher', 'the better teacher', 'the best teacher'; 'the small portion', 'the smaller portion', 'the smallest portion'; 'the beautiful view', 'the more beautiful view', 'the most beautiful view'. (For more detail on comparatives and superlatives, see Chapter 4, p. 138)

Adjectives (and adverbs – see below) can also be used to *grade* something or someone – with such terms as 'fairly', 'rather', 'quite', 'very', 'pretty'. These adjectives are **qualitative**. So we could have 'a fairly mediocre meal', served by 'a rather rude waiter', after 'a quite unpleasant film', in 'a very grim cinema'; all in all, 'a pretty disastrous evening'.

Then there are **classifying adjectives**, which are used to put something or someone into a category or group. They cannot be graded and cannot be used with a comparative or superlative – for example, 'the political situation', 'the northern hemisphere', 'the geography lesson'.

In addition to **descriptive adjectives**, there are **limiting adjectives** – so called because they qualify a particular noun; in other words, they 'limit' it. The main categories of limiting adjectives are **demonstrative, possessive, numerical** and **interrogative**.

A **demonstrative adjective** picks out a specific noun rather than using the more general articles, 'a', 'an' or 'the'. Demonstrative adjectives are 'this', 'that', 'these', 'those' – '<u>this</u> fish is inedible', 'I want <u>that</u> chocolate', '<u>these</u> chips are delicious', '<u>those</u> people are staring at us' are examples of demonstrative adjectives.

A **possessive adjective** is used to show – funnily enough – possession. Possessive adjectives are 'my', 'your', 'his', 'her', 'its', 'our', 'their'. For example, 'here's <u>my</u> idea', 'it's <u>your</u> turn', '<u>our</u> book is progressing'.

A **numerical adjective** – as it says on the tin – is a number used as an adjective. There are two types (a numerical adjective in itself): cardinal (quantity) and ordinal (position). So 'one book', 'two people', 'five gold rings' are cardinal numerical adjectives; 'first place', 'third child', 'tenth rate' are ordinal.

An **interrogative adjective** asks a question about a noun – 'what' or 'which'. 'What DVD are we renting?' 'Which dress are you going to wear?'

*Here are 10 sentences. Decide which type of adjective each is using –
demonstrative, possessive, numerical or interrogative.*

1 Four people boarded the bus.

2 Which train are you catching?

3 His flies are undone.

4 This book is doomed.

5 What film are we going to see?

6 The first taxi is yours.

7 Those cakes are stale.

8 Their home is for sale.

9 Our plan won't work.

10 My idea was rubbish.

Adverbs

An adverb modifies a verb – 'I <u>occasionally</u> smoke'; an adjective –
'the <u>strangely</u> agile girl'; or another adverb – 'the boy walks <u>really
slowly</u>'. Like an adjective, it is a helping word, and answers the
questions how, when or where something is done, and to what
degree. If a word doesn't answer one of these questions, it isn't
an adverb.

Tessa tap-dances tentatively.

How does she tap-dance? 'Tentatively' – so this is an adverb.
However:

Tessa is a tentative tap dancer.

cannot answer any of the questions *how, when* or *where,*
and so 'tentative' is not an adverb (it's an adjective).

Adverbs are often adjectives with an 'ly' tacked on the end – 'bare/barely', 'reckless/recklessly', 'rude/rudely', 'soft/softly' – which make them easy to spot. This isn't a hard-and-fast rule, though: the adverbs 'always', 'ever', 'often', for example, show that 'ly' can't be added to any old thing; some adjectives end in 'ly' anyway – 'friendly', 'lonely', 'lovely' – so when they are used as adverbs, they don't need another 'ly' added ('friendlyly'? no thanks).

Another anomaly: some non 'ly' adverbs are the same as adjectives – 'fast', 'hard', 'later'.

the fast runner (adjective)

she ran fast (adverb)

And to confuse things even more: 'I feel badly' and 'I feel bad' are both adverbs, but the sense is rather different. In the first, I am feeling ill, or my sense of touch has gone up the spout; in the latter, I am feeling bad about something, such as dumping my boyfriend just after he lost his job.

There are four types of common adverb: **time/frequency, place, manner** and **degree**.

Time/frequency adverbs answer the question of *when* and *how many times* – with adverbs such as 'afterwards', 'always', 'before', 'early', 'late', 'never', 'often', 'seldom', 'sometimes', 'still', 'yet'.

My parents often have breakfast in bed at the weekend.

Lucy never missed a lecture in her first year.

Place adverbs answer the question of *where* – with adverbs such as 'abroad', 'anywhere', 'backwards', 'downhill', 'downstairs', 'everywhere', 'forwards', 'here', 'inside', 'near', 'nearby', 'nowhere', 'outside', 'overground', 'there', 'underground', 'uphill', 'upstairs'.

Let's do the show right <u>here</u>!

Lucy went <u>nowhere</u> <u>near</u> the lecture theatre in her second year.

Manner adverbs answer the question of *how* – with adverbs such as 'badly', 'beautifully', 'carefully', 'craftily', 'messily', 'noisily', 'quietly', 'seriously', 'shiftily', 'slowly', 'slyly', 'well'.

Ted read the poem <u>beautifully</u>.

Lucy <u>slyly</u> slipped into a lecture or two in her third year.

Degree adverbs answer the question *to what extent* – with adverbs such as 'absolutely', 'almost', 'barely', 'completely', 'easily', 'entirely', 'extremely', 'fairly', 'hardly', 'just', 'least', 'little', 'most', 'nearly', 'quite', 'scarcely', 'somewhat', 'thoroughly', 'totally', 'utterly', 'very'.

The man was <u>very</u> tall.

Lucy <u>barely</u> scraped a pass degree.

Here are 10 sentences. Decide whether the adverb in each is one of time, place, manner or degree.

1   The crowd cheered enthusiastically.

2   Jack was so exhausted.

3   The teacher spoke too quickly.

4   The train will be leaving soon.

5   We're going to move abroad.

6   Come inside.

7   They walked through the garden.

8   She knocked loudly on the door.

9   They finished at the same time.

10   They were totally unsuitable.

Pronouns

A pronoun is used to take the place of other words – usually nouns – to avoid repetition and long-windedness. Rather than saying or writing 'the boy is playing football and the boy is annoyed because the ref disallowed the boy's goal', it's better to say or write 'the boy is playing football and he is annoyed because the ref disallowed his goal'. And instead of 'this programme is unwatchable, and this programme is also boring', say 'this programme is unwatchable, and it's also boring'.

Pronouns can be divided into eight categories: **personal, possessive, relative, demonstrative, indefinite, interrogative, reciprocal** and **reflexive**.

Personal pronouns are: 'I/me', 'you', 'he/him', 'she/her', 'it', 'we/us', 'they/them'. In 'Jo embarked on this project and then she regretted it', the personal pronoun ('she') replaces the noun ('Jo') used earlier in the sentence. Personal pronouns can be subjective or objective.

I like Jo (subjective)

Jo likes me (objective)

Subject: the main element of a clause or sentence. It comes before the verb, and is what the sentence is about. 'Barbara fed Rover.'

Object: the secondary element of a clause or sentence. It usually comes after the verb and is on the receiving end of whatever that verb is about. 'Barbara fed Rover.'

Possessive pronouns are: 'mine', 'yours', 'his', 'hers', 'its', 'ours', 'theirs'. 'That idea was <u>ours</u>' is an example. Note that possessive pronouns can stand alone, whereas possessive adjectives are always attached to a noun – '<u>my</u> sister is older than <u>yours</u>'.

Relative pronouns are: 'that', 'when', 'where', 'which', 'who', 'whom', 'whose', 'why'. 'The girl <u>whose</u> party it was felt sick after eating too much jelly' is an example. They are called relative pronouns because they are used before a relative clause (or phrase) – 'felt sick after eating too much jelly' being the relative clause in the sentence above.

Demonstrative pronouns are: 'this', 'that', 'these', 'those'. They indicate whether the noun they are replacing is singular or plural, and also suggest location and time – 'this' and 'these' are the singular and plural of something close by in location or time; 'that' and 'those' are the singular and plural of something more distant. '<u>This</u> looks better on me than <u>that</u>', for example. (Demonstrative pronouns might look the same as demonstrative adjectives, but there is a difference – 'this is tasteless' is an example of the former, as it can stand alone; 'This milk is off' is an example of the latter, as it qualifies the noun.)

Indefinite pronouns, as the term suggests, refer to things that are not definite, or precise, or specific. They include: 'all', 'any', 'anybody', 'anyone', 'anything', 'everybody', 'everyone', 'everything', 'few', 'many', 'nobody', 'none', 'no one', 'nothing', 'some', 'somebody', 'someone', 'something'. '<u>Nobody</u> answered the door when I knocked' is an example.

Interrogative pronouns are: 'what', 'which', 'who', 'whom', 'whose'. They are used to form questions, such as '<u>Who</u> has been eating my porridge?' The pronoun here represents the unknown thing, hence the question. 'What' and 'which' can also be used as interrogative adjectives – 'Which yogurt do you want?' (adjective), 'Which is mine?' (pronoun); 'which', 'who' and 'whom' can be used as relative pronouns – 'Whose is this jumper?' (interrogative), 'The girl whose jumper was mislaid' (relative).

Reciprocal pronouns are: 'each other', 'one another'. If Bill loved Ben, and Ben loved Bill, this would be reciprocal – so 'Bill and Ben loved each other'; if Bill loved Ben, but Ben hated Bill, it wouldn't be reciprocal (and Bill would be devastated).

Reflexive pronouns are: 'myself', 'yourself', 'himself', 'herself', 'itself', 'oneself', 'ourselves', 'yourselves', 'themselves'. They are used when the object in a sentence is the same as the subject; they cannot be used as subjects themselves (which is an example of a reflexive pronoun). Each personal pronoun has a reflexive pronoun – 'I/myself', 'you/yourself', 'he/himself', 'she/herself', 'it/itself', 'we/ourselves', 'you/yourselves', 'they/themselves' – such as 'he talked to himself'.

Here are 20 sentences using pronouns. Identify the type underlined.

1 Is this yours?

2 He loved his new trousers.

3 The pony whose rider was too heavy was fed up.

4 Her husband was late.

5 The plumber who did the bathroom was excellent.

6 Which one shall we go for?

7 That's my house.

8 It's down to the two of us.

9 To whom does this belong?

10 The missing diamonds were hers.

11 <u>That</u> was rubbish.

12 She kept the best praline for <u>herself</u>.

13 They followed <u>one another</u> down the stairs.

14 Don't believe <u>everything</u> you read.

15 <u>Whose</u> line is it anyway?

16 The deadline was fast approaching <u>them</u>.

17 The co-stars loathed <u>each other</u>.

18 <u>Nobody</u> said a word.

19 He made <u>himself</u> at home.

20 <u>These</u> are to die for.

Articles

There are only two types of article: definite – 'the' – and indefinite – 'a' or 'an'. The definite article is used when the specific subject is known; the indefinite is used for non-specific subjects. An article comes before a noun, and 'defines' it. '<u>The</u> girl won <u>the</u> race', '<u>a</u> girl is in <u>the</u> race'; '<u>an</u> apple would be nice', '<u>the</u> apple was delicious'.

'a' or 'an'?

On the whole, 'an' goes with any noun starting with a vowel – 'an apple', 'an egg', 'an ice cream', 'an olive' – though not always with 'u' nouns (it depends on how the 'u' is pronounced – it's not 'an unicorn' but it is 'an umbrella'). Although it hasn't always been the case, nowadays an 'h' noun is treated as a consonant (which it is) rather than a vowel – 'a hysteric' and 'a hotel' are more common, and less pretentious, than 'an hysteric' or 'an hotel'.

Upper or lower case?

Definite articles don't need to be upper case when attached to
a proper noun, unless they are part of a title. So it's the Who, the
Arctic Monkeys, the Wolseley, the Stockpot, the Royal Albert Hall,
the Sage Gateshead, rather than The Who, The Arctic Monkeys,
etc. Likewise, newspaper and magazine titles – the *Guardian*,
the *Independent*, the *Lancet* (although it is always *The Times*
for some reason). And yet, it's The Mall, The Cut, The Headrow,
The Bishops Avenue, because in these cases 'The' is part of the
street's name. (In a different vein, there's no article at all attached
to Tate Modern, Tate St Ives, etc., but there is one attached to
the Tate.)

Delete or not?

Should the article be kept with a title when using directly after
a proper noun or pronoun? There's no fixed rule on this, but it
can sometimes sound and look a bit clumsy, as in Shakespeare's
A Midsummer Night's Dream, Dickens's *The Old Curiosity Shop*,
Iris Murdoch's *The Black Prince*; Shakespeare's *Midsummer Night's
Dream*, Dickens's *Old Curiosity Shop*, Iris Murdoch's *Black Prince*
are nicer, and follow the pronoun logic, as in 'his *Midsummer
Night's Dream*' and, her *Black Prince*' ('his *A Midsummer Night's
Dream*' and 'her *The Black Prince*' are pretty horrible).

In the following extract, pick out all the definite and indefinite articles.

The dining-room was inconveniently crowded. There was a KC and his
wife, a Government official and his wife, Mrs Strickland's sister and her
husband, Colonel MacAndrew, and the wife of a Member of Parliament.
It was because the Member of Parliament found that he could not leave
the House that I had been invited. The respectability of the party was

portentous. The women were too nice to be well dressed, and too sure of their position to be amusing. The men were solid. There was about all of them an air of well-satisfied prosperity.

W. Somerset Maugham, *The Moon and Sixpence*

Prepositions

These are 'linking' words. They denote a connection between two words in a clause or phrase, usually relating to time and space, and typically come before the noun or pronoun (or equivalent). These are the most common:

about	but	outside
above	by	over
across	despite	past
after	down	since
against	during	through
along	except	throughout
amid	for	till
among	from	to
around	in	towards
at	inside	under
before	into	underneath
behind	like	until
below	near	up
beneath	of	upon
beside	off	with
between	on	within
beyond	out	without

So:

after you

around teatime

below stairs

in 2012

on fire

without doubt

Prepositions can be **simple** or **compound**. Simple prepositions are single-word ones – as in the list above.

The plate is on the table.

The plate is beside the glass.

The plate was smashed during supper.

Compound prepositions are two or more words, as in the list below.

according to	effect of	in spite of
along with	effect on	instead of
apart from	except for	in the event of
as well as	for lack of	in the face of
away from	for want of	next to
because of	in agreement with	on behalf of
causes of	in between	on top of
close to	in case of	owing to
consequence of	in charge of	up to
due to	in front of	with regard to

The bowl is <u>instead of</u> the plate.

Your supper is <u>next to</u> the cat's.

The cat has eaten your steak <u>as well as</u> his Whiskas.

Prepositions and verbs

There is a school of thought that believes the preposition should come straight after the verb – 'Put on the kettle, I'm parched' rather than 'Put the kettle on, I'm parched'. Either is OK. But this school collapses when the noun becomes a pronoun – 'Put on it, I'm parched' is nonsense, and George Michael and the other one never sang 'Wake up me before you go-go', did they?

In the extract below, pick out all the prepositions.

A vulture flapped and shifted on the iron roof and Wilson looked at Scobie. He looked without interest in obedience to a stranger's direction, and it seemed to him that no particular interest attached to the squat grey-haired man walking alone up Bond Street. He couldn't tell that this was one of those occasions a man never forgets: a small cicatrice had been made on the memory, a wound that would ache whenever certain things combined – the taste of gin at midday, the smell of flowers under a balcony, the clang of corrugated iron, an ugly bird flopping from perch to perch.

Graham Greene, *The Heart of the Matter*

Conjunctions

These are also 'linking' words, joining together other words, phrases or sentences.

There are three types: **coordinating**, **correlative** and **subordinating**.

Coordinating conjunctions connect items that, grammatically, have the same status. Words such as 'and', 'but', 'for', 'nor', 'or', 'so', 'yet' are coordinating conjunctions.

Chocolate or fruit for pudding.

Unpredictable but fun.

We didn't get tickets, so we went for a meal.

Samson had lost his strength, for Delilah had cut off his hair.

Jane took a bus and train to work.

Correlative conjunctions are made up of two or more words working together as a pair, to link two similar items. The most commonly used are 'both/and', 'either/or', 'neither/nor' (don't mix and match, though: 'neither/or', 'either/nor' should never be used, because they're not correlative).

This book is both concise and informative.

We can either go to the supermarket or shop online.

That remark is neither clever nor funny.

Other correlative conjunctions include 'hardly/when', 'if/then', 'no sooner/than', 'not only/but also', 'rather/than', 'scarcely/ when', 'whether/or'.

We had <u>hardly</u> finished our meal <u>when</u> the bill was put on the table.

<u>If</u> you can't find the car keys, <u>then</u> you'll have to walk.

<u>No sooner</u> had Hamlet started his soliloquy <u>than</u> someone's mobile went off.

Roger is <u>not only</u> a good long-distance runner, <u>but also</u> a good sprinter.

I would <u>rather</u> wash my hair <u>than</u> go to their party.

Jim had <u>scarcely</u> had a chance to ride his bike <u>when</u> it was stolen.

They didn't know <u>whether</u> to go to Paris <u>or</u> Brighton for the weekend.

Subordinating conjunctions are used when the two items or clauses being linked are not equal, so there is a 'subordinate' clause and a 'main' one. 'If I'm working [subordinate], I won't answer the phone [main].' The subordinate is dependent on the main clause and cannot work on its own. Words such as 'after', 'although', 'as', 'because', 'before', 'how', 'if', 'once', 'since', 'that', 'then', 'though', 'until', 'when', 'where', 'whether', 'while' are subordinating conjunctions.

<u>Since</u> we've invited them for supper, we had better cook something.

You can take a break <u>after</u> you've done some work.

<u>When</u> you've finished your homework, you can watch TV.

<u>While</u> the cat's away, the mice will play.

<u>Although</u> we liked Jenny, we couldn't stand her husband.

In the extract below, pick out all the conjunctions.

When I found so astonishing a power placed within my hands, I hesitated a long time concerning the manner in which I should employ it. Although I possessed the capacity of bestowing animation, yet to prepare a frame for reception of it, with all its intricacies of fibres, muscles, and veins, still remained a work of inconceivable difficulty and labour.

Mary Shelley, *Frankenstein*

Interjections

Interjections – or exclamations – are stand-alone words, used mainly to show emotion (joy, frustration, pain, etc.), and they are not related grammatically to the rest of the sentence. Examples of interjections include:

aha, alas, boo, bravo, cheers, duh, eh?, goodbye, good grief, ha-ha, hallelujah, hello, hey, hmm, huh?, humph, oh, oh dear, oh my God, oh well, okey-dokey, OMG, oops, ouch, ow, phew, shh, thanks, uh-huh, uh-oh, well, whatever, whoa, whoops, wow, yes, yuk, yum

Supply an interjection for each of the following.

1 The ball whacked Bob on the head. '_____ !' said Bob.
2 The curtain came down on the opera. '_____ !' yelled the audience.
3 '_____ – I hope that wasn't your favourite vase.'
4 '_____ , are you really wearing that this evening?'
5 Marmite? _____ .

In the extract below, pick out an example of each of the nine types of words that make up the English language.

The policeman looked at me for a while without speaking. Then he said, 'I am arresting you for assaulting a police officer.'

This made me feel a lot calmer because it is what policemen say on television and in films.

Then he said, 'I strongly advise you to get into the back of the police car because if you try any of that monkey-business again, you little shit, I will seriously lose my rag. Is that understood?'

I walked over to the police car which was parked just outside the gate. He opened the back door and I got inside. He climbed into the driver's seat and made a call on his radio to the policewoman who was still inside the house. He said, 'The little bugger just had a pop at me, Kate. Can you hang on with Mrs S while I drop him off at the station? I'll get Tony to swing by and pick you up.'

And she said, 'Sure. I'll catch you later.'

The policeman said, 'Okey-doke,' and we drove off.

Mark Haddon, *The Curious Incident of the Dog in the Night-time*

2 | Punctuation

Commas in the *New Yorker* fall with the precision
of knives in a circus act, outlining the victim.

Elwyn Brooks White

I can attest there is only one thing more mortifying
than having an exclamation mark removed by an editor:
an exclamation mark added in.

Lynne Truss

Punctuation clarifies the meaning of sentences and phrases.
Without punctuation, language would make little sense, and
correct punctuation is as crucial in writing as correct grammar
and spelling. It's the written equivalent of the satnav (when it
works) – keeping the writers or readers on the right path, and
telling them where to go.

These are the punctuation marks used in the English
language: **full stops, commas, question marks, exclamation
marks, colons, semicolons, apostrophes, quotation marks,
brackets/parentheses, hyphens, dashes, ellipses** and **solidi.**

Full stop (.)

A full stop – sometimes called a period (though mainly by
Americans) or a full point – indicates the end of a sentence.

A written sentence always begins with a capital letter and ends with a full stop, question mark or exclamation mark: 'Here is a sentence.' 'Here is another sentence.' 'Is this yet another sentence?' 'God, these are boring sentences!'

In the following passage of five sentences, put in the full stops and capitals.

> dolly slammed the door behind her in a fit of temper then
> she realised that was rather a stupid thing to do her keys were
> on the hall table it was pouring outside and she had no coat
> but dolly was damned if she was going to humiliate herself
> by ringing the doorbell

While the full stop has no other function in grammar, it does have a few other uses. It is used after **initials** – for example, A. S. Byatt, J. M. Coetzee, e. e. cummings, k. d. lang, J. K. Rowling, J. R. R. Tolkien, J. M. W. Turner – and **abbreviations** – for example, Co. (Company), Cres. (Crescent), Jan. (January), Mon. (Monday), Prof. (Professor), tel. (telephone), etc. (et cetera). **Contractions**, on the other hand, do not use points – a contraction being a word that begins and ends with the same letters as the word it is 'contracting' – such as contd (continued), Dr (Doctor), Ltd (Limited), Mr (Mister), Mrs (Mistress), Rd (Road), vs (versus). Points after contractions are an old-fashioned practice – they might be seen in some old classics (and also in American works – see Chapter 5) but they are not used today.

Are the following examples contractions or abbreviations?
And what are they contracting or abbreviating?

1 dept	**11** abbrev.
2 Revd	**12** Ave
3 Fr	**13** gall.
4 Dec.	**14** Dr.
5 Wed.	**15** Dr
6 ibid.	**16** fwd
7 e.g.	**17** Jr
8 Rt Hon.	**18** sc.
9 i.e.	**19** edn
10 St	**20** no.

Abbreviations can be **acronyms** or **initialisms**. Both terms use initial letters, but while an acronym forms its own word – Aids, BAFTA, FIFA, Ofcom – an initialism pronounces each letter – aka, asap, MRI, MRSA. Acronyms and initialisms that are made up of upper-case (capital) or a mix of upper-case and lower-case (small) letters nowadays rarely use a point – ADHD, AWOL, BBC, BSc, PhD – but those using only small letters often do have points – a.m., p.m., e.g., i.e. (although equally often they are left out, and that's OK). AD, BC and BCE are not small letters, they are small capitals; they don't use points, and AD always comes before the year, BC and BCE after.

Measurement abbreviations – like kg (kilogram), km (kilometre), mm (millimetre) – don't need points. An abbreviated measurement should only be used with a figure, though, not if it's spelt out – '6 cm' or 'six centimetres' are both fine, but 'six cm' is not.

Similarly, M&S, B&B, A&E, etc., don't need points either, and may or may not have a space either side of the ampersand

(&). Another type of abbreviation which no longer uses a point is a word that *was* an abbreviation, but the abbreviation has now become the more commonly used word – such as A level, gym, info, mac, photo, piano, prefab.

One more use of the full stop is in numbers: to indicate a decimal point (7.5), between units of money (£10.50) and between hours and minutes (10.45 a.m.).

Comma (,)

Ah, the comma . . . While the full stop has one basic function in grammar – to end a sentence – the comma has a multitude of uses. To start with the simplest, a comma is used to make sense of a sentence, by breaking it up into smaller sections. Its key roles are: **to list, to join, to replace, to bracket, to separate** and **to introduce direct speech.**

Listing comma – 'makes things less stilted'

This type of comma is used instead of 'and' and 'or'. It separates items – both words and phrases – in a list. For example, 'James plays cricket, rugby, football and tennis' is less clunky than 'James plays cricket and rugby and football and tennis'. But if there is more than one list in the equation, keep 'and' rather than sticking in a comma: 'On holiday, Joyce is going to play Scrabble and read *War and Peace* and *Anna Karenina*' is clearer than 'On holiday, Joyce is going to play Scrabble, read *War and Peace* and *Anna Karenina*'. (That's one hell of a long holiday Joyce is having . . .)

A little mention here about the serial (or Oxford) comma. This is when a comma is used after the penultimate item in the list, before the 'and' or 'or'. It is standard in US punctuation, but in the UK is really only used to avoid confusion. For example: 'The most popular comedians in the 1970s included Les Dawson, Tommy Cooper, the Two Ronnies, and Morecambe and Wise.' Without that final comma, either the Two Ronnies and Morecambe and Wise could be thought a foursome, or Wise a solo act (and that would never have worked). For more on serial commas (and how annoying they can be), see Chapter 5, p.176.

Joining comma – 'makes things flow more smoothly'

This type of comma joins (or 'splices' sometimes in the US) two sentences to make one. For example, while the following is grammatically correct, it's clunky:

> Charlotte loves watching bad talent shows on television.
> Emily does too. Anne watches more than either of them.

To make things more fluid, it would be better to write:

> Charlotte loves watching bad talent shows on television, and
> Emily does too, but Anne watches more than either of them.

Here, the joining commas and words replace the full stops. Other joining words which can be used in this way are 'or', 'so', 'though', 'while' and 'yet'.

> We could try to finish this inedible stew, or we could give
> it to the dog.

> Polly asked us to rewire the house, so we did.

> Andrew lit up another fag, though there was one still burning
> in the ashtray.

> Joshua slept until midday, while his revision lay untouched.

> Johnny worked through the night, yet he was still
> behind with his maths.

In the examples above, if the joining word were omitted, using the comma wouldn't be correct – either make each one two complete sentences using a full stop, or use a semicolon (see below).

Replacing comma – 'makes things less repetitive'

The replacement comma indicates that a word or words have been left out, to avoid repetition. Such as:

> In the playground, Milly wanted to play on the swings, and Billy, the roundabout.

That final comma replaces 'wanted to play on'. (The first comma, by the way, is a separating one, see below, and the second, a joining one, see above – and essential unless Milly is playing on Billy as well as the swings.)

Separating comma – 'makes things simpler to read'

This type of comma indicates that one section of a sentence is separate from another.

> The lift was out of order, so Mary was late for her interview.
>
> To put her at ease, Mary was offered some tea.
>
> As Mary took the cup, she knocked over the milk.
>
> Flustered, she mopped up the milk with her skirt, the only item to hand.

Without the commas, the sense of the sentences isn't as clear.

While some separating commas are essential, others are more a matter of choice. One person might write 'In 1939, Germany invaded Poland', while someone else might write 'In 1939 Germany invaded Poland'. Both are OK.

Bracketing commas – 'makes things less ambiguous'

These types of commas – and there will usually be two (like brackets, hence the name) – are like a little aside in a sentence. Without the aside, the sentence would make perfect sense – it's just giving a bit more info. Bracketing commas are also called a comma sandwich – which is quite a nice image.

> The yogurt, though past its sell by date, tasted fine.

> The cat, at the age of fifteen, developed diabetes.

> Zachary, who should have known better, went too close to the slippery edge of the pond and fell in.

If the phrase between the commas were removed, each of the above would still make sense, and be a complete sentence. This is the hint for remembering bracketing commas: if the removal of the phrase renders the sentence unintelligible, the commas are either in the wrong place, or redundant.

> Paula loved Picasso, and seeing that there was an exhibition of his work at the Pompidou, booked a ticket for Paris.

> Edward was hungry, and spotting a cafe on the corner, ordered the full English.

These commas are in the wrong place, because 'Paula loved Picasso, booked a ticket for Paris' and 'Edward was hungry, ordered the full English' make no sense. But 'Paula loved Picasso and booked a ticket for Paris' and 'Edward was hungry and ordered the full English' would make sense, so in both instances the comma should come after the 'and', not before.

Paula loved Picasso and, seeing that there was an exhibition of his work at the Pompidou, booked a ticket for Paris.

Edward was hungry and, spotting a cafe on the corner, ordered the full English.

The opposite mistake is also common.

Nonetheless, it was thought, irrelevant to bring this up.

This makes no sense with the bracketing commas. Either of the following, however, would make sense:

Nonetheless, it was thought irrelevant to bring this up.

Nonetheless it was thought irrelevant to bring this up.

Note that use of 'however' and its bracketing commas just before the above examples. This is an example of a bracketing word. Other bracketing words include 'meanwhile', 'nevertheless', 'though'.

The clouds were clearing, however, so we risked a country walk.

We took raincoats, though, as the weather could be unpredictable.

These coats were useless, nevertheless, when the downpour came.

The dog, meanwhile, was having a whale of a time.

Again, the sentences make sense with and without the aside.

Another bracketing comma is used when addressing someone.

'I presume the full English is for you, Edward.'

However, the comma isn't needed if Edward isn't being addressed directly.

> 'I presume the full English is for Edward, and the muesli is for you, Miranda.'

Here, Miranda is being addressed (and Edward is being ignored).

Hence the reason why there should be a comma between an interjection, or similar, and a name: 'Hello, Dolly', 'Goodbye, Mr Chips', 'No, no, Nanette', 'Please, sir'.

Another common mistake is confusing a listing comma with a bracketing comma.

> Alice was a keen, though not very good, Scrabble
> player. (✔)

That second comma is often left out, so the sentence would read:

> Alice was a keen, though not very good Scrabble
> player. (✘)

But if 'though not very good' is an aside – which it is – that second comma is essential. 'Alice was a keen not very good Scrabble player' and 'Alice was a though not very good Scrabble player' don't make sense. 'Alice was a keen Scrabble player' does.

Then there are sentences where bracketing commas will change the meaning, and make sense, but not necessarily the sense intended.

> The students who protested about the cuts were expelled.

> The students, who protested about the cuts, were expelled.

In the first example, it was only the protesting students who were expelled – not all the students. In the second, all the students were protesting, so they were all expelled. The commas are needed to show the difference.

> The dresses that were red were too small.

> The dresses, which were red, were too small.

Again, in the first example it's only the red dresses that are too small (the yellow and green ones were a good fit). In the second, all the dresses are too small (and they were all red).

This also illustrates the **restrictive** and **non-restrictive clause**. The restrictive clause is one that 'restricts' the meaning of a sentence, so there are no commas. The non-restrictive clause says something extra about the subject, but isn't necessary, so there *would* be commas. For more on this, see 'That/which' in Chapter 4, p. 169.

Direct-speech comma – 'makes things easier to follow'

Commas are used to introduce and end speech.

> Rowena said, 'This stuff on commas is quite complicated.'

> 'Yes,' Katherine agreed, 'but we'll get there in the end . . .'

More uses for the comma

Commas are used to separate parts of large numbers – like '1,000' or '50,000,000'. However, they are never used in years – it's '1066', not '1,066'.

Here are 10 sentences. Insert commas where appropriate, and for bonus points name the type of comma.

1 Types of commas include listing, joining, replacing, separating, bracketing and direct speech. ✓

2 Penny and Kathy wrote the book, though Sally took the credit. ✓

3 Despite being up against an unseeded competitor, Andy still managed to lose. ✓

4 Everyone in the play, apart from Lady Macbeth, was really good. ✓

5 'I ate too much cake,' she said, 'so I feel a bit sick.' ✗

6 Charlie likes the chocolate ice cream, and Veronica the vanilla. ✗

7 Olivia, in her orange, pink and red outfit, had no taste. ✓

8 The ratings had gone down, so the show was cancelled. ✓

9 Scarlett has an allergy to wheat, nuts, dairy, eggs and shellfish. Or so her mother says. ✗

10 As Tilly turned the corner, she realised she was completely lost. ✓

As indicated, commas are a vital part of punctuation, but occasionally they can be overused. Is a comma necessary after or before such words as 'but', 'of course', 'too', 'then'? Not really, as the following examples show:

> There was no food in the house, of course, so we went out for supper.
> There was no food in the house of course, so we went out for supper.

> We decided to go to the cinema, too.
> We decided to go to the cinema too.

Let's go, then, or we'll be late.
Let's go then, or we'll be late.

But, the film had already started.
But the film had already started.

Which looks better? – the latter example in each pairing, on the whole.

Similarly, it's not always necessary to insert a comma between a noun and its name, as in 'My wife, Peta, took our dog, Rex, for a walk, so I went for a beer with my mate, Paul' – 'My wife Peta took our dog Rex for a walk, so I went for a beer with my mate Paul' is fine (and less fussy).

Another couple of examples of unnecessary commas: after the house or flat number in an address – '165, Eaton Place' rather than '165 Eaton Place' (the former is now considered old-fashioned); between verbs and adverbs – 'she said, cheerfully' rather than 'she said cheerfully'.

Question mark (?)

Like a full stop, a question mark indicates the end of a sentence. It also indicates that the sentence is a direct question (or interrogative sentence). So does it do exactly what it says on the tin? Yes, it does . . .

What time does my train leave?

Will I be over the border by tomorrow night?

Are the canvases well hidden?

How do you think I should plead if they catch me?

A question mark is *not* needed if the sentence is an indirect question.

> He demanded to know what time his train left.

> The art thief asked if the canvases were well hidden.

But a question mark *is* needed if quoting verbatim speech.

> 'What time does my train leave?' he demanded.

> 'Are the canvases well hidden?' asked the art thief.

Aside from its grammatical use the question mark may also be used to show that something is unknown or doubtful, and is often used in brackets (parentheses).

> Ginny and George agreed (foolishly?) to open a restaurant during a recession.

> Frank Franklin (born 1902?) was a well-known forger during the war.

Contrary to what some people might think, a rhetorical question, despite not requiring an answer, *does* require a question mark.

> 'I told you, didn't I?'

> 'How should I bleedin' know?'

> 'How are you?' (Rhetorical because few people *really* want to know.)

> 'Who cares?'

Exclamation mark (!)

An exclamation mark or point, which is sometimes, weirdly, called a shriek, or a bang, is used at the end of a (usually short) sentence to indicate a depth of feeling. If someone were speaking it, the exclamation mark would probably suggest a raised voice.

> Blimey!

> Ow!

> Stop that right now!

Exclamation marks can be quite effective, but should be used sparingly, and just the one, rather than two or more together ('It's meeeeeeeeeeeeeeeeeeeeeeeeeeeee!!!!!!!!!!!!!!!!!!!!!!!!!!!!!!!!!!' is fine only if you're ten or under). As F. Scott Fitzgerald said, 'Cut all these exclamation points. An exclamation point is like laughing at your own joke.'

Colon (:)

The comma, colon and semicolon are all used to break up sentences. It can be tricky to know when to use the appropriate mark, and it's not always definitive – there are times when it's a matter of choice.

The colon nowadays has three main functions:

> to introduce a list – as in the line above

> ✳ to divide two parts of a sentence – the second expanding on the first

> to introduce direct speech – in the same way as a direct-speech
> ✳ comma

A colon shouldn't function as a longer pause than a semicolon, but not quite such a long pause as a full stop. That's a rather old-fashioned guide to commas, semicolons, colons and full stops, and usually used wrongly.

Listing colon

Gary had been practising several things for his driving test: three-point turns, reversing round corners and pulling out sensibly.

Dividing colon

Gary failed his driving test on one thing: his emergency stop.

Direct-speech colon

The examiner said to Gary: 'Cyclists *are* allowed on the road too, you know.'

Should a colon or a comma be used before direct speech? There is not much difference between them, although the former is more emphatic. A colon also tends to be used more commonly in newspapers and journals.

A few other functions for the colons are in ratios (70:30), citing Bible chapters and verses (1:1–5), classes of university degree (2:1), separating a book title and subtitle (*Eats, Shoots and Leaves: A Zero Tolerance Approach to Punctuation*), and to introduce a passage of text or bullet points.

A no-no: don't put a dash or hyphen after a colon, like :-. It's wrong, and somewhat bizarre, considering the function of each one of those marks. Americans often follow a colon with a capital letter (Brits don't on the whole); they also use it to divide hours and minutes.

Put a colon in each of the following sentences.

1 I have two people to thank for this award: Brad and George.

2 There is only one solution to a dull party: alcohol.

3 And Rhett declared: 'Frankly, my dear, I don't give a damn!'

4 The houses at Hogwarts are: Gryffindor, Ravenclaw, Hufflepuff and Slytherin.

5 Here's an idea: let's have lunch.

Semicolon (;)

The correct use of the semicolon seems to confuse people more than any other punctuation mark, so they avoid them. But in fact it's relatively straightforward (compared to the minefield that is commas), and actually rather useful. Its principal use is to link two sentences of equal weight to make one. The semicolon could, in theory, be replaced with a full stop, or with one of those joining commas – so long as the comma is followed by 'and' or 'or', etc.; if it isn't used with one of those words, the comma is being used erroneously.

The thing to remember is that the two parts of a sentence divided by the semicolon must be sentences in themselves. So:

Matthew was a good tennis player; Mark practised more, though, so Matthew was usually beaten.

Luke liked watching tennis on TV; John couldn't see the point.

In both of the above examples, the semicolon could be replaced with a full stop or with ', but' – that joining comma.

> Matthew was a good tennis player. Mark practised more, though, so Matthew was usually beaten.

> Luke liked watching tennis on TV, but John couldn't see the point.

There are some joining words that *do* need a semicolon rather than a comma – words like 'however', 'meanwhile', 'nevertheless', 'nonetheless' – because they are linked to the second part of the sentence only, not the first.

> Holly loved cheese; however, she was lactose-intolerant.

> Polly, however, was allergic to nuts.

In the second example, 'however' is dividing the two parts of the sentence; in the first example, it isn't – the semicolon is the divider. Change the semicolon to a comma and the sense becomes unclear.

Semicolons are used if a sentence already contains a few commas, and the sense, again, is confusing if more commas are added to the mix.

> I have so many people to thank for making this book what it is – my publisher, Joe Bloggs, my editor, Jim Bloggs, my wonderful friends, Martin, Julian, Ian, Salman and Howard, my husband, Bill, my ex-husband, Ben, my ex-wife, Briony . . .

A bit of a muddle, really. So:

> I have so many people to thank for making this book what it is – my publisher, Joe Bloggs; my editor, Jim Bloggs; my wonderful friends, Martin, Julian, Ian, Salman and Howard; my husband, Bill; my ex-husband, Ben; my ex-wife, Briony . . .

Now we know for sure what the role of each of these people was on the author's journey to publication.

Semicolons are often used in a list following a colon – particularly, yet again, if they avoid ambiguity. However, some people make the mistake of thinking any list introduced by a colon must be divided by semicolons (indeed, some people think that's the semicolon's *only* use).

> These are the men I must thank: Joe; Jim; Martin; Julian; Ian; Salman; Howard; Bill; and Ben.

This is wrong (and pretty irritating). There is no possibility of confusion, and they are all related to the thank-you, so the right marks to use would be commas.

> These are the men I must thank: Joe, Jim, Martin, Julian, Ian, Salman, Howard, Bill and Ben.

Replace some of the commas with semicolons in the following sentences.

✗ 1 Books by Ian McEwan include *First Love, Last Rites*; *On Chesil Beach*; *Atonement*; *Solar*.

✓ 2 The lovers go upstage behind the tree; meanwhile, the jealous husband enters downstage left, with a gun . . .

✓ 3 Sarah was an *Archers* addict; Lionel, however, would turn the radio off at the first note of the theme tune.

✗ 4 The cast includes Romeo, Leonardo DiCaprio; Juliet, Claire Danes; the Nurse, Miriam Margolyes; and Friar Laurence, Pete Postlethwaite.

✓ 5 The spaghetti western trilogy consists of *A Fistful of Dollars*; *For a Few Dollars More*; *The Good, the Bad and the Ugly*.

Apostrophe (')

So much has been written and debated about the apostrophe, and yet it is still worth repeating as nothing will scream 'illiterate' to a reader more than a misplaced, misused, missed-out humble apostrophe.

The two main uses of apostrophes are in **contractions** and **possessives**.

Contractions

These types of apostrophe are the easiest to learn, and are a reflection of spoken English. In speech we elide two or more words to make one shorter one. When writing them down the apostrophe is there just to show there are missing letters (and is placed exactly where the missing letters occur).

> cannot > can't
> could have > could've
> it is/it has > it's
> she would/she had > she'd
> should have > should've
> was not > wasn't
> we shall/we will > we'll
> will not > won't
> would not > wouldn't

Not using an apostrophe in such words might make a phrase meaningless – 'she'd' would be 'shed', 'can't' would be 'cant', which are both perfectly acceptable words but nonsense in the context.

There are some contraction apostrophes which have become the standard form of a word and the full versions are never used, such as:

fo'c's'le – forecastle
o'clock – of the clock
sou'wester – southwester

Then there are words which used to have a contraction apostrophe,
to indicate a missing part of the word, but the abbreviated form
is so common that to use an apostrophe just looks odd (or like an
affectation), such as:

'flu – influenza
'phone – telephone
'bus – omnibus
'bye – goodbye

Another common contraction is 'n', as in:

rock 'n' roll
pick 'n' mix
stitch 'n' bitch
surf 'n' turf

Both of these are apostrophes – *not* quote marks – they are
replacing *a* and *d*, not highlighting *n* – so 'n', not 'n'.

One more use for the contraction apostrophe is in dates – the
class of '66 (for 1966). An apostrophe isn't necessary in '1960s
and '70s'; it's better to write '1960s and 70s' or '1960s and 1970s'.
Likewise, an apostrophe with 'seventies is redundant (and horrid),
though not technically wrong. However, using an apostrophe
with 'seventy's' or '1970's' would be nonsensical (unless that
particular year is possessing something – see immediately below).

Possessives

These apostrophes show when something belongs to something, someone or some people, and these are the apostrophes which cause most of the problems. But they really shouldn't, because the rule isn't actually that difficult or complicated.

In the singular form, instead of 'the computer belonging to Simon', which is rather long-winded, simply say 'Simon's computer'.

The plural form has the apostrophe *after* the 's', to show that it is plural. Instead of saying 'the car which belongs to the boys', say 'the boys' car'. However, the apostrophe goes *before* the 's' with nouns whose plurals don't end with 's', because 'men' is already the plural of 'man' – so, 'the men's car', not 'the mens' car'.

Put the apostrophe in the correct place in the following.

√ **1** the girl's dress   √ **6** wits' end

√ **2** the dog's bollocks   √ **7** donkeys' years

√ **3** Vicky's violin   √ **8** Women's Institute

✗ **4** the children's party   √ **9** season's greeting

√ **5** the cat's whiskers   √ **10** Mother's Day

(Handy hint: would you say 'compliments of the seasons' or 'I'm at the end of my wit'? Hopefully not . . .)

There can be a problem with names ending in 's', but write it as it's pronounced, so: 'Morris's wallpaper', 'Iris's house', 'Dickens's book', '*The Times*'s conservative leaning'. However, because this is a modern practice, and it was formerly customary to leave off that extra 's', classical and historical names still omit them on the whole. So: 'Aeschylus' plays', 'Oedipus' mother', 'Moses' toes', 'Jesus' sandals'.

If there is shared ownership, or similar, the possessive is attached only to the last person in the list, such as: 'His aunt, uncle and cousin's house' (they share one house); 'Rick and Roland's civil partnership' (they are joined in one civil partnership). However, if there is separate ownership, or similar, the possessive is attached to each person in the list, such as: 'His aunt's, uncle's and cousin's houses' (they live in separate houses – perhaps the aunt and uncle finally got divorced when the cousin left home); 'Rick's and Roland's parents met for the first time at the reception' (they each have a set of parents).

Never put possessive apostrophes in pronouns, because they already denote possession – 'which is hers?' (*not* her's), 'this is ours' (*not* our's), 'that's yours' (*not* your's) 'whose house is this?' (*not* who's). Which is why there is no apostrophe in the possessive 'its' – 'the canary left its cage'. An apostrophe is only in 'it's' when it is a contraction of 'it is'. This is a rule which seems to flummox many people. Try saying 'the canary has left it is cage'. Nuff said.

> Nouns which you think would have apostrophes but don't:
>
> Achilles heel, Hundred Years War, Thirty Years War, Earls Court, Queens (NY), All Souls College, Goldsmiths College, Johns Hopkins University, *Howards End*, *Finnegans Wake*, St Albans, St Andrews, St Stephens (House of Commons), Prince of Wales Island.
>
> Many well-known institutions probably had apostrophes originally, as they were derived from the founder – Butlin's, Harrod's, Selfridge's, Woolworth's – but now either they don't have an apostrophe or they don't exist. Waterstones is a more recent example, although maybe it's Waterstone's again if they've had a rethink by the time this is published.

Quotation marks (' ' or " ")

Quotation marks (or inverted commas, or quote marks, or speech marks) are punctuation marks used to highlight a word or words in the text. Primarily, they indicate quotations (hence 'quotation marks') and direct speech (hence 'speech marks').

There are two types of quotation marks: 'single' and "double". In the UK, on the whole, single quotation marks are used, although double quotation marks are frequently used in newspapers, journals and children's books. In the US, however, double quotation marks are used.

(Bear in mind that as well as preferring the double type, US punctuation with quotation marks is not the same as UK punctuation. See Chapter 5 for the differences between the two.)

So, that's what the marks indicate; now comes the thorny issue of where to put the full stops, commas and any other punctuation with the quotation marks.

Direct speech

In simple direct speech, the punctuation marks come before the closing (') quotation mark. Here are some variations on a theme:

'If I have to read any more of this bilge, I'll weep,' said Rose.

Rose said, 'If I have to read any more of this bilge, I'll weep.'

'If I have to read any more of this bilge,' said Rose, 'I'll weep.'

All quite straightforward. Now:

The editor said in the meeting that 'the author is refusing to rewrite the ending'.

The editor said in the meeting, 'The author is refusing to rewrite the ending.'

Why does the first example's final punctuation point come outside the closing quote mark, but the second example's inside? Because in the first there is no punctuation mark – such as a comma or colon – before the opening quote mark, and the first word of the quote is lower case. In the second, there is a comma before the opening quote mark and the quote starts with a capital letter. What if there is no punctuation mark before the opening quote mark, but the first word in the quote is upper case? Well, some people would put the final punctuation mark inside the closing quote mark, but our preference is still for it to go outside the quote mark.

> The editor said in the meeting that 'Julia is refusing to rewrite the ending'. (✔)

> The editor said in the meeting that 'Julia is refusing to rewrite the ending.' (✘)

Yet there are occasions when the final punctuation mark would go before the closing quote mark even without punctuation before the opening quote mark, and that is when the quote ends with a question mark, exclamation mark, ellipsis or dash. Yet if the question mark is not part of the quote, it would go after the closing quote mark.

> Despite the ridiculous plot, the editor told the author that it was 'marvellous, but would it be all right to perhaps tweak the ending a tiny bit?'

> Did the author really say 'I'm not doing any rewrites'?

These make sense (really, they do). However, there is one time when standard practice rather than sense takes precedence.

> 'The author,' the editor said in the meeting, 'is refusing to do any rewrites.' (✔)

'The author', the editor said in the meeting, 'is refusing to do any rewrites.' (✘)

The reasoning behind the second example is that the quoted material does not include a comma after 'author' – the speech is 'The author is refusing to do any rewrites', *not* 'The author, is refusing to do any rewrites'. *But* the standard rule nowadays for this type of quote is always to follow the first example. Some people have a hissy fit about this – and it's understandable – but for conventional, aesthetical, stylistic reasons, that's the rule now.

If the quote has no punctuation mark before its opening and starts with a lower-case word, but there is another full sentence in the quote, the closing quote mark comes after the final punctuation mark.

> The editor said in the meeting that 'the author is refusing to do any rewrites. However, I've threatened to publish the manuscript with all her mistakes and ridiculous plot holes, so let's hope she's having a rethink.'

If one person is speaking more than one paragraph, a closing quote mark is used only at the end of the final paragraph, whereas there should be an opening quote mark for each one.

> 'Well,' said the chairman, 'I think we can all agree that was a fascinating discussion on pensions, so we'll conclude the meeting.
>
> 'It just remains for me to say a big thank-you to Kiki for providing our delicious refreshments.
>
> 'And one more thing, don't forget the next meeting is at Hector's on 5 November.'

Reported speech does not have quote marks.

> The editor said, 'The author is refusing to do any rewrites.'

> The editor said that the author was refusing to do any rewrites.

> Clare said, 'The book is really boring and the ending's predictable.'

> Clare said that the book was really boring and the ending was predictable.

Note the difference: no quote marks for the second example of each and the whole sentence is in the past tense.

Here is an either/or. In the following example, some people wouldn't put a comma before the closing-quote mark, but some would.

> 'Well, I'm disappointed' was what Rose said after her meeting with the author.

> 'Well, I'm disappointed,' was what Rose said after her meeting with the author.

We think the comma is unnecessary because the quote is part of the whole sentence, while retaining the comma suggests something is missing from the quote, but both are OK.

Quotations

The rules applying to direct speech also apply to quotations. So, when quoting a piece of text, be aware of the original punctuation. If the quote includes the punctuation, it should come inside the quote marks; if it doesn't, put it outside.

Michael was learning the speech that begins 'All the world's a stage'.

But:

If Michael learns a bit more than the opening line, he might say 'All's the world's a stage, / And all the men and women merely players: / They have their exits and their entrances; / And one man in his time plays many parts, / His acts being seven ages.'

See the difference? The reason the full stop is before the closing quote mark for the latter is because it is part of the original quotation. In the former, the line ends in a comma, so the full stop goes after the closing quote mark.

With a longer passage of quoted material, it is better to 'display', or indent, without quote marks. So:

Michael had learned the whole of Jaques' speech, the first few lines of which are:

All's the world's a stage,
And all the men and women merely players:
They have their exits and their entrances;
And one man in his time plays many parts,
His acts being seven ages. At first the infant,
Mewling and puking in the nurse's arms.
And then the whining schoolboy, with his satchel,
And shining morning face, creeping like snail
Unwillingly to school.

Irony

Ironic or 'finger' quotes marks are used to suggest scepticism, cynicism, distance or 'don't blame me'.

Fiona claimed she was 'exhausted', but since she'd been watching telly all day, this seemed highly improbable.

If Cora is the 'talented' one in the family, God help the rest of them.

Cherry sold the product on its 'health-giving' properties.

The president 'regretted' the loss of life.

Titles

To highlight titles of books, films, newspapers, etc., they are usually put in italics or in quotation marks. Italics are standard practice for print, but when writing by hand the latter are used (or caps, or underlining) since italics can't really be written. Informally, on the computer, all are fine – although don't overdo the caps, BECAUSE IT CAN LOOK AS IF THE RECIPIENT IS BEING SHOUTED AT.

As well as for books, films and newspapers, in print italics are used for the titles of albums, computer games, long poems, magazines, operas, orchestral works, paintings, plays, sculptures, ships, radio and TV programmes. Quote marks, however, are used for the titles of articles, essays, individual episodes of a radio or TV programme, short poems, reports, short stories and songs. For example:

Robin Robertson's book of collected poems, *The Wrecking Light*, includes the poems 'Law of the Island' and 'Hammersmith Winter'.

Julian Barnes's short-story collection, *Pulse*, begins with 'East Wind' and ends with 'Pulse'.

The album *Aerial* by Kate Bush features the single 'King of the Mountain'.

Quotes within quotes

If there is a quote within a quote, or a speech within a speech, use double quotation marks within the usual single quotation marks.

'He said to me, "Will you buy me the album for my birthday?" So I did.'

'My favourite song on that album is "Picture This".'

If there is a quote within a quote within a quote, use single quotes within double within single –

'He said to me, "And what are you going to sing for the audition?" I said, "I'm going to sing 'Somewhere Over the Rainbow' from *The Wizard of Oz*." "Well, that's original," muttered the pianist.'

– but hopefully there won't be very often . . .

Put quotation marks in the following sentences.

1   The disc she decided she would run to save from the sea was I Will Survive.

2   Babs said, There's a short-story competition in the *Guardian*. I think I might enter Dolly in Denial.

3   I'll have to resend the document, as Fred claimed he never received my email with the info.

4   Shouldn't it be for whom the bell tolls, not for who the bell tolls?

5   It could be argued that there is just too much to take in on quote marks. However, it will sink in eventually.

6   I don't think I can make it in to work today, Colin croaked, I've got really bad flu.

7 Colin had really bad flu, though actually it was a bit of a sore throat.

8 This is perhaps the most famous opening line of a Shakespeare play: Now is the winter of our discontent.

9 William said, Let's call it a day.

10 Do you think you could stop playing with your mobile phone? We're trying to watch the play, Wendy whispered to the boy next to her. She was told to eff off.

Brackets / Parentheses (( ) [ ])

Brackets, or parentheses, are always used in pairs and contain an aside which adds extra information or explains something in the sentence in which they are used. There are two types: round and square.

Round brackets (parentheses)

Round brackets have a similar function to bracketing commas and dashes (see above and below), but brackets are generally less ambiguous and can withstand stronger interruptions. So:

> Charles (also known as Chas) first came to work here in November last year.

> The World Cup attracted a large television audience (2 billion worldwide).

> The French word *'oui'* (pronounced 'wee') means 'yes'.

If the sentence is grammatically correct it will make sense without the bracketed interruption, which is a good way of testing to see whether the use of brackets is right or wrong.

Charles first came to work here in November last year.

The World Cup attracted a large television audience.

The French word *'oui'* means 'yes'.

As with a few of the punctuation marks described in these pages, use brackets sparingly because overuse quickly becomes irritating for the reader.

Square brackets

Square brackets are used to show an interruption by the author to point out a mistake which is not his, or to supply missing information, and they are almost always used in quoted passages.

'He learnt me [*sic*] how to speak,' said Dorothy.

In this quotation, *'sic'* (meaning 'thus, so') has been inserted in square brackets to indicate that this is what Dorothy actually said, even though it is grammatically wrong.

'They [Mary and Joseph] were fed up with the estate agent.'

In this quotation, the bracketed information is supplied to avoid confusion over who 'they' might be.

Brackets and punctuation

Unless the bracketed text is a complete sentence, punctuation – if there is any – always comes after the closing bracket, not before.

E. M. Forster (full name Edward Morgan Forster) wrote six novels.

E. M. Forster wrote six novels (though one was published posthumously). His best known is probably *A Passage to India*.

E. M. Forster wrote six novels. (*Maurice* was published posthumously.)

Hyphen (-)

Much has been written about the hyphen – there seem to be as many 'rules' as there are grammar books. And in the end much of it boils down to personal preference and a war of the dictionaries. Here are the bare bones.

A hyphen is used to link two or more words together to make a new word – a **compound word** – or to split long words if they run over at the end of a line of text. Hyphens are attached to the words they are joining – i.e. there are no spaces before or after them (except in one special case, explained below). And it's already been mentioned, but there's no harm in reiterating it: a hyphen never immediately follows a colon.

Compound nouns

Whether or not this new word is hyphenated depends on a number of things, much of it to do with changing fashion (and geography, e.g. America, see Chapter 5). While compound nouns were on the whole hyphenated in the past, the practice nowadays is often to have either two words or one – such as 'letter box' or 'letterbox', 'tail light' or 'taillight', 'river bank' or 'riverbank', 'cell phone' or 'cellphone'. Some people might write 'letter-box' or 'tail-light', 'river-bank' or 'cell-phone', and it wouldn't be wrong, just a bit old-fashioned, and therefore rather odd with a word like 'cellphone'. So there's no hard-and-fast rule, but whatever style is selected for a particular piece of writing, keep it consistent. If 'cellphone' is chosen, for instance, stick to it – don't write 'He threw her cellphone in the swimming pool. She was furious – her world didn't exist beyond that cell phone. Then he realised it was his cell-phone.'

Compound verbs

Generally, a hyphen should be used when joining **nouns** of two or more words together to form a **verb**. So 'a test drive' becomes 'to test-drive', 'the fox hunt' becomes 'to fox-hunt', 'a tap dance' > 'to tap-dance', 'a machine gun' > 'to machine-gun', 'a tightrope walk' > 'to tightrope-walk', 'the speed date' > 'to speed-date', etc., etc.

With verbs that are made up of two words, one of which is a preposition (also known as phrasal verbs), hyphens are not needed in the basic verb – such as 'to break up', 'to comb over', 'to take off' – but are needed if those verbs are made into nouns. So: 'The break-up came as a shock to him', 'Before shaven heads became fashionable balding men had to make do with a comb-over' and 'The take-off was traumatic for Trevor – which was a calamity for the crew as he was the captain'.

Compound adjectives

Compound adjectives are made up of a **noun** and an **adjective** – 'world-famous', 'fat-free', 'age-related', 'knee-deep', 'sky-high'; a **noun** and the past or present participle of a **verb** – 'tongue-tied', 'arse-licking', time-wasting', 'home-made', 'asset-stripping'; or an **adjective** and the past or present participle of a **verb** – 'good-looking', 'hard-working', 'deep-fried', 'cold-blooded', 'hot-tempered'.

Compound adverbs

Compound adverbs are generally not hyphenated – 'the brightly coloured dress', 'the dimly lit room'. The exceptions are adverbs like 'well' and 'half', but *only* if the compound word *precedes* the noun; if it *follows* the noun, it shouldn't be hyphenated.

the half-finished chapter *but* the chapter was half finished

the well-known actor *but* the actor is well known

Compound modifiers

These use hyphens, or not, to avoid ambiguity – because they modify (change) the sense. Take the sentence:

Myra was a short story writer.

Does this mean a) Myra was a short woman who wrote stories, or b) Myra was a writer of short stories? The hyphen will tell you: a) Myra was a short story writer, and b) Myra was a short-story writer. (Though she could, of course, have been a short, short-story writer . . .) There's a similar ambiguity in this sentence:

Thirty odd people attended the meeting.

Does this mean a) there were roughly thirty people at the meeting, or b) the thirty people were a bit strange? Again, the hyphen will avoid confusion. So: a) Thirty-odd people attended the meeting, and b) Thirty odd people attended the meeting.

Hyphens with prefixes

If a prefix (like 'mini', 'post', 'pre', 're', 'sub', etc.) is attached to a word a hyphen is often not needed – 'minibar', 'postmodern', 'prefix', 'rearrange', 'subplot' – unless the prefix ends in an 'e' and the word attached begins with an 'e' – such as 'pre-exist' and 're-edit'. However, as always, there are exceptions – such as 'mini-break', 'post-mortem', 'pre-shrunk', 're-release', 'sub-zero'.

The prefix 're' should also have a hyphen following it if the meaning would otherwise be ambiguous, so we have 're-present', meaning to present again, and 'represent', meaning to depict or act for. Other such words are: 're-form' (form again), 'reform' (correct or improve); 're-mark' (mark again), 'remark' (comment); 're-sort' (sort again), 'resort' (holiday place, recourse); 're-sign' (sign again), 'resign' (quit).

The prefix 'ex' – e.g. 'ex-husband' – should always have a hyphen, as should words with the prefix 'self' – e.g. 'self-expression' (except for 'selfless' and 'selfish').

Prefixes joined to proper nouns need a hyphen – 'un-British', 'pre-Norman', 'post-World War II'. Otherwise, 'un' doesn't need to be followed by a hyphen, even when the following word begins with 'n', as in 'unnamed', 'unnerving' and 'unnatural'.

Hyphens in numbers, ages and dates

All compound-word numbers need hyphens – 'twenty-one', 'forty-four', 'sixty-two', etc.

Hyphens should be used with ages and numbers expressed as adjectives, so 'Rachel's dog is three years old' becomes 'Rachel has a three-year-old dog'. This is important for clarity; '150-year-old tortoises' does not mean the same as '150 year-old tortoises', that is to say several tortoises which are 150 years old and 150 tortoises only a year old. Likewise, a twentieth-anniversary present means something different from a twentieth anniversary present. The first means Bill got one present for his twentieth anniversary, the second means Bill got twenty presents for an unspecified anniversary (lucky ol' Bill).

Hyphens in double-barrelled names

The use (or not) of a hyphen is entirely down to the owner (or giver) of the name. So we have Sarah Jessica Parker, but Mary-Louise Parker; Rowena Skelton-Wallace, but Helena Bonham Carter. Even within one family, it might be inconsistent – hence Cecil Day Lewis, but his son Daniel Day-Lewis. (Go figure . . .)

Hyphens and part-words

If a word has a prefix which isn't a 'word' in its own right, a hyphen is needed – so 'Anglo-American' and 'Afro-Caribbean', but 'African American' and 'French Canadian' ('Anglo' and 'Afro' are prefixes, 'African' and 'French' are not). If listing words with a repeated element, use a hyphen with a space following it (the special case!), so 'pre-production and post-production' becomes 'pre- and post-production' which is less pedestrian.

> The film had extremely long pre- and post-production times,
> so the budget increase was more dramatic than the film (which
> was really dull).

Similarly, rather than writing 'himself and herself', another option is to go for 'him- and herself' – the hyphen showing that the 'him' is incomplete – or 'him and herself' – the argument here being that 'himself' has no hyphen in the whole word. Both, however, are acceptable, and a matter of personal choice. (One of us, for example, prefers the former; the other prefers the latter.)

Hyphens and splitting words

As printed text is mostly justified left and right into a block of text (for example, in a newspaper, magazine or book – though not this one), it is sometimes necessary to break long words over two lines to make the best use of the space. Try to break words at obvious points, such as at a syllable end or after one part of a compound word, and try to keep the sound of the fragment the same as for the full word, so the word isn't misread before you discover on the next line what it really is. A few examples: 'sheath-ed', not 'sheat-hed'; 're-address', not 'read-dress'; 'thera-pist', not 'the-rapist'; 'earn-est', not 'ear-nest'.

> Compound adjectives which you might think would have hyphens but don't:
>
> air traffic control, car boot sale, New Age traveller, old boy network, old wives' tale, port wine stain, Six Day War, South East Asia, Twentieth Century Fox (though it's Twentieth Century–Fox in the US), wild goose chase.

Insert hyphens, if necessary, in the following sentences.

1 The examples given in the grammar book were rather ✓ old-fashioned.

2 The gauge's pointer showed the racing driver had to leave the ✓ track for a fill-up.

3 Dave's dog trampled all over Dolly's dahlias in the flower-bed. ✗ flower bed

4 For an optimist the glass is always half-full. ✗ *(handwritten)* half full

5 Captain Bligh was a tall-ships' captain. ✓

6 The pre-Roman artefacts went unnoticed by the kids in the museum owned by my ex-husband, because they were really ✓ boring.

7 The war lasted for six days, so it became known as the Six Day War.

8 The TV series *Upstairs Downstairs* depicts above-and below-stairs life in one house in Edwardian England.

9 The badly organised event was a cock-up from the outset.

10 The waiter had to reserve the potatoes because the first batch was stone-cold.

Dash (–)

A dash – or en dash, or en rule (so called because it is the width of a typeset capital 'N') – is twice the length of a hyphen, but their uses have no connection. In fact, the dash has a similar function to the comma, colon and semicolon, though possibly a more informal – and emphatic – one.

Bracketing dash

This works in the same way as brackets and bracketing commas, i.e. there should be two. Also like brackets and bracketing commas, make sure the sentence still works without the text between the dashes. If it doesn't, the dashes aren't being used correctly.

> She really hated listening to her daughter practising the violin – and with good reason – as the child was tone-deaf.

Expanding dash

This is, funnily enough, an expansion of what has come before.

> Let's change to a different Internet service provider, Gwen – ours is hopeless.

Interrupting dash

This is generally only used to indicate cut-off speech.

> There was silence in the auditorium as the envelope was opened.
> 'And the winner is –' began the presenter.
> But before he could finish, Gwyneth was up on her feet and weeping with joy.
> '– er, Angelina,' he finished.

Replacing dash

This type of dash has no space either side, unlike the first three. This is because it is replacing the word 'and' or 'to' – such as 'French–Swiss border', 'Iran–Iraq War', 'A–Z', '2011–12'.

Em dash

Occasionally, an 'em' dash (the width of a typeset capital 'M') is used instead of an 'en' dash. In the UK, it might be used for interruption instead of the more usual en, particularly if it is interrupting a word – 'Don't eat those mushrooms, they're pois—'. They might also appear in those more discreet classics, such as 'Lord L— from the county of F— leered lasciviously at young Fanny on the milking stool', either to tease or to avoid libel.

In the US, however, the em dash is used instead of the en – see Chapter 5, p. 178.

Ellipsis (...)

The ellipsis (plural 'ellipses') is shown by three dots with spaces in between, like . . . this. (The only time there isn't a final space is when the ellipsis comes before a closing quote mark – then the quote mark comes directly after dot 3, 'like . . .' this, 'not . . . ' this.) It has two functions.

1 It may be used to replace omitted material if a passage of text is being quoted but the omission is irrelevant to the main point – the written equivalent of 'blah blah blah' perhaps. So, those first three verses of the Bible:

> In the beginning God created the heaven and the earth . . .
> And God said, Let there be light: and there was light.

Rather than writing the verses in full, the ellipsis has replaced 'And the earth was without form, and void; and darkness was upon the face of the deep. And the Spirit of God moved upon the face of the waters.'

Sometimes square brackets are inserted around the ellipses (particularly in academic books) to show that the ellipsis is not part of the text, though this isn't usually necessary. However, if a word needs to be added for the sense of the passage to be conveyed, but it's not part of the original, square brackets around that word should be used.

> Gentleness, docility, and a spaniel-like affection are, on this ground, confidently recommended as the cardinal virtues of the sex . . . She [woman] was created to be the toy of man, his rattle, and it must jingle in his ears whenever, dismissing reason, he chooses to be amused.
>
> Mary Wollstonecraft, *A Vindication of the Rights of Woman*

Because we are missing the text that came before this passage where 'woman' was mentioned, we need it here to know who 'She' is.

2 The other function of an ellipsis is to indicate an unfinished sentence – a fade-out, though, rather than an abrupt cut-off when a dash would be more appropriate.

> Ooh, I don't really know if I should tell you this . . .

It can be used in a similar way to the exclamation mark – though it's rather more subtle, avoiding the 'Hey! I'm making a funny comment!' when it's blindingly obvious.

Note that an ellipsis consists of only three dots. Don't get carried away and put in any more. (But see Chapter 5, p. 181, for the American variation.)

Solidus (/)

The solidus (plural 'solidi') – also known as the oblique, stroke or slash (the latter two commonly used in speech for giving websites or email addresses) – has several functions.

1 To divide alternatives, such as:

> Each competitor will be drug-tested after the race, and he/she must provide his/her own sample and not someone else's.

> The successful candidate will have good A-level grades and/or a parent able to pull a few strings.

2 To indicate a period of time, such as:

> The Metropolitan Opera House has announced its 2012/13 season.

> February/March is the best time to see the daffodils.

3 In abbreviations, such as:

> a/c (air conditioning), c/o (care of), c/s (cycles per second), n/a (not applicable), w/e (weekend), w/o (without)

And date abbreviations, such as:

1/1/12 (1 January 2012), 25/12 (Christmas Day)

4 In fractions, such as:

½, ¼, ¾ (and so on . . .)

5 To indicate a new line if quoting a passage of poetry, such as:

> To be, or not to be; that is the question: / Whether 'tis nobler
> in the mind to suffer / The slings and arrows of outrageous
> fortune, / Or to take arms against a sea of troubles, / And by
> opposing end them?

In this last example, each solidus has a space either side – if the letters and punctuation are 'closed up', it can look a little crowded.

So that's the essence of British punctuation. More to come in the American chapter.

Here are unpunctuated extracts from three published novels. Insert punctuation and capital letters as appropriate. (See if your choices match the authors' . . .)

george has just gulped nearly a quarter of his scotch to drown out
a spasm which started when he talked about jim and the animals now
he feels the alcohol coming back on him with a rush it is exhilarating
but it is coming much too fast
    you dont realise how many kids my age just dream about the kind
of setup youve got here i mean what more can you want i mean you dont
have to take orders from anybody you can do any crazy thing that comes
into your head
    and thats your idea of the perfect life
    sure it is

honestly

whats the matter sir dont you believe me

what i dont quite understand is if youre so keen on living alone how does lois fit in

lois whats she got to do with it

now look kenny i dont mean to be nosey but rightly or wrongly I got the idea that you and she might be well, considering

getting married no thats out

oh

she says she wont marry a caucasian she says she cant take people in this country seriously she doesnt feel anything we do here *means* anything she wants to go back to Japan and teach

A Single Man, Christopher Isherwood

i was staring at the ends of her hair against the rock an inch or two from my eyes and trying to bring myself to the point of confession but it seemed like treading on a flower because one cant be bothered to step aside i pushed up but she held me by the shoulders so that i had to stare down at her i sustained her look its honesty for a moment then I turned and sat with my back to her

whats wrong

nothing i just wondered what malicious god made a nice kid like you see anything in a shit like me

that reminds me a crossword clue I saw it months ago ready i nodded shes all mixed up but the better part of nicholas six letters

i worked it out smiled at her did the clue end in a fullstop or a questionmark

it ended in my crying as usual

and the bird above us sang in the silence

The Magus, John Fowles

gerber whistles lotta stuff in here *drug use cache of semi automatic*
weapons inappropriate behaviour with children

see thats what im thinking if we

not much for us here really though gerry on the gun stuff a dozen
or so semiautomatic pistols an assault weapon or two some hunting rifles
christ half the basements and rec rooms in texas are better armed than
that the guys hardly fucking rambo

yeah but theyre not his its unlawful possession

technically yeah but

i know what youre saying boss but listen the fbi have been keeping
a loose eye on this guy hes made a bunch of public pronouncements in
favour of legalising marijuana talked openly about using it and if you
look here on the aerial shots cauldwell leaned across the table and pointed
with his pen theyve indicated what might be a possible marijuana patch
now none of this interests the feds too much but they do want to take a
look at the childabuse claims so i was thinking

a multiagency effort

you got it

The Second Coming, John Niven

And just to ram home the point once again:

> An English lecturer wrote the words 'A woman without her
> man is nothing' on the blackboard and asked the students to
> punctuate it correctly.

> All the men in the class wrote: 'A woman, without her man,
>   is nothing.'

> All the women in the class wrote: 'A woman: without her,
>   man is nothing.'

. . . which is why punctuation is important.

3 | Spelling

I have a spelling chequer
It came with my pee see
It plainly marks four my revue
Miss takes I cannot sea
I've run this poem threw it
I'm shore your pleased two no
Its letter perfect in it's weigh
My chequer tolled me sew.

Anon.

There are some people who don't think we should get too hung
up about correct spelling, just as they don't think we should get
too hung up about correct punctuation. But as shown in the
previous chapter, correct punctuation avoids confusion, ambiguity,
misunderstanding, bewilderment, etc., etc. Exactly the same applies
to spelling. If the wrong spelling of a word is used, not only does
the writer appear illiterate, but the reader's flow is broken, as he/
she tries to work out just exactly what the sense is.

This chapter highlights homonyms – words spelt (or spelled)
differently but pronounced the same and words spelt the same
way but with different pronunciations – common confusions,
common misspellings, preferred spellings and pronunciation.

The following emails show why correct spelling is a good idea.

> Hi A
>
> Just to let you know I've booked you an isle seat for the play
> as I know you're claustrophobic.
>
> B x

Now A may be slightly claustrophobic, but would nevertheless still like to be in the theatre, not on her own island watching the play via satellite. What B meant was, of course, an *aisle* seat – 'aisle' meaning gangway, not 'isle' meaning island.

> Hi Gran
>
> I won a meddle at sports day today!!!
>
> ☺ xxx

Well, it's lucky the boy's good at something, because he certainly wouldn't win one for his spelling.

> After the ceremony, refreshments will be served in the marquis.

A marquee would probably be more useful than a French nobleman.

Words spelt differently but pronounced the same way

Here is a pretty comprehensive list of words that sound the same (or as near as dammit) but are spelt differently and have different meanings.

> **adapter** (person) / **adaptor** (device)
> **aid** (help) / **aide** (helper)
> **ail** (ill) / **ale** (beer)
> **air** (gas, song) / **ere** (before) / **heir** (successor)

aisle (gangway) / **isle** (island)
allowed (permitted) / **aloud** (audibly)
alms (charity) / **arms** (limbs, weapons)
altar (church table) / **alter** (change)
ante (before) / **anti** (against)
arc (curve) / **ark** (boat, chest)
ascent (going up) / **assent** (agree)
auger (tool) / **augur** (fortune-teller)
aural (relating to ear) / **oral** (relating to mouth)
away (distance) / (anchors) **aweigh**
awe (wonder) / **oar** (paddle) / **or** (alternative) / **ore** (mineral)
aye (yes) / **eye** (used for seeing) / **I** (pronoun)

bail (scoop water, surety) / **bale** (bundle)
ball (posh dance, spherical object) / **bawl** (cry)
balmy (soothing) / **barmy** (bonkers)
bare (naked) / **bear** (animal, carry)
barren (bleak, devoid) / **baron** (title)
base (foundation) / **bass** (low pitch)
bask (chill out) / **basque** (corset)
be (verb) / **bee** (buzzing insect)
beach (sand) / **beech** (tree)
beat (hit) / **beet** (vegetable)
beau (male lover) / **bow** (knot, used with arrows and
    stringed instruments)
beer (drink) / **bier** (coffin support)
berth (bed for person and ship) / **birth** (born)
bevvy (drink) / **bevy** (flock)
bight (inlet) / **bite** (tear with teeth) / **byte** (computer unit)
blew (past tense of blow) / **blue** (colour)
bloc (political alliance) / **block** (solid mass, restrict)
boar (animal) / **bore** (make hole, past tense of bear, tedious
    person or thing)

board (plank) / **bored** (uninterested, restless)
boarder (lodger, not a day pupil) / **border** (edge)
bole (tree trunk) / **bowl** (utensil)
boos (catcalls) / **booze** (alcohol)
bootee (little boots) / **booty** (bottom, stolen goods)
born (product of birth) / **borne** (past participle of bear)
bough (branch) / **bow** (bend, front of ship)
boy (male youth) / **buoy** (float)
brake (slow down) / **break** (pause, change, smash)
breach (break) / **breech** (part of gun, trouser, tricky birth)
bread (food) / **bred** (past tense of breed)
broach (bring up) / **brooch** (ornamental clasp)
brows (eyebrows, summits) / **browse** (look)
bruit (rumour) / **brut** (very dry sparkling wine) / **brute** (thug)
but (conjunction) / **butt** (target, wallop, American for 'bum')
buy (purchase) / **by** (preposition) / **bye** (goodbye, sporting term)

cache (store, hide items) / **cash** (money)
callous (cruel) / **callus** (hard skin)
calmer (more tranquil) / **karma** (doctrine, luck)
cannon (gun) / **canon** (cleric, collection)
canvas (cloth) / **canvass** (campaign)
carat (unit of weight) / **carrot** (vegetable)
carol (Christmas song) / **carrel** (cubicle)
caught (past tense of catch) / **court** (place of law)
caw (birdcall) / **cor!** (exclamation) / **core** (centre) / **corps**
        (body of people)
cede (give up) / **seed** (part of plant, competitor's position)
cell (small room in prison or monastery, American for 'mobile
        phone') / **sell** (trade)
cellar (basement) / **seller** (someone who sells)
censer (incense container) / **censor** (assessor)
cent (money) / **scent** (perfume) / **sent** (past tense of send)

cereal (breakfast food, but not exclusively at breakfast time) / **serial** (story in instalments)

cession (giving up) / **session** (meeting)

cheap (inexpensive) / **cheep** (bird noise)

check (verify) / **cheque** (bank order)

chilli (hot) / **chilly** (cold)

choir (singers) / **quire** (paper)

chord (musical term) / **cord** (string, parts of string-like anatomy – spinal cord, vocal cords)

choux (pastry) / **shoe** (footwear) / **shoo** (chase away)

chute (channel, slide) / **shoot** (aim to kill or wound)

cite (refer to) / **sight** (vision) / **site** (area)

coarse (rough, vulgar) / **course** (route, part of meal, studies)

cocks (more than one male bird, more than one penis) / **cox** (coxswain)

colonel (army officer) / **kernel** (seed)

come (move closer, arrive) / **cum** (combined with)

compare (and contrast, make comparison) / **compère** (host)

complacent (smug) / **complaisant** (agreeable)

complement (complete, improve) / **compliment** (praise, flatter)

coo (bird sound, exclamation) / **coup** (takeover, triumph)

council (legislative body) / **counsel** (advice, barrister)

cue (signal, prompt, stick for snooker) / **queue** (line of people)

curb (restrain) / **kerb** (pavement edge)

currant (dried grape) / **current** (contemporary, flow)

cymbal (percussion instrument) / **symbol** (sign)

dam (barrier, block) / **damn** (curse, denounce, give a toss)

days (more than one day) / **daze** (stun, stupor)

dear (expensive, darling, precious) / **deer** (animal)

dependant (hanger-on) / **dependent** (conditional on)

descendant (successor) / **descendent** (going downwards)

descent (going down, decline) / **dissent** (disagree)

dew (little drops of water) / **due** (expected, required)

diaeresis (mark on a vowel for pronunciation) / **diuresis** (increased production of wee)

die (croak, singular of dice) / **dye** (alter colour)

disc (flat, round object) / **disk** (computer-related)

discomfit (unease) / **discomfort** (slight pain – but as verbs both can mean to embarrass)

discreet (tactful, careful) / **discrete** (separate)

doe (animal) / **doh** (musical note) / **d'oh** (© Homer Simpson) / **dough** (pastry)

draft (early version, bank order) / **draught** (air current, drink)

draw (sketch) / **drawer** (sliding bit of desk or chest)

dray (cart for horse) / **drey** (home for squirrel)

drier (more dry) / **dryer** (device for drying)

dual (double) / **duel** (fight)

earn (acquire) / **urn** (container)

eave (edge of roof) / **eve** (day before)

eerie (creepy) / **eyrie** (nest)

er (hesitate) / **err** (make a mistake)

ewe (lady sheep) / **yew** (tree) / **you** (pronoun)

exercise (physical activity, task) / **exorcise** (drive out spirits)

faint (pass out, indistinct) / **feint** (pretend)

fair (average, light-coloured, impartial, just, fete) / **fare** (food, ticket price)

farther (further) / **father** (male parent, leader)

fate (destiny) / **fete** (fair)

faze (disconcert) / **phase** (stage of development)

feat (achievement) / **feet** (plural of foot)

feta (cheese) / **fetter** (shackle)

file (document, store, line, smooth) / **phial** (bottle)

fishing (catch a fish) / **phishing** (illicit emailing)

flair (aptitude, style) / **flare** (blaze, widen – as in trousers)
flaw (fault) / **floor** (ground, level)
flea (insect) / **flee** (scarper)
flocks (crowd) / **phlox** (plant)
floe (floating ice) / **flow** (run)
flour (milled grain) / **flower** (part of plant)
for (preposition) / **fore** (in front) / **four** (number)
forceable (can be forced) / **forcible** (done by force)
forego (precede) / **forgo** (go without)
foreword (introduction) / **forward** (towards the front)
forth (forward) / **fourth** (number)
foul (disgusting, dirty tackle) / **fowl** (poultry)
freeze (turn into ice) / **frieze** (wall picture)

gage (fruit) / **gauge** (measure)
gait (style of walking) / **gate** (barrier)
gamble (bet) / **gambol** (prance about)
geezer (bloke) / **geyser** (hot spring)
genes (unit of heredity) / **jeans** (trousers)
gild (paint gold, elaborate) / **guild** (association)
gilt (covered in gold paint) / **guilt** (responsible for crime,
    feeling responsible for wrongdoing)
gnaw (chew) / **nor** (and not)
gorilla (animal) / **guerrilla** (fighter)
grate (irritate, shred, part of fireplace) / **great** (excellent,
    powerful)
grill (cooking method) / **grille** (grating)
grisly (gruesome) / **grizzly** (bear, moaning)
groin (part of anatomy) / **groyne** (barrier on seashore)

hail (frozen rain, greeting) / **hale** (healthy)
hair (fur, head of) / **hare** (big bunny)
hall (room) / **haul** (drag)

hangar (large building) / **hanger** (for clothes, person
  who hangs things, group of trees on a hillside)
haw (fruit) / **hoar** (frost) / **whore** (prostitute)
hay (dried grass) / **heigh** (ho) / **hey!** (exclamation)
heal (make better) / **heel** (part of foot, part of shoe)
heard (past tense of hear) / **herd** (crowd)
heroin (drug) / **heroine** (intrepid woman, female
  starring role)
hi (greeting) / **high** (tall, top)
higher (comparative of high) / **hire** (employ, rent)
him (pronoun) / **hymn** (song)
hoard (store) / **horde** (crowd)
hoarse (croaky) / **horse** (animal)
hole (opening) / **whole** (complete, entire)
holey (full of holes) / **holy** (religious) / **wholly** (completely,
  entirely)
humerus (bone) / **humorous** (funny)

idle (lazy) / **idol** (icon, heart-throb)
in (preposition) / **inn** (tavern)
incite (stir up) / **insight** (intuition)
ion (molecule) / **iron** (metal, domestic chore that apparently
  can be shared . . .)

jam (tailback, tricky situation, preserve) / **jamb** (a post)
jewel (precious stone) / **joule** (unit)

key (entering device) / **quay** (ships' dock)
knave (scoundrel) / **nave** (part of church)
knead (pummel dough) / (knock-) **kneed** / **need** (must have)
knew (past tense of know) / **new** (not old)
knight (person of rank) / **night** (dusk to daybreak)
knit (make with wool) / **nit** (insect, twit)

knot (fastening device) / **not** (negative)
know (be aware, understand) / **no** (negative)

larva (baby insect) / **lava** (volcanic rock)
leach (seep) / **leech** (parasite)
lead (metal) / **led** (past tense of lead)
leader (chief) / **lieder** (German songs)
leak (drip, disclosure) / **leek** (vegetable)
leant (leaned) / **lent** (past tense of lend)
lessen (to shrink) / **lesson** (education)
levee (embankment) / **levy** (tax or toll)
liar (fibber) / **lyre** (stringed instrument)
licence (UK noun) / **license** (UK verb and US noun)
lichen (algae) / **liken** (compare)
light (illumination, not dark, not heavy) / **lite** (low in
     calories / simple version)

'Introducing "Lite" – the new way to spell "Light", but with
twenty per cent fewer letters'

Jerry Seinfeld

lightening (getting lighter) / **lightning** (flash preceding
     thunder)
literal (word for word) / **littoral** (shore)
load (carry, lots of) / **lode** (seam of metal ore)
loan (to lend) / **lone** (on its own)
loot (to steal, contraband) / **lute** (stringed instrument)
lumbar (lower back) / **lumber** (useless stuff, timber)

made (past tense of make) / **maid** (female servant)
mail (post) / **male** (half the population)

main (primary) / **mane** (hair on horse and lion)

maize (cereal) / **maze** (labyrinth)

mall (boulevard, shopping centre) / **maul** (rip to shreds)

mantel (mantelshelf) / **mantle** (hooded cloak)

marquee (big tent) / **marquis** (French nobleman)

massif (mountain range) / **massive** (enormous)

material (cloth) / **materiel** (army equipment)

maw (mouth) / **moor** (heathland) / **more** (additional)

mean (intend, average, stingy, nasty) / **mien** (person's appearance)

meat (flesh) / **meet** (come together) / **mete** (give out)

medal (award) / **meddle** (interfere)

metal (hard material) / **mettle** (spirit)

meter (device for measuring) / **metre** (unit of measurement, poetic rhythm)

mews (little street, cat sound) / **muse** (creative influence, ponder)

might (maybe, strength) / **mite** (insect)

miner (pit worker) / **minor** (junior, insignificant) / **mynah** (bird)

missed (past tense of miss) / **mist** (fine spray)

moan (grumble) / **mown** (past participle of mow)

moo (cow sound) / **moue** (pout)

morning (before noon) / **mourning** (bereavement period)

muscle (part of body, strength) / **mussel** (shellfish)

naught (nothing) / **nought** (zero)

naval (maritime) / **navel** (belly button)

nay (no) / **née** (put before a woman's maiden name) / **neigh** (horse sound)

none (not one) / **nun** (bride of Christ)

oar (for rowing) / **or** (conjunction)

one (number) / **wan** (pale) / **won** (past tense of win)

pail (bucket) / **pale** (wan)

pain (suffering) / **pane** (sheet of glass)

pair (two things) / **pare** (trim) / **pear** (fruit)

palate (roof of mouth) / **palette** (painter's tool) / **pallet** (mattress, platform)

parse (grammatical term) / **pass** (move, go by, as opposed to 'fail')

passed (past tense of pass) / **past** (history)

pastel (crayon) / **pastille** (lozenge, sweetie)

patience (stoicism) / **patients** (ill people)

pause (hiatus) / **paws** (animals' feet)

paw (animal's foot) / **poor** (impoverished) / **pore** (scrutinise, tiny hole) / **pour** (chuck it down, flow)

pawky (sardonic) / **porky** (fat, lie)

pawn (chess piece, puppet) / **porn** (erotica)

pea (vegetable) / **pee** (wee)

peace (between wars) / **piece** (a bit)

peak (top) / **peek** (glimpse) / **pique** (annoyance)

peal (chime) / **peel** (remove vegetable or fruit skin)

pec (pectoral muscle) / **peck** (jab, nibble, kiss)

pedal (lever) / **peddle** (sell)

peepul (tree) / **people** (us)

peer (look, equal, titled person) / **pier** (jetty)

petrel (bird) / **petrol** (fuel)

pi (3.14159 approx., Greek letter) / **pie** (enclosed food in pastry)

pidgin (language) / **pigeon** (bird)

place (position) / **plaice** (fish)

plain (simple, flat land, grown-ups' chocolate) / **plane** (aircraft, shave, tree)

plum (fruit) / **plumb** (precisely, measure depth)

pole (post) / **poll** (vote)

populace (the people) / **populous** (heavily populated)

practice (noun and US verb) / **practise** (verb, and also adjective)

pray (entreat) / **prey** (hunt, the hunted)
premier (important) / **premiere** (first performance)
principal (chief) / **principle** (belief)
prise (lever open) / **prize** (reward)
profit (surplus) / **prophet** (seer)
program (computer-related) / **programme** (list of
    events, show)
pseud (pretentious person) / **sued** (past tense of sue)

rack (framework, anguish, torture) / **wrack** (wreck, seaweed)
rain (wet weather) / **reign** (rule) / **rein** (horse harness)
raise (lift) / **raze** (destroy)
rap (knock, music) / **wrap** (enfold)
rapt (engrossed) / **wrapped** (past tense of wrap)
raw (uncooked) / **roar** (loud animal noise)
read (past tense of read) / **red** (colour)
read (peruse) / **reed** (plant)
real (genuine) / **reel** (bobbin, dance)
rec (recreation ground) / **wreck** (derelict, destroy)
reek (stink) / **wreak** (inflict)
retch (gag) / **wretch** (pitiful creature, scoundrel)
reverend (worthy of reverence, clergyman) / **reverent**
    (showing reverence)
review (analysis) / **revue** (stage entertainment)
rhyme (verse) / **rime** (frost)
right (correct, not left) / **rite** (tradition) / **write** (transcribe)
ring (circular enclosure) / **wring** (twist)
road (thoroughfare) / **rode** (past tense of ride) / **rowed**
    (past tense of row)
roe (fish eggs) / **row** (line, using oars)
role (acting part, function) / **roll** (rotate)
roo (kangaroo) / **roux** (sauce thickener) / **rue** (regret, plant)
root (basis) / **route** (direction)

rote (repetition) / **wrote** (past tense of write)
rough (irregular, imprecise) / **ruff** (neck wear)
rung (ladder foothold) / **wrung** (past tense of wring)
rye (cereal) / **wry** (crooked, sardonic)

sail (boat-related) / **sale** (selling, knockdown prices)
sauce (dressing, cheeky) / **source** (origin)
sawed (past tense of saw) / **sword** (blade)
sea (ocean) / **see** (look, perceive)
seam (join) / **seem** (appear)
seamen (sailors) / **semen** (sperm)
set (put, solidify, collection) / **sett** (badger's home)
sew (a needle pulling thread) / **so** (conjunction) / **soh** (musical
    note) / **sow** (plant)
shake (jiggle about, tremble) / **sheikh** (Arab chief)
shear (cut) / **sheer** (total, see-through)
shore (water's edge) / **sure** (certain, true)
sic (as original) / **sick** (not well)
sink (basin, go down) / **sync** (synchronisation)
slay (kill) / **sleigh** (sledge for Father Christmas)
sleight (cunning) / **slight** (small, insult)
sloe (fruit) / **slow** (not fast, bit thick)
soar (fly up) / **sore** (painful)
sole (only, part of foot, part of shoe) / **soul** (spirit, person)
some (unspecified number) / **sum** (maths, total)
son (male offspring) / **sun** (big yellow thing in sky)
sort (arrange, type) / **sought** (past tense of seek)
staid (unadventurous, stiff) / **stayed** (past tense of stay)
stair (step) / **stare** (gaze)
stake (post, assert) / **steak** (meat)
stationary (motionless) / **stationery** (desk stuff)
steal (nick) / **steel** (metal, screw up courage)
step (stair, walk) / **steppe** (grassy plain)

stile (steps) / **style** (particular way, fashion, luxury)
storey (level) / **story** (tale)
straight (not bent) / **strait** (passage of water, difficulty)
suite (set of rooms or objects) / **sweet** (confectionery, sugary, nice)
summary (brief statement) / **summery** (summer-related)
surplice (church clothing) / **surplus** (excess)
swat (hit) / **swot** (work hard)

tail (at end of animal) / **tale** (story)
taught (past tense of teach) / **taut** (tight) / **torte** (cake)
te (musical note) / **tea** (drink, meal) / **tee** (golf term)
team (group) / **teem** (swarming with, pouring down)
tenner (ten quid) / **tenor** (singer)
their (of them) / **there** (that place) / **they're** (they are)
threw (past tense of throw) / **through** (preposition)
throne (regal chair) / **thrown** (past participle of throw)
thyme (herb) / **time** (period)
tic (spasm) / **tick** (correct mark, parasite)
tire (weary) / **tyre** (wheel casing)
to (preposition) / **too** (also) / **two** (number)
toe (part of foot) / **tow** (pull)
told (past tense of tell) / **tolled** (past tense of toll)
traffic (vehicles) / **traffick** (deal)
troop (group) / **troupe** (group of actors)
tuba (brass instrument) / **tuber** (root)
tuna (fish) / **tuner** (someone or something that tunes)

vain (egotistical) / **vane** (wind indicator) / **vein** (blood vessel)
vale (glen) / **veil** (covering)
verses (stanzas) / **versus** (opposition)
vial (glass bottle) / **vile** (horrible) / **viol** (stringed instrument)

wail (moan) / **whale** (sea mammal)
waist (part of body) / **waste** (rubbish)
wait (hiatus) / **weight** (heaviness)
waive (do without, brush aside) / **wave** (gesture, ripple, curl)
wander (roam) / **wonder** (awe, ponder)
warrior (soldier) / **worrier** (person who worries)
watt (unit of electricity) / **what** (question)
way (route) / **weigh** (measure weight)
we (pronoun) / **wee** (small, urine)
weak (not strong) / **week** (seven days)
weals (marks on skin) / **wheels** (on the bus go round and round)
weather (meteorological conditions) / **whether** (conjunction)
which (pronoun) / **witch** (sorceress)
while (during) / **wile** (stratagem)
whine (drone) / **wine** (drink)
whither (to where) / **wither** (fade)
whoa (stop) / **woe** (unhappiness)
who's (who is) / **whose** (belonging to whom)
wood (timber) / **would** (auxiliary verb)

yoke (neck brace) / **yolk** (yellow part of egg)
your (owned by you) / **you're** (you are)

In the following sentences, select the correct spelling.

1 Stuart was on the beers/biers last night, and came in to work this morning/mourning completely waisted/wasted.

2 The heroin/heroine in the storey/story died/dyed of a heroin/heroine overdose.

3 The seamen/semen were hoping for a good hall/haul of place/plaice and sole/soul, but the weather/whether was foul/fowl and they returned with naught/nought caught/court.

4 The none/nun had been standing at the altar/alter all morning/mourning, singing hims/hymns and praying/preying, and was now feeling faint/feint as well as rather board/bored.

5 The author had finished the final draft/draught, but before she could put it in the draw/drawer, a draft/draught blew/blue the hole/whole storey/story away/aweigh.

6 The council/counsel was in the final faze/phase of building the knew/new dam/damn, which hopefully wood/would not leak/leek like the last one/won.

7 The principal/principle tenner/tenor and base/bass were exercising/exorcising their/there/they're vocal chords/cords, practicing/practising for the premier/premiere of the review/revue.

8 The ceded/seeded player ceded/seeded play.

9 The currant/current was against them in the rough/ruff sea/see as the thunder and lightening/lightning continued apace, so they brought the ship in to berth/birth.

10 It was poring/pouring with rain/reign/rein, and the raining/reigning/reining Queen rained/reigned/reined in her hoarse/horse hoarse/horse, but in vain/vane/vein, as she was throne/thrown to the flaw/floor.

Words spelt the same way but pronounced differently

Now, here is a somewhat shorter list of words that are spelt the same way but are pronounced differently.

> **abuse** (rhyming with 'loose' – noun / rhyming with 'fuse' – verb)
> **alternate** (stress on second syllable – adjective, every other / stress on third syllable – verb, occurring by turns)

bass (rhyming with 'ass' – fish / rhyming with 'ace' – low pitch)

bow (rhyming with 'go' – knot, used with arrows and stringed instruments / rhyming with 'cow' – bend, front of ship)

buffet (rhyming with '[Miss] Muffet' – strike / rhyming with 'muff' and 'eh' – help-yourself food)

close (rhyming with 'dose' – adjective, near / rhyming with 'doze' – verb, to shut)

commune (stress on first syllable – noun, collective / stress on second syllable – verb, bit spiritual)

compound (stress on first syllable – noun, enclosed area, comprising two or more parts / stress on second syllable – verb, to mix, make worse)

console (stress on first syllable – noun, control panel / stress on second syllable – verb, to comfort)

consort (stress on first syllable – noun, companion / stress on second syllable – verb, to associate)

construct (stress on first syllable – noun, theory / stress on second syllable – verb, to build)

consummate (stress on first syllable – adjective, skilled / stress on third syllable – verb, archaic or legal term for sealing a marriage with sexual intercourse)

contrary (stress on first syllable – opposite / stress on second syllable – stroppy)

converse (stress on first syllable – noun and adjective, the opposite / stress on second syllable – verb, to have a conversation)

convict (stress on first syllable – noun, prisoner / stress on second syllable – verb, to pronounce guilty)

desert (stress on first syllable – noun, barren land / stress on second syllable, sounding like 'assert' – verb, to run away)

elaborate (stress on second syllable – adjective, intricate / stress on fourth syllable – verb, to expand on)

entrance (rhyming with 'sentence' – entry / rhyming with 'perchance' – delight, hypnotise)

estimate (stress on first syllable – noun / stress on third syllable – verb)

frequent (stress on first syllable – adjective / stress on second syllable – verb)

house (rhyming with 'louse' – noun, dwelling / rhyming with 'cows' – verb, to shelter)

invalid (stress on first syllable – noun, sick or disabled person / stress on second syllable – adjective, not valid)

lead (rhyming with 'bed' – metal / rhyming with 'seed' – to guide)

live (rhyming with 'hive' – adjective, having life / rhyming with 'give' – verb, to be alive)

minute (rhyming with 'innit' – sixty seconds / sounding exactly like 'my newt' – very small)

moderate (stress on first syllable – adjective, average, mediocre / stress on third syllable – verb, to arbitrate, to curb)

object (stress on first syllable – noun, a thing / stress on second syllable – verb, to disagree)

pasty (pronounce with a short 'a', like 'gas', or 'nasty' if you live in the north – noun, pie / rhyming with 'hasty' – adjective, pale complexion)

permit (stress on first syllable – noun, authorisation / stress on second syllable – verb, to allow)

Polish / polish (sounding like 'bloke-ish' – language, nationality / sounding like 'abolish' – shine)

present (rhyming with 'pheasant' – noun, gift, now / rhyming with 'dissent' – verb, to deliver, to give)

project (stress on first syllable – noun, venture / stress on second syllable – verb, to predict, to convey)

read (rhyming with 'deed' – to comprehend writing / rhyming with 'red' – past tense of read)

rebel (rhyming with 'pebble' – noun, resister / rhyming with 'lapel' – verb, to revolt)

recount (stress on first syllable – noun and verb, count again / stress on second syllable – verb, to narrate)

refuse (stress on first syllable – noun, rubbish / stress on second syllable – verb, to decline)

reject (stress on first syllable – noun, substandard article / stress on second syllable – verb, to turn down)

resent (rhyming with 'dissent' – to feel indignant / rhyming with 'he went' – to send again)

row (rhyming with 'cow' – argument, noise / rhyming with 'go' – line, move through water)

second (rhyming with 'fecund' – one-sixtieth of a minute, / rhyming with 'respond' – transfer)

separate (rhyming with 'desperate' – noun, adjective / rhyming with 'decorate' – verb)

sow (rhyming with 'cow' – pig / rhyming with 'doe' – to plant)

subject (stress on first syllable – noun, a topic / stress on second syllable – verb, to put through)

tear (rhyming with 'air' – rip / rhyming with 'beer' – drop of liquid from eye)

transport (stress on first syllable – noun / stress on second
   syllable – verb)

use (rhyming with 'deuce' – noun / rhyming with 'fuse' – verb)

wind (rhyming with 'sinned' – noun, current of air / rhyming
   with 'lined' – verb, to coil)
wound (rhyming with 'mooned' – injury / rhyming with
   'found' – coiled, past tense of wind)

*In the following sentences, underline the stressed syllable in each
italicised word for the correct meaning.*

1 The *refuse* collector *refused* to take away the rubbish as the
   paper and plastics weren't in *separate* bags.

2 The portions in the restaurant were so *minute* that the main
   course lasted less than a *minute.*

3 The *buffet* was barely worth a *second* glance.

4 The *elaborate* front *entrance* was a *contrast* to the more *moderate*
   servants' door round the back, which was far less *entrancing.*

5 The *rebels deserted* and set up a *separate* party.

6 The winner *objected* to a *recount*, even though there was very
   little to *separate* him from the others.

7 The *invalid* found to her distress that her parking *permit* had
   expired, and was *invalid.*

8 With *consummate* skill, he *consummated* the marriage.

9 She, however, didn't think it was quite so *consummate*, and
   went for their *entrancing Polish* builder instead.

10 The builder felt a bit like a sex *object*, though, and rather
   resented being used in this way.

Common confusions

Now, here's a list of words that are often mistaken for each other (though one or two are common typos rather than actual confusions).

accept (receive) / **except** (excluding)

acute (sudden and severe pain) / **chronic** (persistent and intermittent pain)

advice (noun) / **advise** (verb)

aesthetic (tasteful) / **ascetic** (austere)

affect (verb, to have an effect on) / **effect** (noun, result; verb, bring about)

affront (insult) / **effrontery** (insolence)

agnostic (believes there is no god, unless there is proof) / **atheist** (*knows* there is no god)

allegiance (loyalty to someone) / **alliance** (pact between two parties)

allergy (hypersensitivity) / **elegy** (funeral song or poem)

alliterate (same letter or sound) / **illiterate** (unable to read or write)

all together (all at once) / **altogether** (in total)

allude (refer to) / **elude** (evade)

allusion (reference to) / **illusion** (mistaken impression)

alternate (every other) / **alternative** (another)

amend (revise) / **emend** (correct)

amiable (friendly – people) / **amicable** (friendly – things)

amoral (not bothered with right and wrong) / **immoral** (knowingly doing wrong)

annex (verb) / **annexe** (noun)

annual (once a year) / **perennial** (lasting several years – so you don't need to plant those daffs every year)

annunciation (announcement) / **enunciation** (clear speech)

antisocial (against the norms of society) / **unsociable** (not
keen on others' company) / **unsocial** (outside the normal
working day)

anyone (meaning 'any person', e.g. 'Anyone could do this') /
any one (meaning 'any single person or thing', e.g. 'Any one
of you could do this')
anyway (an emphasis, meaning 'in any case', e.g. 'It's too
late now anyway') / **any way** (meaning 'in any manner',
e.g. 'This isn't going to work in any way')

appraise (assess) / **apprise** (inform)
assure (reassure) / **ensure** (make certain) / **insure**
(underwrite)
astrology (nonsense about signs of the zodiac) / **astronomy**
(study of the universe)
astronaut (spaceman) / **cosmonaut** (Russian spaceman)

bathos (something that goes unintentionally from the
sublime to the ridiculous) / **pathos** (something that
arouses compassion or sadness)
bazaar (fete) / **bizarre** (rather strange)
biannual (twice a year) / **biennial** (every other year)
blond (male) / **blonde** (female)
bona fide (genuine) / **bona fides** (sincere intention, credentials)
bought (past tense of buy) / **brought** (past tense of bring)
breath (noun) / **breathe** (verb)
Britain (place) / **Briton** (person)

calendar (almanac) / **colander** (sieve)
canapé (finger food) / **canopy** (awning)
canter (between a trot and gallop) / **cantor** (religious singer)

carousal (booze-up) / **carousel** (merry-go-round)
catarrh (phlegm) / **guitar** (instrument)
chafe (rub) / **chaff** (husk)
choose (present tense) / **chose** (past tense)
cinch (easy) / **sync** (synchronisation – don't shorten to 'synch')
climactic (big finish) / **climatic** (climate-related)
collage (mixed-media artwork) / **college** (place of education)
complex (hard to understand, but intriguing) / **complicated**
(hard to understand, but irritating)
compulsive (obsessive) / **compulsory** (obligatory)
confidant *or* **confidante** (a male *or* female adviser) /
confident (sure)
contagious (spread by physical contact) / **infectious**
(spread by air)
continual (repeated) / **continuous** (uninterrupted)
crumble (disintegrate) / **crumple** (crush)

dairy (housing or selling milk products) / **diary**
(appointments book)
decent (respectable) / **descent** (going down)
defuse (make safe) / **diffuse** (spread out)
deprecate (disapprove of) / **depreciate** (belittle *or* go down
in value)
desert (barren land) / **dessert** (pudding)

> Although 'just deserts' is the spelling, 'just desserts' is the
> pronunciation – because it means a person is getting what she
> 'deserves', rather than meaning only pudding is on the menu.

detract (take away) / **distract** (divert attention)
diacritic (sign on letter for pronunciation) / **diuretic** (causing
increased need to pass water)

diagnosis (identifying the disease) / **prognosis** (outlook for the disease)

dinghy (boat) / **dingy** (gloomy)

disassemble (dismantle) / **dissemble** (disguise)

disburse (pay out money) / **disperse** (scatter)

disinterested (impartial) / **uninterested** (not interested)

distrust (noun) / **mistrust** (verb)

doner (kebab) / **donor** (giver)

dystopia (nightmare of a place – horrible) / **utopia** (dream of a place – ideal)

egoist (self-interested) / **egotist** (conceited)

elegy (poem for the dead) / **eulogy** (speech of praise – for the living or the dead)

elicit (draw out) / **illicit** (illegal)

emigrant (person moving away) / **immigrant** (person moving in)

emanate (spread out) / **eminent** (renowned) / **immanent** (intrinsic) / **imminent** (impending)

empathy (able to identify with another's feelings) / **sympathy** (feel pity for another)

emulate (copy by following the example of) / **imitate** (copy more blatantly, impersonate)

Perhaps it would be truer to say 'emulation is the sincerest form of flattery' . . .

endemic (regularly found in an area or group of people) / **epidemic** (outbreak) / **pandemic** (widespread)

enervate (tire) / **innervate** (supply with nerves – biological term) / **innovate** (introduce something new)

enquiry (general questioning) / **inquiry** (official questioning)

entomology (study of insects) / **etymology** (history of words)

envelop (surround) / **envelope** (wrapping for letter)

epigram (clever remark) / **epigraph** (quote at start of book or chapter) / **epitaph** (inscription) / **epithet** (sobriquet)

erupt (explode) / **irrupt** (enter suddenly)

eschatology (area of religion concerning death and destiny) / **scatology** (fascination with shit)

everyday (commonplace) / **every day** (each day)

everyone (every person) / **every one** (each one)

evoke (bring to mind) / **invoke** (refer to)

explicit (direct, no holds barred) / **implicit** (indirect, fundamental)

explode (blow up) / **implode** (cave in)

famous (well known) / **infamous** (notorious)

farther (more distant) / **further** (more distant, in addition, promote)

ferment (brew) / **foment** (incite)

flammable *and* **inflammable** (both mean combustible – the opposite is non-flammable)

flaunt (show off) / **flout** (defy)

forever (continuously) / **for ever** (for always)

gourmand (glutton) / **gourmet** (connoisseur of good food)

grisly (gruesome) / **gristly** (tough) / **grizzly** (bear, moaning)

homogeneous (uniform) / **homogenous** (common ancestry, used only in biology)

however (adverb – 'However, despite my bad knee I finished the marathon') / **how ever** (emphasising 'how' – 'How ever did you manage to finish the marathon with your bad knee?)

impracticable (unworkable) / **impractical** (unrealistic)
inchoate (partly formed) / **incoherent** (unintelligible)
indistinguishable (no distinction) / **undistinguished**
(unexceptional)
ingenious (inspired) / **ingenuous** (naive)
inimitable (unique) / **inimical** (harmful)
interment (burial) / **internment** (imprisonment)

into (preposition – meaning 'to a place in something', e.g. 'She fell into his arms') / **in to** (adverb and preposition – meaning 'inwards and towards', e.g. 'He would not give in to the calls for his resignation')

judicial (legal) / **judicious** (sensible)

libel (written defamation) / **slander** (spoken defamation)
liqueur (sweet-flavoured alcoholic spirit) / **liquor** (alcoholic
drink, liquid made or used in cooking)
liquidate (wipe out) / **liquidise** (purée)
literally (exactly – your eyes were not popping out of your
head literally . . .) / **literary** (well read, written)
loath (reluctant) / **loathe** (detest)
loose (baggy) / **lose** (misplace)
luxuriant (strong and healthy) / **luxurious** (expensive)

mandatary (person receiving a mandate) / **mandatory**
(compulsory)
marinade (noun) / **marinate** (verb)
masochist (takes pleasure in pain) / **sadist** (takes pleasure
in inflicting that pain)
massage (rub-down) / **message** (communication)
maybe (perhaps) / **may be** (might be)

momentary (fleeting) / **momentous** (important)
moral (ethical) / **morale** (state of mind)
motif (repeated image) / **motive** (reason)
mucous (adjective) / **mucus** (noun)

naturalist (studies natural history) / **naturist** (likes going
    around naked)
negligent (careless) / **negligible** (trivial)
noisome (smells disgusting – the Under 15s changing room on
    a wet Wednesday afternoon) / **noisy** (rowdy – the school
    playground at going-home time on a Friday afternoon)

obsolescent (declining) / **obsolete** (outdated)
odious (repulsive – derives from 'odium', not 'odour') /
    odorous (having an odour – not necessarily a bad one)
Olympic (concerning Olympia or the Olympic Games) /
    Olympics (Games) / **Olympiad** (a staging of the Games) /
    Olympian (being similar to a god, competitor of the
    Games)
oral (spoken) / **verbal** (spoken and written)

onto (preposition – meaning 'to a place on something',
e.g. 'The actor walked onto the stage') / **on to** (adverb and
preposition – meaning 'onwards and towards', e.g. 'Let's
move on to the next scene')

perquisite (privilege, hence 'perk') / **prerequisite** (prior
    requirement)
persecute (torment) / **prosecute** (take to court)
personal (relating to an individual) / **personnel** (people)
picaresque (episodic fiction about a lovable rogue) /
    picturesque (attractive)

plaintiff (litigant) / **plaintive** (piteous sound)
practical (realistic, helpful) / **practicable** (feasible)
precede (go before) / **proceed** (start)
precedence (predominance) / **precedents** (earlier examples)
prescribe (dictate, suggest) / **proscribe** (ban)
prevaricate (to act or speak evasively) / **procrastinate** (to put off doing something)
prophecy (noun) / **prophesy** (verb)
prostate (gland) / **prostrate** (lying flat)
psych (mentally prepare) / **psyche** (spirit)
pubic (concerned with the pubis) / **public** (populace)

rare (uncommon at all times) / **scarce** (uncommon temporarily, a shortage)
ravage (destroy) / **ravish** (violate)
relation (connection between people, groups or countries, so 'Relations broke down between the union and the company bosses – as per'; *but* relations are also family members, so 'Relations broke down sobbing when they heard I'd married the man they all loathed') / **relationship** (friendship with romantic connotations) / **relative** (as noun, family member – same as relation)
repertoire (stock of skills, stock of plays performed alternately in a season) / **repertory** (stock of plays performed one after the other)
revers (turned-back edge of garment) / **reverse** (go back)
riffle (search through pages) / **rifle** (search through anything)

salvage (rescue) / **selvedge** (edge of cloth)
same (identical) / **similar** (resembling)
scald (liquid burn) / **scold** (berate)
scared (past tense of scare) / **scarred** (marked with a scar)

sceptic (doubter) / **septic** (infected)

sculptor (one who sculpts) / **sculpture** (the product of the sculptor)

serial (story in instalments, making a series) / **series** (self-contained stories, serials combined)

sheath (noun) / **sheathe** (verb)

shoulder (part of body) / **solder** (join) / **soldier** (army person)

silicon (chemical element) / **silicone** (compound of silicon and oxygen)

sing (la la) / **singe** (lightly burn)

solecism (grammatical mistake) / **solipsism** (self-absorption)

sometime (at some point in time) / **some time** (a certain amount of time)

sooth (archaic word for truth) / **soothe** (pacify)

speciality (forte) / **specialty** (branch of medicine, US version of speciality)

suit (part of a deck of cards, a matching jacket and trousers or skirt) / **suite** (set of things)

systematic (structured) / **systemic** (affecting a whole system)

terminal (meeting point for arrival or departure – so airport terminal) / **terminus** (end or start of a line – so railway terminus)

tortuous (twists and turns) / **torturous** (like torture)

triannual (three times a year) / **triennial** (every three years)

vicious (violent) / **viscous** (sticky liquid)

whinging (whining) / **winging** (flying, improvising)

whiskey (US and Irish whisky) / **whisky** (Scotch)

wreath (ring of flowers) / **wreathe** (decorate)

zeros (plural) / **zeroes** (verb)

In the following sentences, fill in the blanks.

1 Let's find an altern— explanation, to —sure there's no confusion.

2 The only way to stop her contin— requests was to —cept an invitation to one of Maureen's dull parties.

3 Alison's advi— was ignored as usual; her role as confid— is obviously superfluous.

4 She was loath— to ask the gour— for supper as she was an unconfid— cook.

5 Despite the musicians being out of syn— with the conductor, the last movement of the symphony was clima—.

6 My —nent operation is to be performed by an —nent surgeon.

7 The moral— of the Olymp— was low as he was the Brit— who mucked up the 400 metres relay.

8 The vi—ous thug was thrown head first into the vat of vi—ous oil.

9 The soup sc—ded the gour— because he was too greedy to let it cool.

10 As he was on death row, he knew that his inter— would end with his inter—.

Common misspellings

Now, here's a list with no alternatives – no different meanings, no different pronunciations – just quite important to get right. (Many of the following may seem ridiculous or unlikely, but we've come across all of the misspellings – including 'mispellings' – at some point or other.)

absorption *not* absorbtion
accommodate *not* acommodate, accomodate
acquire *not* aquire
acquaintance *not* aquaintance
adamant *not* adament
ancillary *not* ancilliary
anemone *not* anenome
annihilate *not* anihilate, annilate
assessment *not* asessment, assesment

battalion *not* batallion, battalian
bankruptcy *not* bankrupcy
barbecue *not* barbeque
believable *not* believeable
berserk *not* beserk
bony *not* boney
bourgeois *not* bourgois
broccoli *not* brocolli, broccli, broccolli

Caribbean *not* Carribean
carnivorous *not* carniverous
cemetery *not* cemetary, cematery
chrysanthemum *not* crysanthemum, chrysanthemun
committal *not* comittal, commital, committall
committee *not* comittee, commitee
condemn *not* condem
contributor *not* contributer
conveyor *not* conveyer
corduroy *not* cordroy
courageous *not* couragious
courteous *not* curteous
curiosity *not* curiousity
curriculum *not* curicculum, curiculum

daiquiri *not* daquiri
deceive *not* decieve

That familiar 'i' before 'e' except after 'c' rhyme works here, but is not a rule to follow generally. Think of 'deficient', 'proficient', 'science', and 'albeit', 'heinous', 'forfeit'.

definite *not* definate
desiccate *not* dessicate
deodorant *not* deodorent
desperate *not* desparate
dexterous *not* dextrous
diaphragm *not* diaphram
diarrhoea *not* diarhhoea
disappoint *not* dissapoint
disastrous *not* disasterous
discoloration *not* discolouration

dissatisfaction *not* disatisfaction
dissect *not* disect
dissipate *not* disippate
drunkenness *not* drunkeness
duffel *not* duffle
duress *not* durress

ecstasy *not* extasy
eczema *not* exema
eighth *not* eigth
⤙ **embarrass** *not* embarass, embarras
exaggerate *not* exagerrate
exhilarate *not* exilarate, exhilerate

February *not* Febuary
fluorescent *not* flourescent
foreboding *not* forboding
forsake *not* foresake
forty *not* fourty
fulfilment *not* fulfillment, fullfillment

gauge *not* guage
government *not* goverment
gruesome *not* grusome
guerrilla *not* guerilla

haemorrhage *not* haemorrage
haemorrhoids *not* haemorroids
harass *not* harrass
height *not* heigth
honorary *not* honourary
humorist *not* humourist
humorous *not* humourous

idiosyncrasy *not* idiosyncracy
impresario *not* impressario
inane *not* innane
incomprehensible *not* incomprehensable
infallible *not* infallable
innate *not* inate
innocuous *not* inocuous
innovate *not* inovate
inoculate *not* innoculate
iridescent *not* iridiscent
irresistible *not* irresistable, iresistible

knowledge *not* knowlege

laborious *not* labourious
laudable *not* laudible
leisure *not* liesure
liaise *not* liase
liaison *not* liason
lustrous *not* lusterous

maintenance *not* maintainance
manoeuvre *not* manouvre, maneuver
Mediterranean *not* Mediterrenean, Mediteranean
memento *not* momento
millennium *not* millenium, milennium
miniature *not* miniture, minature
minuscule *not* miniscule
moccasin *not* mocassin

Neapolitan *not* Neopolitan
necessary *not* neccesary
niece *not* neice

ninety *not* ninty
non-committal *not* non-comittal, non-commital,
  non-committall

obscene *not* obsene
obsession *not* obssession
occasion *not* ocassion
occurrence *not* ocurrence, occurence

pantomime *not* pantomine
parallel *not* parralel, paralell
parliament *not* parliment
patient *not* paitent, paitient
pejorative *not* perjorative
playwright *not* playright, playwrite
pneumonia *not* pnumonia
Portuguese *not* Portugese
prerogative *not* perogative
privilege *not* privelege, privilige, privelige, priviledge
puerile *not* purile

questionnaire *not* questionaire

rambunctious *not* rambunctuous, rambumtious
recommend *not* reccomend, recomend
reconnaissance *not* reconaissance
religious *not* religous
renaissance *not* rennaissance
repetitious *not* repititious
restaurateur *not* restauranteur
rhododendron *not* rhodedendron, rododendron
rhythm *not* rythym, rythm
rumbustious *not* rumbunctious, rumbustuous

sacrilegious *not* sacriligious, sacralegious, sacreligious
satellite *not* satallite, sattelite
scrumptious *not* scrumptuous
seize *not* sieze
separate *not* seperate
shaky *not* shakey
sherbet *not* sherbert
sheriff *not* sherriff, sherrif
siege *not* seige
spaghetti *not* spagetti
spaghetti bolognese *not* spagetti bolognaise
sporadic *not* sparodic
squalor *not* squalour
stony *not* stoney
straitjacket *not* straightjacket
strait-laced *not* straight-laced
stripy *not* stripey
✗ **stupefy** *not* stupify
sumptuous *not* sumptious
supersede *not* supercede
surprise *not* suprise

tariff *not* tarrif
tenterhooks *not* tenderhooks
tomorrow *not* tommorow, tomorow
tragedy *not* tradegy
tremor *not* tremour
twelfth *not* twelth, twelvth

umbrella *not* umberella
unanimous *not* unanimus, unaminous
unbelievable *not* unbelieveable

unctuous *not* unctious
unnecessary *not* unecessary, unneccesary

vaccinate *not* vaccinnate, vacinnate
vacuum *not* vaccum, vacumm
vermilion *not* vermillion
veterinary *not* vetinary
villainy *not* villany
vineyard *not* vinyard
visible *not* visable
vocabulary *not* vocablary
vocal cords *not* vocal chords

Wednesday *not* Wendsday, Wensday
weird *not* wierd
whittle *not* wittle
wholly *not* wholy

And here are a few examples of those prefixes and suffixes frequently confused and misspelt, those uns and ins, ibles and ables, ants and ents, cians, cions, sions and tions.

hospitable, irritable *but* indestructible, illegible

defendant, incessant *but* despondent, independent

commentary, monetary *but* monastery, confectionery
but accessory, purgatory

dietician, musician *but* coercion, suspicion *but* decision,
tension *but* attention, superstition

indefensible, insolvent *but* unsociable, unequal (*but* inequality)

If in doubt (as with all spellings), look it up.

In the following sentences, fill in the correct prefix or suffix.

1 A scientist works in a laborat—. *[orium]*

2 You didn't have to join the scheme – membership was volunt—. *[voluntary]*

3 The trains were intermitt— due to the wrong weather yet again. *[ent]*

4 The fish had no use for the bicycles – the machines were completely redund—. *[ant]*

5 Maria had the tuna melt as usual. The waitress said, 'You're so predict—.' *[able]*

6 Wayne could feel the wind in his hair – his new car was a convert—. *[ible]*

7 The serg— was despond— when the defend— was found not guilty. *[eant] [ent] [ant]*

8 George was feeling irrit— because the weeds in his garden were proving indestruct—. *[able] [able]*
[irritable ✗ / indestructible]

9 The courtroom was silent after the barrister's formid— summing-up, and the tens— was palp—. *[able] [ion] [able]*

10 Luckily the por—s in the cafe were pretty mean, as the chef's cooking was generally indigest—. *[tion] [ible]*

Watch out for anomalies when nouns ending in -ic or -i become verbs or adjectives. Words such as 'colic', 'frolic', 'mimic', 'panic', 'picnic', 'plastic', 'shellac', 'traffic' have a 'k' added after the 'c' when they become verb participles or adjectives – 'colicky', 'frolicking', 'mimicking', 'panicking', 'picnicking', 'plasticky', 'shellacking', 'trafficking'. Words ending in 'i' – 'graffiti', 'ski', 'taxi' – retain that 'i' when they become verb participles – 'graffitiing', 'skiing', 'taxiing'.

Preferred spellings

This is a list of words that have more than one spelling, but there is a preferred or standard form (by KF and RK anyway).

adrenalin *rather than* adrenaline
adviser *rather than* advisor
all right *rather than* alright
amid *rather than* amidst
among *rather than* amongst
bougainvillea *rather than* bougainvillaea
Caesarean *rather than* Caesarian
curtsy *rather than* curtsey
dispatch *rather than* despatch
encyclopedia *rather than* encyclopaedia
focused/focuses *rather than* focussed/focusses
grandad *rather than* granddad
gypsy *rather than* gipsy
hello *or* hallo *rather than* hullo
likeable *rather than* likable
lovable *rather than* loveable
medieval *rather than* mediaeval
naive *rather than* naïve
naivety *rather than* naïvety *or* naïveté
nonetheless *rather than* none the less
no one *rather than* no-one *and definitely not* noone
nosy *rather than* nosey
OK *rather than* okay
pricey *rather than* pricy
protester *rather than* protestor
racket *rather than* racquet
Shakespearean *rather than* Shakespearian

swap *rather than* swop
tsar *rather than* tzar *or* czar
unmistakable *rather than* unmistakeable
unshakeable *rather than* unshakable
veranda *rather than* verandah
while *rather than* whilst
yogurt *rather than* yoghurt

In addition, where it can be either, -ise endings are preferred
to -ize endings – words such as 'antagonise', 'civilise', 'realise',
'recognise', etc., *rather than* 'antagonize', 'civilize', 'realize',
'recognize', etc. (The latter style is favoured by the *Oxford English
Dictionary* and the Americans.)

With -t or -ed endings, there is no preference, just be consistent,
although there is an obvious difference in pronunciation with some.

burned / burnt
dreamed / dreamt
kneeled / knelt
leaned / leant
leaped / leapt
learned / learnt
smelled / smelt
spelled / spelt
spilled / spilt
spoiled / spoilt

But there is no such word as 'earnt'.

Pronunciations

Apart from one or two words, this is nothing to do with regional variations or accents – northern English short and southern English long 'a' sounds, etc., are fine – but rather to do with standard emphases and stresses.

Let's start with 'pronunciation' itself – look at the spelling, it's pro<u>nun</u>ciation, *not* pro<u>noun</u>ciation. Here are a few more words that often puzzle people (and irritate others when they are mispronounced).

> **amenity** – ah-<u>meen</u>-iti, rather than ah-<u>men</u>-iti (which is the
>   American pronunciation)
> **analogous** – hard 'g', an-nal-o-gus
> **anchovy** – stress on first syllable, <u>an</u>chovy, rather than
>   an<u>cho</u>vy
> **appreciate** – appre-<u>shee</u>-ate, not appre-<u>see</u>-ate
> **argot** – the 't' is silent, so 'argo'
>
> **buffet** – another silent 't', buff-ay, when referring to the meal
>
> **centenary** – sen <u>teen</u> ary, rather than sen-<u>ten</u>-ary
> **cerebral** – stress on second syllable, ser-<u>ree</u>-brul, is more
>   common, though stress on first syllable, <u>ser</u>-ri-brul,
>   is also OK
> **cervical** – stress on first syllable, <u>ser</u>-vik-le, is more common,
>   though stress on second syllable, ser-<u>vy</u>-kle, is used in
>   medicine
> **chimera** – hard 'c', ky-meer-a
> **clematis** – stress on first syllable, <u>clem</u>atis, rather than
>   clem<u>ay</u>tis
> **clerk** – rhyming with 'dark', not rhyming with 'jerk'
> **comparable** – stress on first syllable, <u>com</u>parable, rather than
>   com<u>par</u>able

controversy – stress on second syllable, con<u>tro</u>versy, is more common, though stress on first syllable, <u>con</u>troversy, is more traditional

data – day-ta, rather than dah-ta
-day – as in Mon-day, rather than Mon-dee
debacle – stress on second syllable, day-<u>bark</u>-cul
debris – stress on first syllable, <u>deb</u>-ree; <u>day</u>-bree is also OK but avoid duh-<u>bree</u>
decade – <u>deck</u>-aid, rather than dick-<u>aid</u>
desultory – four syllables, stress on first, <u>dez</u>-ul-tor-i
detritus – stress on second syllable – de-<u>try</u>-tus
dilemma – di<u>lem</u>ma is more traditional, but <u>dy</u>lemma is OK too
dour – sounding more like 'do-er' than 'dower'
drawing – note, there is only one 'r': it's not 'drawring'
due – not 'Jew', pronounce the 'd'

economic – eko-<u>nom</u>-ic is more common, though eeko-<u>nom</u>-ic is OK
either – <u>eye</u>-ther is more traditional, but <u>ee</u>-ther is OK
envelope – <u>en</u>-ve-lope is more common, but <u>on</u>-ve-lope is OK too
err – er, rather than air
espresso – 's'presso, not 'x'presso
et cetera – exactly as it's spelt, not ek cetera or eggs cetra

feral – stress on first syllable, <u>fair</u>-ul
finance – <u>fy</u>-nance, rather than fi-<u>nance</u>
forehead – four-head these days, rather than forrid
furore – three syllables – few-roar-i – rather than two – few-roar

gala – gah-la, rather than gay-la
genealogy – stress on third syllable, jeanie-<u>al</u>-ogy

glacier – rhyming with 'lass' is more common, though rhyming with 'face' is not wrong

h – pronounced 'aitch', not 'haitch', as in 'aitch$(H)_2O$', not 'haitch$(H)_2O$', 'W. Aitch Auden', not 'W. Haitch Auden' (ignore, though, if you're Irish where it's fine, to be sure, so it is)

harass – stress on first syllable, ha̲rass, is more traditional, but stress on second syllable, hara̲ss, is becoming increasingly common (it's the American pronunciation)

homage – hom-ij, rather than om-arge

homosexual – hom-oh-sexual or hoe-mo-sexual

hyperbole – four syllables with stress on second, hype̲rbolee, rather than three syllables, hyperbowl

ideology – eye-di-o̲l-ogy, rather than id-i-o̲l-ogy

idyllic – id-i̲ll-ik, rather than e̲ye-dil-ik

inclement – stress on second syllable, incle̲ment

innovative – stress on first syllable, i̲nnovative, rather than innova̲ytive or inoh̲vative

integral – stress on first syllable, i̲n-te-grul, though stress on second syllable, in-te̲g-rul, is OK

irreparable – four syllables, not five, with stress on the second, irre̲p-rabble, rather than irrepai̲rrable

irrevocable – five syllables, with stress on second, irre̲vocable, rather than irrevo̲keable

issue – ish-you, rather than iss-you

italic – i-tal-ik, not eye-tal-ik

kilometre – stress on second syllable, ki-lo̲m-eter, is more common, though stress on first syllable, ki̲ll-ometer, is more traditional

lamentable – stress on first syllable, <u>la</u>-mentable, rather than la-<u>ment</u>-able

lido – lee-do, rather than ly-do

lieutenant – left-tenant, not loo-tenant (that's strictly US)

litotes – ly-toe-tees

loath – rhyming with 'both', not rhyming with 'cove'

longevity – soft 'g', lon-jev-ity

magus – hard 'g', may-gus, but the plural, 'maji', soft 'g', may-jy

migraine – <u>mee</u>graine is more traditional, but <u>my</u>graine is OK (though don't give yourself a headache over it)

nadir – nay-dear, though nad-ear is OK

née – nay, not knee

neither – see 'either' above

nomenclature – stress on second syllable, no-<u>men</u>-clature

nonpareil – stress on last syllable, non-pa-<u>rail</u>, rather than non-pa-<u>rile</u>

non sequitur – stress on second syllable, non <u>sek</u>-wit-ur

often – offen, rather than offten

paean – <u>pee</u>-un, rather than <u>pay</u>-un

papaya – stress on second syllable, pa-<u>pie</u>-ya (or call it a pawpaw)

paprika – stress on first syllable, <u>pap</u>-ri-ka, rather than pap-<u>ree</u>-ka

patriot – <u>pay</u>-triot, rather than <u>pat</u>-riot

pedagogy – ped-a-gog-i, but ped-a-goj-i is OK

plaid – plad, not played

privacy – <u>priv</u>-a-see, rather than <u>pry</u>-va-see

project – first syllable rhyming with 'dodge', not with 'dough'

promenade – stress on third syllable, prom-i-<u>nard</u>

quagmire – <u>kwog</u>-mire, though <u>kwag</u>-mire is OK
quasi – kway-zye, rather than kwar-zye or kwar-zi

racist – ray-sist, not ray-shist
reliquary – stress on first syllable, <u>rel</u>-i-quarry
respite – spite, not spit
revelatory – stress on third syllable, rev-el-<u>ay</u>-tory

scallop – skollop, though skallop is OK
schedule – shedyule, rather than skedyule
scone – KF would rhyme it with 'con' because she's a
    southerner; RK would rhyme it with 'cone' because she's
    a northerner – reluctantly, we have to agree both are fine
sewage – soo-ij, rather than see-you-ij
skeletal – stress on first syllable, <u>skell</u>-i-tle, rather than
    ske-<u>lee</u>-tal
sojourn – stress on first syllable, <u>soj</u>-earn
species – spee-shees, rather than spee-sees
stereotype – <u>stair</u>-e-o-type, not <u>steer</u>-e-o-type
subsidence – sub-<u>sy</u>-dense, rather than sub-<u>si</u>-dense
sudoku – sue-<u>doe</u>-coo
synecdoche – sin-ek-ducky
syzygy – <u>scissor</u>-ji (two connecting things, not a Polish
    pop group)

tête-à-tête – tet-ah-tet, rather than tayte-ah-tayte
the – when this little word is before a vowel, it's pronounced
    'thee' (so 'thee apple', not 'thuh apple')
theatre – theer-ter, not the-et-her
tissue – tish-you, rather than tiss-you
tortoise – tortus, rather than tortoys
transparent – rhyming with 'apparent', not rhyming
    with 'parent'

turquoise – turk-woyz, rather than turk-ois or turk-wahz
tyrannical – tee-ran-ikle, rather than ty-ran-ikle

urine – yoor-in, not yoor-ine

venal – vee-nul, rhyming with 'penal', not rhyming with
    'fennel'
via – rhyming with 'dire', not rhyming with 'deer'
vice versa – vy-sah ver-sah, not vycee ver-sah or vycee ver-see
vitae – vee-tie, rather than vee-tay
viva – vy-va, rather than vee-va (España)

A few strange place names that are quite often mispronounced:
Bicester – Bister; **Dun Laoghaire** – Dun Leery (well, bugger me);
Holborn – Ho-bun; **Keighley** – Keith-lee; **Kirkcaldy** – Ker-coddy;
Marylebone – Marry-le-bun; **Plaistow** – Plah-stow; **Shrewsbury** –
Shroes-bury; **Pontypridd** – Ponty-preeth. And a few across
the pond: **Adirondack** – Addy-ron-dack; **Arkansas** – Ar-kan-saw;
St Louis – Saint Lewis; **Yosemite** – Yoh-sem-itty.

Just to get a couple more spellings and pronunciations off our
chests: It's 'Katherine' with a 'K', not a 'C', and 'Fry' as in 'small' –
really not that difficult. It's 'Roweena' rhyming with 'hyena',
not 'Rowenna' rhyming with 'henna', and 'Kirton', not things
drawn together or apart.

> Always read stuff through before sending (and check who you
> are sending to – don't send the grouchy gripe about your boss
> to everyone in the building, including your boss), and don't use
> textspeak or rely on a spellchecker – if in doubt, use a dictionary.

In the following extracts, correct the spelling mistakes and confusions.

Her experiance had been of a kind to teach her, rightly or wrongly, that the doubtfull honor of a brief transit threw a sorry world hardly called for efusiveness, even when the path was suddenly eradiated at sum half-way point by daybeams rich as hers. But her strong sense that niether she nor any human being deserved less than was given, did not blind her to the fact that there were others recieving less who had deserved much more. And in being forced to class herself among the unfortunite she did not cease to wander at the persistance of the unforseen, when the won to whom such unbroken tranquility had bean acorded in the adult stage was she who's youth had seamed to teach that hapinness was but the ocassional episode in a general drama of pane.

Thomas Hardy, *The Mayor of Casterbridge*

Ironicly, it was Begbie who was the quay. Ripping of your mates was the highest offense in his book, and he would demand the severist penulty. Renton had used Begbie, used him to burn his boats compleatly and utterly. It was Begbie who insured he could never return. He had done what he wanted to do. He could now never go back to Lieth, to Edinborough, even to Scotland, ever again. There, he could not be anything other than he was. Now, free from them all for good, he could bee what he wanted to bee. He'd stand or fall alone. This thought both terrified and exited hymn as he contemplated live in Amsterdam.

Irvine Welsh, *Trainspotting*

As the saint was born away, the people, in an agony of suspence, scrutinized the patience in order to sea if their had bean any change. Some one spotted Socrates and pointed. He was shaking his soldiers like an athlete about to throw a javelin, and he was starring with amazement at his hands, moving his fingers in order one by one. He looked up sudenly, saw that every one was watching him, and waived shyly. An unatural howl went up from the crowd, and Socrates' mother fell to her knees, kissing her sun's hands. She stood up, through up her arms to the wide sky, and called, 'Praise to the saint, praise to the saint,' so that in know thyme at all the hole assembly was histerical with exhilirated awe. Dr Iannis pulled Pelagia away from the inpending crush, and wiped the swet from his face and the tiers from his eyes. He was trembling in every part of his body, and so, he saw, was Pelagia. 'A purely sychological phenomonen,' he muttered to himself, and was struck suddenly by the sensasion of being an ingrate. The bell of the church began to peel out wildly as nuns and priests decorously fort each other for the tug of the wire.

Louis de Bernières, *Captain Corelli's Mandolin*

4 | Beyond the Basics

When I split an infinitive, god damn it,
I split it so it stays split.

Raymond Chandler

Verbing weirds language.

Bill Watterson, *Calvin and Hobbes*

While the first three chapters cover the more straightforward stuff (OK, quite a bit isn't *that* straightforward), this chapter deals with more quirky, more tricky, more nuanced, more divisive issues, things off the beaten track, why to use this rather than that. Extra bits and bobs that make people stop short, because they know one path is correct and one isn't, but can't remember which one, or why. And just to complicate matters, in a few cases, both paths might be correct, or neither.

Accents and diacritics

Accents and diacritics are marks above and below letters indicating how a word is pronounced. They are not native to the English language, but many words we have incorporated from Europe do use accents. Some words are now so ingrained that we no longer need the mark, while others are retained because without the accent either the word is ambiguous – such as 'pate' (head), 'pâte' (paste for porcelain) or 'pâté' (paste of meat, fish, etc.) – or the pronunciation is debatable – 'soufflé' (a familiar, not always successful, fluffy egg concoction) might be mistaken for 'souffle' (a rather obscure name for the sound heard via a stethoscope).

Here are some words that no longer need accents. (None of them should cause any problems re pronunciation.) To put an accent on them can look old-fashioned or, worse, pretentious.

cafe	eclair	melee
debacle	elite	naive
decor	facade	naivety
denouement	fete	premiere
divorcee	matinee	role

Here are some other words, though, that should always have accents or diacritics.

André	déjà vu	omertà
aperçu	doppelgänger	outré
appliqué	éclat	papier mâché
attaché	émigré	passé
Béarnaise (sauce)	entrée	pâte
bête noire	exposé	pâté
blasé	fiancé(e)	pièce de résistance
Brontë	fin de siècle	pietà
cafetière	flambé	plié
caffè latte	Fräulein	protégé(e)
canapé	Führer	purée
Champs-Elysées	Guantánamo	raison d'être
Chloë	idée fixe	répétiteur
cinéma-vérité	ingénue	retroussé
Citroën	jeté	risqué

cliché	maître d'	rosé (wine)
compère	manqué	rösti (potato)
consommé	marinière	roué
cortège	maté	sauté
coup d'état	ménage à trois	Schrödinger's cat
coup de grâce	métier	señor
coup de théâtre	meunière	señora
coupé	Moët & Chandon	señorita
crèche	Motörhead	soirée
crème de la crème	naïf	soufflé
crêpe	né/(e)	soupçon
Dáil	(salad) Niçoise	tête-à-tête
décolletage	objet trouvé	touché
devoré	olé!	Zoë

The marks on Chloë and Zoë Brontë (those lesser known, illiterate sisters) are not umlauts, which are used on German words, they are diaereses. Most Zoës spell their name with one, though not all, and occasionally it's then pronounced 'Zo', which as all keen Scrabble players will know is a useful two-letter word meaning a Himalayan animal similar to a yak or cow.

Although/though

These words are often interchangeable – although 'although' is more formal, and sounds nicer at the start of sentence. 'I'm quite full, although I could probably manage a piece of that apple cake' and 'I'm quite full, though I could probably manage a piece of that apple cake' are both fine. There are really no instances where 'though' cannot substitute for 'although', but there are instances where only 'though' is appropriate. For example, 'although' cannot be used with 'as' and 'even' – it makes no sense to say 'Even although I'm quite full, I could probably manage a piece of that apple cake' (it should be 'Even <u>though</u> I'm quite full . . .'). Neither can it be used as an adverb – 'She had eaten too much although, and it would have made her sick to run for the bus' (it should be 'She had eaten too much <u>though</u> . . .').

In the following sentences, should 'although' or 'though' be used?

1 Even — Daisy was one of the smallest girls in her class, she could run very fast and won the 400-metre race. *though*

2 — James would rather be watching the telly, he hadn't finished his homework. *Although*

3 Her books are unreadable, — that doesn't stop the gullible public buying them. *although / though*

4 Michael claimed he was far too busy to see his relatives; he could still find the time to play solitaire on the computer, —. *though*

5 Ben wanted to leave his job, — he decided it was better to wait until he'd got his bonus. *although*

6 Fred bought a coat for his wife, — the shop said he could bring it back if she didn't like it. *though*

7 William started to make a Christmas list, — it was only January. *although*

8 — he suffered from acrophobia, Archie braved it up the Eiffel Tower. *Although*

9 If I were you, —, I wouldn't do that. *though*

10 It looks as — it's going to snow again. *though*

'And' at the start of a sentence

Despite what you might have been taught at school – or what your children are still being taught at school – it's fine to use this little word at the beginning of a sentence; just look at most of Genesis, or indeed most of the Bible. It can, in fact, be quite effective, even stylish, although avoid overdoing it (only the Bible/God's scribes can get away with it for page after page). Similar aversion has been applied to 'but'. But, again, there is no reason not to use it to start a sentence – 'But, soft! what light through yonder window breaks?' for example.

Around/round

These words are often interchangeable – 'He put the noose round his neck' or 'He put the noose around his neck' – but there is in fact a difference. 'Round' is more specific and precise, 'around' more abstract: 'The house is round the corner', 'They worked round the clock'; 'She looked around the room, before finding an available seat', 'We walked around ten miles today'.

American usage is the opposite (see Chapter 5) – hence the film (or movie) *The Shop Around the Corner* and Bill Haley's 'Rock Around the Clock'.

(And of course a ball is always round, not around – unless it's a rugby ball, which is neither.)

In the following sentences, should 'around' or 'round' be used?

1 — and — the garden like a teddy bear . . .

2 There isn't enough food to go —.

3 — the windows the roses were in full bloom.

4 She slipped her arm — his waist, and smirked at his ex-girlfriend.

5 What's a girl supposed to do to get a drink — here?

6 David is hanging — with the wrong people.

7 Go — the —about, take the second exit, then first left, and the optician's is — there, I think.

8 The tradesmen's entrance is — the back.

9 We're meeting — eight o'clock.

10 There were red faces all — when the wrong version of Jonathan Franzen's *Freedom* was published.

Avoiding pronouns

Nowadays, it seems rather old-fashioned and pompous to use 'one' – as in 'One should learn grammar if one is to write properly'. But, at the same time, 'You should learn grammar if you are going to write properly' sounds rather patronising and bossy. And using 'he/she', or the even more irritating 's/he', is cumbersome and smacks of political correctness – 'It will help him/her to write properly if he/she learns some grammar.' So, if possible, try to avoid the use of such pronouns in these types of sentences. 'In order to write properly, it is a good idea to learn grammar' or 'Learning grammar will make it easier to write properly' are more neutral statements, but manage to convey the same message in a less heavy-handed way. Unless, of course, heavy-handedness is what one/you/he/she needs . . .

Between you and me

Using 'I' instead of 'me' after 'between' is a mistake people often make. This is sometimes because they think 'I' is more 'correct English'. Well, it is if 'I' is being used as a subjective pronoun, but not as an objective one. Yes, 'you and I are baking a cake', but 'between you and me, we are baking a cake'. This is the hint: it's 'between *us*' (i.e. you and me), not 'between *we*' (i.e. you and I). If in doubt, try the phrase in the plural – us – first and the error will be avoided. So: 'Between us, we managed to push the car up the hill', or 'Between Matthew, Mark, Luke and me, we managed to push the car up the hill', but *not* 'Between Matthew, Mark, Luke and I, we managed to push the car up the hill'.

Bored

It is 'bored by' or 'bored with', *not* 'bored of'. 'I'm bored by these stupid people' and 'I'm bored with this physics lesson' are fine, but 'I'm bored of waiting in all day for my delivery' is not (though common in both respects).

Can/may

These are often blurred, but there is a distinction (although some might think it an old-fashioned one). 'Can' is the *capability* of doing something; 'may' is the *possibility* of doing something. The difference is to do with permission. If Bill says, 'Can I borrow this book?' he's not really asking the right question. Of course he's capable of borrowing it, but he should be asking if it's possible to borrow it (I might not have finished reading it, or I might know that Bill never gives books back), so technically it should be, 'May I borrow this book?'

Clarity and concision

Think about this when writing – in both ordinary communication and for more literary purposes. Long-windedness can obscure the meaning or simply bore the reader. Don't use six words when one will do – particularly with adjectives. It may be a cliché (all right, one or two are permissible – see 'Clichés' below), but less is more . . .

Aim for simplicity –

> This piece of work was a lazy, inferior, worthless, poorly
> constructed, substandard, unsatisfactory, second-rate effort

is verbose.

> Your work was very disappointing

conveys the point more succinctly and is probably more
devastating for its brevity.

Avoid ambiguity –

> I felt sick – someone muttered something about the food from
> the kebab van I'd eaten earlier.

The speaker is probably feeling queasy as a result of the shish
kebab he's eaten, but from the way the sentence is constructed,
it sounds as though he's eaten the van.

> He wore a dirty priest's collar around his neck.

Is the priest dirty or the collar?

And try not to show off – the occasional obscure word can be
stylish, instructive even, but if a reader is spending more time
looking up words in the dictionary than on the piece of writing,
something's wrong.

Clichés

Avoid like the plague . . . But sometimes it's easier said than
done . . . And occasionally they can be worth their weight in
gold (to coin a phrase) . . . And that's probably enough of flogging
a dead horse.

Collective nouns

Do collective nouns (see Chapter 1, p. 7) take a singular or plural verb? In the UK either is fine, with the plural more common, although the US practice is to go for the singular. Whichever is used, however, make sure any related pronouns follow the same form. For example, 'The audience *was* so distracted by the mobile-phone conversation in the fifth row, *it* missed the director's coup de théâtre' or 'The audience *were* so distracted by the mobile-phone conversation in the fifth row, *they* missed the director's coup de théâtre' are both fine. However, 'The audience *was* so distracted by the mobile-phone conversation in the fifth row, *they* missed the director's coup de théâtre' and 'The audience *were* so distracted by the mobile-phone conversation in the fifth row, *it* missed the director's coup de théâtre' are not. RK's preference is the singular form (because it is *one* audience), KF's for the plural (because an audience is made up of more than one person – with any luck).

In the following sentences, put in the correct verb or pronoun.

1 The government — ruining the country and they will be voted out at the next election.

2 Random House always treats — authors well.

3 The choir — out of sync with the orchestra and so they got a bollocking from the conductor after the performance.

4 The football team performed so badly that even their fans booed — off.

5 The flight of swallows — feeling a bit cold, so it decided it was time to head south.

6 The cast were gloomy when — play closed early.

7 That family — had enough of this intrusion into its privacy.

8 The flock of sheep were making so much noise — frightened the dog away.

9 The army — fed up with having its budget cut yet again.

10 England has improved — performance since the last Test match.

Comparative and superlative

An adjective in its basic form is an *absolute*, but it also has a *comparative* and a *superlative* form, such as 'bright', 'brighter', 'brightest', or 'dim', 'dimmer', 'dimmest'. However, a few comparatives and superlatives are irregular (that old chestnut), the most common being 'good', 'better', 'best' and 'bad', 'worse', 'worst'.

The general rule is if the adjective is one syllable – 'thick', for example – add '-er' and '-est' to the absolute to form the comparative and superlative ('thicker', 'thickest'), but if the adjective has three or more syllables, use 'more' and 'most' with the absolute, otherwise it sounds pretty clunky – so 'more beautiful' and 'most beautiful', rather than 'beautifuller' and 'beautifullest'. If the adjective has two syllables, take your pick: 'chunkier' or 'more chunky', 'chunkiest' or 'most chunky', 'bouncier' or 'more bouncy', 'bounciest' or 'most bouncy'. Don't use both together though: 'more better' and 'most best' make no sense.

Compare to / compare with

On the whole, 'compare to' is used when two things are similar, 'compare with' when two things are different. For example: 'The chorus girls were compared to a herd of elephants'; 'The national A-level results were fantastic compared with last year's.' (This seems to be an annual tradition nowadays . . .)

Comprise

'Comprise' means to 'consist of', and tradition dictates that therefore it should never be used with 'of' because it's already included – so 'The publishing house comprises many imprints' rather than 'The publishing house comprises of many imprints'. But like so many traditions, this is not always the case today – particularly when used *passively* rather than *actively*. 'The book comprises fifty chapters' or 'The book is comprised of fifty chapters' are both fine.

Could / might

Like 'can' and 'may', the distinction between these two slightly longer words is often blurred, but, again, there is one. 'Could' suggests *ability* (like 'can') – 'Harry could watch the football match' because he has eyes and a TV. 'Might' means *perhaps* – 'Harry might watch the football match' – if his team is playing, if he's finished his homework, if his mum isn't watching another channel, etc.

Could of, should of, would of

Do not use. The terms are 'could have', 'should have', 'would have' (or 'could've', 'should've, would've). Macbeth doesn't say 'She should of died hereafter', does he? And even Eliza doesn't sing 'I could of danced all night' . . .

Danglers

A dangler – or technically a dangling participle – occurs when two clauses of a sentence are not obviously connected. With the subject missing from the first clause, the subject of the second clause is forced to apply to both parts, but makes no sense.

> Eating my sandwich still, the train pulled into the platform.

To the reader, this could sound like the train is eating the passenger's sandwich, which is obviously not what the writer intends. What he probably means is:

> I was still eating my sandwich as the train pulled into the platform.

Or another way of putting it:

> As the train pulled into the platform, I was still eating my sandwich.

Another example:

> Serving an ace, the fans cheered the new Wimbledon champion.

This sounds as though the entire Centre Court served the ace, and not Roger Federer. Instead, the writer should say:

> The fans cheered the new Wimbledon champion when he served an ace.

A dangler should be avoided as it's not related grammatically to the rest of the sentence, can be ambiguous and wastes readers' time as they try to puzzle out the sense.

Different from, different to, different than

All three constructs are permissible – though some people will be horrified to hear this. In UK English, 'different from' is traditionally the correct form – as in 'The hotel is different from the one we stayed at last time'. Purists might disagree, but 'different to' is also acceptable in the UK – as in 'My coffee looks different to yours'.

While 'different than' is seldom used in the UK, in the US it is the favoured option, and 'different to' is almost never used. If push came to shove, 'different from' is the one that still probably sounds best.

Dr or Mr / Mrs / Miss

When is a doctor a Dr? A physician is always a 'Dr'; a surgeon is not, however, so use 'Mr', 'Mrs' or 'Miss' (unless your physician or surgeon is a professor or knighted, then it's Prof., Sir or Dame). In the US, however, there is no difference – your surgeon is a 'Dr'.

Double negatives

Don't use two negatives when one is intended for the sense.
'I didn't do nothing' actually means 'I did everything' – but that's not what's usually meant. It should be either 'I didn't do anything' or 'I did nothing'.

In addition to 'not' and 'nothing', other negative words, like 'barely', 'hardly', 'rarely', 'scarcely' shouldn't be doubled up – 'I didn't hardly touch her' would be no defence, as well as ungrammatical. Rather than confess, what the accused probably intended to say was 'I hardly touched her' or 'I didn't touch her'.

Other words to watch out for include 'decline', 'deny', 'refuse' – 'Suzanne declined not to be interviewed for the *Today* programme' suggests that Suzanne was eagerly awaiting that call from John Humphrys when in fact she'd turned puce at the very thought of it, and 'declined to be interviewed'.

However, there are a couple of instances when a double negative is acceptable. One is when a negative word is linked to another with a negative prefix, like 'dis-', 'non-', 'un-'. 'Your idea is not unappealing' is more understated than 'Your idea is appealing'. And 'Your short story is not uninteresting' is a more polite way of saying 'Your short story is not very good'. Another instance is in a construct such as 'We can't not go to the wedding – you are the best man, after all' – because both negatives are required for the sense. The best man clearly doesn't want to go to the wedding (does he hate/love the bride?), so 'We can go to the wedding' wouldn't work as a response to his little tantrum. One more instance is for literary effect. 'I wasn't sure her eyes were not filling with tears' is a bit more subtle than 'I was sure her eyes were filling with tears'.

Elder/older

As an adjective, 'older', meaning 'more old', is the term to use, so: 'My edition is older; let's use yours instead.' 'Elder' can be used with family relationships, such as 'my elder sister', but even here 'older' is now preferred. However, 'elder' as a noun cannot be replaced with 'older' – there are no tribal or church 'olders'. 'Elder' is also retained in certain set phrases – 'elder statesmen', 'elders and betters'. Another use is to differentiate between famous fathers and sons from days gone by – Pieter Bruegel the Elder, Pieter Bruegel the Younger; Pitt the Elder, Pitt the Younger. Nowadays they would probably be called Pitt Senior and Pitt Junior – like those Bushes.

Fewer/less

These two words are often muddled up, but there is a difference. 'Fewer' applies to things that can be counted; 'less' applies to things that can't be counted and fixed amounts.

'Fewer people went to see the play after the reviews came out', *not* 'Less people went to see the play after the reviews came out'. 'Fewer tickets were sold, so the show closed early', *not* 'Less tickets were sold, so the show closed early'. 'Fewer people meant less popcorn sold', *not* 'Less people meant fewer popcorn sold'. 'Tickets were being flogged for less than five quid in the final week of performances – which was actually less than a month after it opened', *not* 'Tickets were being flogged for fewer than five quid in the final week of performances – which was actually fewer than a month after it opened'.

In the following sentences, should 'fewer' or 'less' be used?

1 There were — disruptive children in the class so the teacher ~fewer / less~ was — distracted.

2 The rugby team scored — tries than they did last season.

3 The author sold — books than he thought he would, as there ~fewer / less~ was — of a crowd than expected at the literary festival.

4 — is more ... ~less~

5 Standing in the queue for five items or —, Carmen ~fewer / less~ was — than pleased to see the man in front had six items in his basket.

6 The door was — than ten metres away, so Don decided ~less~ to make a quick exit.

7 It will take about three hours or — to get there. ~less~

8 There are — police on the streets these days. ~less~

9 You'll consume — calories if you eat — food. ~fewer / less~

10 — than a year after they married, the couple split up. ~less~

First / firstly

Either is OK, but be consistent in a list, so 'first, second and third'; or 'firstly, secondly and thirdly' (or even 'firstly, secondly and lastly'); but *not* 'first, secondly, third' (or 'firstly, second and last').

Foreign names

Surnames with the prefixes d', da, de, du, van, von, etc., are usually lower case in French, German and Spanish names, and upper case in Flemish, while the Dutch and Italians seem to swing both ways.

Generally, non-anglicised European names with a prefix lose it when referred to just by the surname – as in Manuel de Falla (Falla), Marquis de Sade (Sade), Ludwig van Beethoven (Beethoven), Johann Wolfgang von Goethe (Goethe), and that is where they are listed in the hypothetical phone book. (There are exceptions – as usual – like de Gaulle and de Beauvoir, von Sternberg and von Trapp.) However, if they are anglicised, particularly from the French, the practice seems to be to retain the prefix, as in Walter de la Mare (de la Mare), Olivia de Havilland (de Havilland), Daphne du Maurier (du Maurier).

With the Dutch and Flemish (and South African), the prefixes vary – both in case and in where they are listed in that hypothetical phone book. Vincent Van Gogh is always Van Gogh, not Gogh; Jan Van Eyck is Van Eyck, not Eyck; Rembrandt van Rijn, just to muddle things up even more, is Rembrandt, not van Rijn or Rijn; F.W. de Klerk is de Klerk, Willem de Kooning is de Kooning.

Italian prefixes, likewise, vary in case and listing – Catherine de' Medici (Medici *or* de' Medici), Giovanni Pierluigi da Palestrina (Palestrina), Leonardo da Vinci (Leonardo), Lorenzo da Ponte (da Ponte), Dino de Laurentiis (de Laurentiis), Vittorio De Sica (De Sica). And watch out for those Italian Americans, as there's no consistency there – Don DeLillo, Robert De Niro, Danny DeVito, Leonardo DiCaprio, Vincent D'Onofrio.

In the same way, the Scottish have variations on the theme of Mac and Mc, but the listing is always under 'Mac' even if spelt Mc, so 'Adam McBeth' comes before 'Eve MacBeth'.

Lower-case prefixes should be used with or without the first name – it's always 'de Beauvoir', 'von Trapp', 'du Maurier', not

'De Beauvoir', 'Von Trapp', 'Du Maurier' – unless the sentence begins 'De Beauvoir . . .', 'Von Trapp . . .', 'Du Maurier . . .'.

Foreign places

Some places have an English translation, so stick to that – don't say 'We're going to Firenze for the weekend on easyJet', or 'Tom's having his stag week in München and Praha'. Other names, however, keep the original, so it's 'Aix-en-Provence', not 'Aix in Province', and 'Baden-Baden' not 'Bath-Bath'.

Foreign words now English

These are words taken from other languages, but which are now common enough to be considered part of ours. So there is no need to emphasise them – either by italicising or putting in quote marks – when writing. French words now familiar in English include: ballet, cul-de-sac, en suite, faux pas; German words: dachshund, kindergarten, lager, zeitgeist; Italian: cappuccino, opera, paparazzi, pizza; Latin: ad infinitum, curriculum vitae, decree nisi, et cetera; Spanish: flamenco, paella, poncho, tapas; Russian: bolshie, gulag, tsar, vodka; Yiddish: bagel, chutzpah, schlep, shtum; Chinese: chop-chop, chow mein, lychee, t'ai chi; Indian: curry, jodhpurs, kedgeree, khaki; Japanese: karaoke, origami, sudoku, tsunami; et cetera, et cetera, ad infinitum . . .

Former and latter

Only use these words when referring to two things – former being the first, latter the second. Don't use if referring to three or more things, or only one. Also, they work best in quick succession; otherwise, the readers may lose their way (and their will to live) trying to search for that 'former' three pages back.

From/to

In a list, 'from' and 'to' should be used only with two things or types of things, otherwise the list becomes clumsy and unintelligible. 'This music reference book covers everything from Abba to Zappa', *not* 'This music reference book covers everything from Abba to the Beatles to Coldplay to Zappa', *and not* 'This music reference book covers everything from Abba and from the Beatles, to Coldplay and to Zappa'. Also watch out for long-windedness. 'This music reference book covers everything from Abba to the Beatles, from Blur to Coldplay, from the Dandy Warhols to Elbow, from Joy Division to the Kaiser Chiefs, from the Smiths to Tinie Tempah, from Rufus Wainwright to X-Ray Spex, from the Yeah Yeah Yeahs to Zappa' is accurate but deadly dull. If using three things is unavoidable, connect with 'via' or 'through' – 'The gallery covers modern art from impressionism via surrealism to postmodernism' or 'His oeuvre went from the thriller through science fiction to romcom'. Again, not ideal, and a little verbose. Best to follow the succinct Dorothy Parker on Katharine Hepburn: 'She ran the whole gamut of emotions from A to B.'

From/to, between/and

Don't mix these up. The construction is 'Her holiday was from Saturday to Wednesday' or 'Her holiday was between Saturday and Wednesday', or 'Her holiday was Saturday–Wednesday', *not* 'Her holiday was between Saturday to Wednesday', or 'Her holiday was from Saturday–Wednesday', etc.

Fused participle

'Your mentioning it reminded me that I had no idea what a fused participle was' is in fact an example of a fused participle. In the past, this construction seems to have been the subject of much heated debate – one side considering it grammatically hideous, the other side not really seeing the problem. Nowadays, most people would be in the latter camp.

A fused participle is when '-ing' is added to a verb – like a **gerund** (see below) – and it is preceded by a possessive noun or pronoun. A few examples: 'His missing the penalty meant we lost the match'; 'Kate's forgetting to add the eggs resulted in a rather disappointing Victoria sponge'; 'Your not knowing is very strange – she is your wife after all'; 'Stand not upon the order of your going, / But go at once'. These make sense to us (and the last one certainly did to Shakespeare). Sometimes it may sound less formal to leave off the possessive with a noun, as in: 'Miles breaking his leg left the team in chaos' instead of 'Miles's breaking his leg left the team in chaos'; 'The headmaster entering the room sent a wave of terror across the class' instead of 'The headmaster's entering the room sent a wave of terror across the class'. Both are fine (that is, if you are one of those who is fine with the concept of the fused participle).

However, there are times when using the fused participle can be clunky or ambiguous – and if that's the case, rephrase to avoid. For example, 'I don't think John's driving is a good idea.' This could mean John's driving is always terrible, or that it's just not a good idea this evening because he's about four times over the limit. If it's the former sense, perhaps rephrase as 'It's never a good idea for John to drive'; if it's the latter, 'It's not a good idea for John to drive, since he can barely stand up.'

Gender/sex

Unlike many other languages, English doesn't differentiate between genders. So we have 'the small man and the small woman', as opposed to *'le petit homme et la petite femme'*. However, there are a few words which do have a gender divide – a 'confidant' is male, a 'confidante' is female; 'fiancé' is male, 'fiancée' is female; 'né' is rare but male, 'née' is female. In UK English a 'divorcee' is both male and female, but in the US it's 'divorcé' and 'divorcée'. Conversely, 'blond' usually covers both male and female in the US, but in UK English it's 'blond' for the boys and 'blonde' for the girls. A 'masseur' covers both male and female in English, but if you want to be pedantic, or American, and the person who is giving you a rub-down is female, call her a 'masseuse'.

Then there is the slightly more controversial area of male and female job descriptions. These days we can all agree to ditch the 'adventuress', 'authoress', 'chairwoman' (though we're not that keen on 'chairperson' either – go for 'chair'), 'comedienne', 'manageress', 'poetess', 'sculptress', 'villainess'. But there are others which are not so straightforward. Some headmasters and headmistresses might prefer 'head', but others not. Most waiters and waitresses don't care what they're called so long as they're not shouted at and get a decent tip at the end of the shift. Likewise, the actor/actress – some women prefer the non-sex specific, others prefer 'actress', and it does depend on context. If a casting director asks a clueless agent to send 'actors' up for a new production of *The House of Bernarda Alba*, that agent could be wasting a lot of people's time when ten blokes from the agency turn up. And isn't it simpler to award the 'best actor' and 'best actress' rather than the 'best male actor' and the 'best female actor' at the Oscars? (Or abolish such awards altogether?) Like the waitresses, most actresses are more interested in the work than what they're called (so long as it's not 'luvvie').

And what to do with the lord mayor who is a woman? Apparently, she's still the lord mayor (which seems bizarre in the twenty-first century), because 'lady mayoress' is out as that's what is used for the female consort, and 'lady mayor' is deemed too weak. (Her husband is not called 'lady mayoress' or 'lord mayoress', by the way – it's the 'lord mayor's consort'.) Similarly, Elizabeth Butler-Sloss was known as the 'Lord Justice of Appeal'.

Meanwhile, at the other end of the sex scale, it still seems obligatory to attach the prefix 'male' to 'nurse' for all nurses who are men, and are there terms for the male 'dinner lady' and 'midwife'? But nothing is consistent, is it? Look at the cat world: why 'lioness' and 'tigress', but not 'cheetahess' or 'catess'?

And will the British go the same way as the French, who are waving *adieu* to 'mademoiselle'? A nice idea to abolish the distinction between 'madam' and 'mademoiselle', 'Mrs' and 'Miss', but someone come up with a better word than 'Ms', please.

Gerund

A gerund is formed by adding '-ing' to a verb, and it can function as a *verb*, but also as a *verbal noun* (another name for this type of gerund). 'The children enjoyed singing in the school concert' (here, 'singing' is a verb); 'The singing in the school concert was dismal' (and here, 'singing' is a verbal noun). A few more examples: 'She bottled out of diving into the pool as the board was giving her vertigo' and 'Time held me green and dying' (both verbs); 'No diving, jumping, spitting or surfing allowed in the pool' and 'Rage, rage against the dying of the light' (all verbal nouns).

Get (got)

This little word is often redundant and clumsy – particularly in writing. 'When Alec boarded the train, Laura was distraught but stoical' sounds better than 'When Alec got on the train, Laura was distraught but got over it quite quickly'. 'Elizabeth mounted her horse and when she reached Tilbury she made her famous speech' sounds better than 'Elizabeth got on her horse and when she got to Tilbury she made her famous speech'. Colloquially and in speech it's difficult to avoid, but some people consider it abhorrent even informally. Here are some variations on a theme for those who care, and those who don't: 'Do you have your PE kit?' or 'Have you got your PE kit?'; 'If we walk it will take us twenty minutes, but twice as long if we go by car using the satnav you were given for Christmas' or 'It will take twenty minutes to get there if we walk, but twice as long if we go by car using the satnav you got for Christmas'.

Hence

'Hence' means 'from here', 'from now', 'from there', so don't say or write 'from hence' – the 'from' is already included. (The same applies to similar constructions – 'henceforth', 'henceforward', 'thence', 'thenceforth', 'whence', 'whither' – though most of these are obsolete and archaic.) So, 'The book is to be published six weeks hence' or 'The book is to be published six weeks from now' but *not* 'The book is to be published six weeks from hence'. It can also mean 'for this reason' or 'therefore'.

Hoi polloi

This Greek phrase literally means 'the masses' or 'the common people'. As 'hoi' therefore equals 'the', pedants will insist on referring to 'hoi polloi' rather than 'the hoi polloi'. However, because it has become one of those foreign words that is now ours (see above), it sounds like showing off to use the original. Note that definition of 'hoi polloi' – it is often mistakenly used to mean 'toffs'.

Hung / hanged

'Hung' is the past tense and past participle of 'hang', unless you've been strung up, in which case you are 'hanged'.

I/me

When is it correct to use 'I' and when 'me'? If there is no verb in a statement, it should be 'me'.

'Who's going to do the washing-up tonight?' 'Me.'

'Guess who ended up doing the drying as well.' 'Me.'

To say 'I' instead of 'me' in both instances would sound affected. However, if a verb were to be added, 'me' would become 'I' – because to say 'Me will' and 'Me did' is obviously nonsense. With a verb such as 'to be', though, it is not so clear-cut. 'Is that a photo of Great-Auntie May?' 'No, it's me, aged twelve!' To say 'No, it's I' is perhaps what Great-Auntie May would have said, but it is far more natural nowadays to say 'me'.

In the following sentences, should 'I' or 'me' be used?

1 Since the dishwasher packed up, it seems to be — doing the dishes every night.

2 Are you and — going to get a new dishwasher?

3 Who was the last person to be picked for the team?   was.

4 The last person to be picked for the team was —.

5 Who is doing this exercise – you or —?

6 — love you – will you marry —?

7 It wasn't — who messed up our marriage.

8 For an early-morning swim, Minnie and — broke the ice on the pond.

9 Who's going to Barbados on holiday? My husband and —!

10 My grandmother really loathed my brother and —.

Irritating expressions

Avoid these even more than clichés (see above). At least clichés were at one time original, and they do have a purpose when reiterating a timeless truism. Irritating expressions, however, are either irritating because they add nothing to what is being said or written, or because they are so overused. A brief pause is better than the pointless 'at the end of the day', 'at this moment in time', 'best practice', 'blue-sky thinking', 'due to the fact that', 'grass roots', 'have a nice day' (if you're British), 'heads-up', 'I'm going to give you 150 per cent' (and variations thereof), 'in my humble opinion', 'in the final analysis', 'it's a game of two halves', 'it's six of one, half a dozen of the other', 'step up to the plate', 'the fact of the matter is', 'think outside the box', 'when push comes to shove'. And yes, OK, like, basically, we all say them, like, but 'absolutely', 'basically', 'empowered', 'gutted', 'iconic', 'like', 'like, you know', 'literally', 'second-guess', 'totally', 'you know', 'you know what I mean' are pretty trite.

I was sat/sitting

It is either 'I sat' or 'I was sitting' – not a combination of the two, so no 'I was sat' please, and definitely no 'I was sat sitting'. Likewise, it's not 'you were stood waiting for the number 12 bus'; it should be 'you stood waiting', or 'you were standing waiting'. See more on auxiliary verbs in Chapter 1, p. 11.

Kind of, sort of, type of

To be grammatically correct, the pronoun should dictate whether 'kind', 'sort', 'type' is singular or plural. 'This kind of chair is comfortable' or 'these kinds of chairs are comfortable', rather than 'these kind of chairs are comfortable'. However, all sorts of (or sort of) highly regarded writers have used that last type of construction for hundreds of years, so while it's best to avoid if possible, it wouldn't be the worst grammatical error to commit. (*But* 'kinda', 'sorta', 'typa' come close.)

Lend/borrow

'Lend' means to give something and 'borrow' means to take something. So 'I lent her a fiver' or 'she lent me a fiver' would mean, correctly, 'I gave her a fiver' and 'she gave me a fiver' (though hopefully I'll/she'll get it back). Similarly, 'I borrowed a fiver' or 'She borrowed a fiver from me' would mean 'I took a fiver' and 'she took a fiver from me' – again, correct. But to say 'I borrowed her a fiver' or 'she borrowed me a fiver' or 'I lent a fiver from her' wouldn't be correct, as well as sounding rather horrible.

Lie, lay, laid, lain

'Lie', meaning *to be horizontal*, is a simple word, as is 'lay', meaning *to put things down*, but they seem to cause a bit of confusion in their various tenses. These are the correct forms: 'I lie down' (present), 'I am lying down' (present continuous), 'I lay down' (past), 'I had lain down' (pluperfect); 'I lay the table' (present), 'I am laying the table' (present continuous), 'I laid the table' (past), 'I had laid the table' (pluperfect).

The mistake people make is using 'lay' in the present when they mean 'lie'. But 'lay' in the present can only be used when it is followed by an object – 'I lay the fire', 'I lay the mash on top of the fish' (both present); 'I laid the fire', 'I laid the mash on top of the fish' (both past). Don't say: 'Now, lay on the floor, everyone' or 'She was laying on the bed to avoid the party'. They should be: 'Now, lie on the floor, everyone' and 'She was lying on the bed to avoid the party'.

In the following sentences, fill in the correct form and tense of 'lie' or 'lay'.

1 We — under the blanket, because we were hiding from Rupert.

2 Don't — on that side of the bed.

3 The books had — unread on the bedside table for months.

4 Why do they always have to — concrete at six o'clock in the morning?

5 The presents were — under the Christmas tree.

6 — on her back during a massage always sent her to sleep.

7 Lizzie was exhausted after — carpet for ten hours and went for a — -down.

8 She had — for too long in the sun and was burnt to a crisp.

9 Camping is no fun in Wales – have you ever tried — a fire in the rain?

10 The cat proudly — the mouse at my feet.

And of course just to confuse matters further, there are the lies we tell. Here, 'lie' can be a noun or a verb, and the past tense is 'lied', not 'lay' or 'laid'. As in: 'I lied about laying the table.'

Like

'Like' (among other things) is a preposition – it compares similar things. Such as 'Caroline was spending money like a lottery winner', 'Ian swam like a fish', 'I've got a dress just like yours'.

'Like' can also be a conjunction – meaning 'in the same way that' – but only informally. The more appropriate words to use are 'as' or 'as if' or 'as though'. 'I felt as if I'd been hit over the head with a hammer after his rant' and 'I felt like I'd been hit over the head with a hammer after his rant' are both fine, though the first is clearly more formal (correct) than the second. Likewise, 'The essay seemed as though it had been written overnight' and 'The essay seemed like it had been written overnight'.

Lots of/a lot of

These are phrases we were no doubt all told to avoid at school – because they were considered to be too vague? too colloquial? too lazy? (lots of reasons!) – and it is still probably best to avoid them in formal writing – 'Dear sir, I have had lots of jobs, and lots of experience, so please employ me and pay me lots of money' – but they are fine to use colloquially.

May have/might have

Although usage is often blurred today, there is a slight difference. Traditionally, 'may have' is used as a present or past option; 'might have' only a past one. For example, 'I may have a run if it's not pouring with rain' (present), 'I might have gone for a run but it was pouring with rain' (past), 'She may have bought lunch yesterday, but it might have been my turn – I can't remember' (both past). It's a little distinction, and OK to ignore, but worth noting nonetheless.

Myriad

The noun 'myriad' means an infinite number or a vast quantity of something – the definition coming from the Greek for 'a unit of 10,000'. There is a school of thought that considers it should be treated along the same lines as 'comprise' (see above), but it is in fact fine to use 'myriad' with 'of' when it's a noun, as in 'Myriads of words have been written on the subject of grammar' or 'A myriad of words have been written on the subject of grammar'. As an adjective, it means 'many' and this is when it is incorrect to add 'of'.

'Myriad words have been written on the subject of grammar', *not* 'Myriad of words have been written on the subject of grammar', just as 'Many of words have been written on the subject of grammar' wouldn't be right.

Myself

When should 'myself' be used? – Not as often as you might think from the myriad times you hear it. It shouldn't be used as a substitute for 'me', as in 'The report needs to be written by Bob and myself for tomorrow's meeting' or 'The gardening has been left to Pippa and myself'. These should be 'The report needs to be written by Bob and me for tomorrow's meeting' and 'The gardening has been left to Pippa and me'. 'Myself' should only be used reflexively – 'I went to the cinema by myself', 'I whistled to myself on the way home' – or for emphasis – 'I baked it myself', 'There was no one else in the office, so I told him myself he was sacked'.

The same principles apply to all the other '-self' and '-selves' – like 'yourself', 'themselves'.

In the following sentences, fill in the correct pronoun.

1 That was a damn good meal, if I say so —.

2 — — admitted it was a mistake to marry him, so don't blame your bridesmaid for spilling the beans.

3 If it were up to —, I'd say no.

4 The children were left to — while the teacher went for a fag break.

5 His badly made suit did nothing for —.

6 We only had — to blame.

7 She said she'd made it —, but I saw the Waitrose packet in the bin.

8 They can do the rest of the clearing-up — tomorrow, we've done enough.

9 She — came to the decision that the job was beyond her.

10 He asked — if I needed a brandy after the shock.

Nice

Another word banned at school (see 'Lots of/a lot of' above). It is fine – in fact, quite nice – when the context is right and it's not overused.

None

There is some debate over whether 'none' should take a singular or plural verb when it refers to more than one thing. Those who insist on the singular believe that 'none' equals 'nobody', 'no one', 'no person', but in fact it derives from 'not one', so either can apply. It depends on context and, to a degree, personal choice. 'None of those apples is edible' and 'None of those apples are edible' are equally correct, but the latter sounds less mannered. With 'None of us is bothered' and 'None of us are bothered', however, the former seems to trip more easily off the tongue. So, to reiterate, it's personal choice, and don't flinch if someone uses the plural when you would use the singular.

Not only . . . but also

Two things to remember here: 1) use both parts of the construction, and 2) make sure they work grammatically by being positioned correctly in a sentence. The following two sentences are incorrect because the verbs are in the wrong place:

The film not only was too long but also too dark.

She wrote not only the film, but also starred in it.

They should be:

> The film was not only too long but also too dark.

> She not only wrote the film, but also starred in it.

Correct, because 'too long' and 'too dark' are both objects of 'the film' in the first, and because 'the film' and 'it' are both objects of 'she' in the second.

In other words, 'not only' and 'but also' follow the subject and the verb, if the verb applies to both constructs (example 1), but they come before, if the verbs are different (example 2).

Number of

'The number of' and 'a number of' may look very similar, but grammatically they are different. When a plural noun is added to 'the number of', the verb is singular – 'The number of spectators attending the match was unexpected.' This is because 'the number of' is singular and the principal noun in the sentence. With 'a number of', though, the verb is plural – 'A number of spectators are leaving the match because they are bored' – because the principal noun is 'spectators', not 'a number of'. A way to remember this is 'a number of' equals 'some' or 'several' (both plural constructs), while 'the number of' equals 'the sum total' (a singular construct).

Number, quantity, amount

The meanings of 'number', 'quantity' and 'amount' are sometimes confused. A 'number' can be applied to countable animate and inanimate objects; a 'quantity' is used usually for inanimate objects, also countable but often less specific; an 'amount' can't be countable. For example:

A small number of people attended the demo, but the police fired large quantities of teargas over them.

I took a huge amount of pleasure from the enormous quantity of money I made selling dodgy mortgages to a vast number of people.

Numbers – figures or spelt out?

No hard-and-fast rules, but for literary purposes, it's probably nicer to spell out numbers up to a hundred, then use figures – 'ninety nine', '199'. For general purposes, spell out numbers up to nine, then use figures – 'nine-year-old', '19-year-old'. One little rule, though: don't start a sentence with a figure. Either spell it out, or rewrite the sentence – preferably the latter, particularly if it's a date or a very long number. 'Eighteen fifty-nine saw the publication of *A Tale of Two Cities*' and 'Two hundred and twenty-one b Baker Street is Sherlock Holmes's address' look much better as '*A Tale of Two Cities* was published in 1859' and 'Sherlock Holmes's address is 221b Baker Street'. While 'four hundreds' or 'five thousands' or 'six millions' might seem technically correct, it's more common, standard in fact, to leave it in the singular. Only pluralise when the number is non-specific, so: 'Hundreds of people took part in the concert, thousands of people attended, and it was watched on TV by millions.'

Objective / subjective

'Objective' is impartial – you are not influenced by personal feelings and views when assessing something. 'Subjective' is the opposite – you *are* influenced by personal feelings and views. Quite straightforward, really, but frequently mistaken for each other.

Owing to / due to

Both mean 'because of', but pedants argue that 'due to' is incorrect, because 'due' is an adjective, and therefore can't be used as a preposition. However, most people would probably agree that these two phrases are interchangeable nowadays: 'Owing to poor attendance, the concert was called off'; 'Due to poor attendance, the concert was called off'. If in doubt, use 'because of' . . .

Oxymoron

This means the juxtaposition of two seemingly contradictory ideas, as in the well-known 'famous Belgians', 'virtual reality' and 'military intelligence'. A few more for the collection: 'the fascinating marketing meeting', 'the thought-provoking Channel Five programme', 'the healthy vegan', 'the hard-up banker', 'the intelligible instruction manual', 'the short game of cricket', 'the useful managing consultant', 'the discreet journalist', 'the charismatic accountant', 'the humble *Apprentice* candidate', 'the underpaid Premiership footballer', 'the fat catwalk model', 'the efficient British transport system', 'rush hour', '*I'm a Celebrity* . . .'. Or some more literary examples: 'Fair is foul, and foul is fair' (*Macbeth*), 'parting is such sweet sorrow' (*Romeo and Juliet*), 'I must be cruel only to be kind' (*Hamlet*).

Prepositions at the end of a sentence

Another topic for the pedants, but sentences can end up sounding far more awkward and unnatural in an effort to avoid. 'What did you do that for?' is easier on the ear and eye than 'For what did you do that?' Similarly, 'Where did you get the bus from?' sounds less pompous than 'From where did you get the bus?' Or: 'Are you

the new boyfriend I've heard so much about?' rather than
'Are you the new boyfriend about whom I have heard so much?'
As Churchill famously said: 'This is the sort of English up with
which I will not put.' (Pedants: this was a joke.)

Proverbs

More useful than clichés (see above), but again watch out for
overkill, and remember that some contradict each other: 'Absence
makes the heart grow fonder' *but* 'Out of sight, out of mind'.

Quite

'Quite' has two senses: it can mean either 'very', 'completely':

> 'Are you quite sure your keys aren't in your pocket?'

> 'This is quite inedible.'

or 'rather', 'somewhat':

> 'I'm quite drunk, but I think I could manage another half.'

> 'His girlfriend wasn't quite what I expected.'

For the Americans, however, it only ever means 'very'. So don't
use it when meaning 'rather', or if attempting subtlety – it will
confuse them. Quite so.

Scotch

Don't annoy the Scots by calling them Scotch – use the term
only for broth, eggs and whisky, or, if it's lower case, to dismiss
something like a rumour – otherwise you might find yourself
on the receiving end of a Glasgow kiss . . .

Shall / will

Traditionally, 'shall' is the future tense with first-person pronouns ('I' and 'we'), and 'will' is the future tense with second- and third-person pronouns ('you', 'he', 'she', 'it', 'they'): 'I shall be finished in about five minutes', 'It will all be over very soon'. However, this is reversed for emphasis or bossiness: 'We will not be moved', 'You shall go to the ball'. The practice is, of course, often blurred by the use of contractions – 'I'll', 'you'll', 'we'll', 'they'll' – so people either don't care about or don't understand the distinction. But the difference is worth remembering, nevertheless.

Should / would

We thought we should cover this too – though nowadays most people would probably say, 'We thought we would cover this too.' Tradition follows a similar pattern to 'shall/will' (see above), although 'should' is dying out, and 'shan't' is pretty much buried.

Since / from

Watch the tenses when using these words. With 'since', the main clause is the present perfect, or sometimes the present; with 'from' (it can also apply to 'when'), it is the past.

> Since we started writing this book, time has flown by.

> From the time we started writing this book, time flew by.

Or:

> She has developed a high opinion of herself since she was accepted at Cambridge.

> She developed a high opinion of herself when she was accepted at Cambridge.

In the following sentences, is the missing word 'from', 'since'
or 'when'?

1 He has become a nightmare to deal with — he married the boss.

2 — he stopped fiddling the books, our profits went down.

3 She was on duty — six o'clock.

4 — the birth of her triplets, she has had no sleep.

5 They didn't speak to each other — that day on.

6 Letter-writing, — the advent of the email, has fallen by the wayside.

7 That child was trouble — the day he was born.

8 The nice teacher who has taught us — September has been sacked.

9 — the moment our eyes met across the library, we were destined to be together.

10 She put on rather a lot of weight — the ice-cream parlour opened next door to the office.

Singular or plural?

Most of the time singular and plural verb agreement is straightforward, but there are a few areas where things are not so clear-cut.

First, when two things combine to make one, the verb should be singular. Such as: 'Her drink and drug habit is rather worrying', or 'The screaming and banging from the flat next door is driving me mad'. Here, drink and drug is treated as one habit, or item, not two; likewise, the screaming and banging.

Second, when the word is clearly plural, but the sense is in fact singular, such as in the following examples with numbers and periods of time. 'Ten pounds is not much to lend me', 'Three is too many in a marriage', 'Seven years of Olympic hype was more than enough for most people', 'Two weeks is a very long time in politics'.

Third, when the subject is singular and the object plural, but the two are easily confused. 'Steak and chips is her favourite meal' ('her favourite meal' is the subject), 'What the teacher couldn't bear was lazy students' ('the teacher' is the subject), 'What she wants for her birthday is lots of presents' ('she' is the subject), 'Among the subjects being discussed is grammar' ('grammar' is the subject).

-size / -sized

These are both adjectives, and often interchangeable, as in 'The chocolate bars are king-size' and 'The chocolate bars are king-sized'. But it's better to use '-sized' when the compound is attributive: 'bite-sized portions', 'medium-sized eggs', 'king-sized chocolate bars'; although the attributive 'life-size' and 'life-sized', as in 'life-size statue' or 'life-sized statue', work equally well.

Sleepwalk

The past tense is 'sleepwalked', not 'sleptwalk' or 'sleptwalked'.

Split infinitives

Splitting an infinitive means putting a word between 'to' and the stem – and it is probably the issue that causes the most heat under the pedant's collar. While there are certainly times when a split infinitive is horrible – 'her choice was not to go to the party' is much nicer than 'her choice was to not go to the party'; and 'he has no right not to let you speak' is also nicer than 'he has no right to not let you speak' – there are just as many times when going round in circles to avoid the split makes a phrase ambiguous, clunky or pompous. 'To really understand this problem, you need to do more work' clearly means you need to do more work. 'Really to understand this problem, you need to do more work' is quite vague, the 'Really' perhaps implying only if you can be bothered. And these sentences mean different things: 'Charles asked Elizabeth to graciously relinquish the throne' and 'Charles asked Elizabeth graciously to relinquish the throne'. In the first, Charles is asking Elizabeth to go quietly, and in the second, he's being gracious in his asking. You can move that 'graciously' around the sentence – 'Charles asked Elizabeth to relinquish the throne graciously' or 'Charles asked Elizabeth to relinquish graciously the throne' – but only in the first example is Charles unambiguous in his desire to finally get (split infinitive alert) a job.

To split or not to split? Ultimately, it's personal choice. The main thing to remember in this thorny area is clarity and fluidity.

Spring-clean

The past tense is 'spring-cleaned', not 'sprung-clean' – it's derived from the season, not something a bouncy bunny rabbit does.

Subjunctive

The subjunctive is part of everyday language in Continental Europe, and is commonly heard in the US. In UK English, however, it is not much used these days, and the issue seems to worry people, so they avoid it at all costs. But in its simplest form, it's not that difficult and is quite useful. The subjunctive mood conveys hypothesis – something that is unlikely to happen – or something imagined, as well as something recommended, demanded, proposed. The easiest way to spot the subjunctive is an unfamiliar past tense after the first and third person. Instead of the standard 'was', the verb is 'were'.

If I *were* you, I wouldn't marry him.

Were she to be promoted, the rest of the department would resign.

I need to go back to subjunctive school, if only that *were* possible.

If it *were* done when 'tis done, then 'tw*ere* well it *were* done quickly. (Three for the price of one.)

The similar 'oddity' happens in the present – there is no 's' added to the third-person singular, and the base form of the verb (such as 'be') is used with the first, second and third singular and plural.

I suggest that she *be* given the job.

The actors request that the person in the audience talking on his mobile *switch* it off or *leave* now.

It is vital that the mother *come* to the parents' evening to discuss Alfie's behaviour.

We demand that the council *turn* down the planning application.

And people do in fact use the subjunctive unconsciously, such as in these familiar phrases:

As it were.

Perish the thought.

Far be it from me . . .

Suffice it to say . . .

Suffice (it) to say

Talking of which, this is another of those phrases some people are unsure about. Well, no need. Both 'suffice to say' and 'suffice it to say' are fine.

Tautology

This means saying the same thing twice in a slightly different way – 'the biannual meeting was twice a year' – and is obviously best avoided. Here are some familiar examples:

4 a.m. in the morning
added bonus
baby infant
close proximity
cold ice cream
continue on
couple together
crispy crisps
enclosed within
espresso coffee
free gift
hot sauna
husband-and-wife duo
new beginning
new innovation
repeat again
they walked in single file one behind the other
two of a pair

A **pleonasm** overlaps with **tautology,** as it also means using more words than necessary, but it is more often associated with verbosity and purple prose. Such as: 'it was pouring down with rain' – well, what else really? Or 'the illustrated picture book', or 'the fictional fairy tale', or 'the unaccompanied a cappella group', or 'that phrase was a tautologous pleonasm'.

Tenses with two murky pasts . . .

These are the verbs with two past tenses, and they are often confused. Some of these are past participles, not just the straightforward past tense; and in some cases one form is favoured by the Americans, the other by the British.

> mow: the past tense is 'mowed' – 'he mowed the lawn' – but the grass can be 'mown' or 'mowed'.

> ring: 'he rang the bell', 'the bell was rung'.

> saw: 'he sawed the firewood', 'the firewood was sawn'; *but* in the US 'the firewood was sawed' and 'the man was injured with a sawed-off shotgun'.

> shine: 'she shined her shoes', 'she shone in the play'.

> sing: 'they sang the chorus in harmony', 'the chorus was sung harmoniously'.

> sink: 'she sank to the bottom of the pool', 'she was sunk in the swimming lesson'.

> sow: 'we sowed the seeds', 'the seeds were sown', *but* 'the seeds were sowed' is also OK.

> speed: 'sped' means moved quickly, 'speeded' means you've exceeded the legal limit – 'she sped up on the quiet road, and speeded past the police car'.

> spring: 'he sprang to his feet', 'the boat has sprung a leak'. The past tense is chiefly 'sprang' in the UK, 'sprung' in the US; the past participle is 'sprung'.

string: the past is 'strung', never 'strang'.

The past participle can also be an adjective – 'sawn log', 'sprung mattress', 'mown lawn', 'sown seeds'. The past tense of 'spin' is 'spun' – 'span' is archaic.

Than I/than me

Which is correct? The guideline here is similar to 'I/me' (see above). Traditional grammar would opt for the former – 'David is shorter than I' – the reason being that the full statement would be 'David is shorter than I am', and 'than' is a conjunction so should be followed by a subjective personal pronoun (I, he, she). But it does sound rather old-fashioned, wrong even. The counter-argument is that 'than' here is a preposition, not a conjunction, and therefore should be followed by an objective personal pronoun (me, him, her) – 'David is shorter than me' – which sounds more natural. In short: if the statement ends with the verb ('am' or whatever), use 'I', as 'me am' is nonsense, but if it ends with the pronoun, go for the objective form – 'me'. (The Americans, by the way, opt for tradition.)

That . . . that

Avoid overusing. 'The girl put on the dress *that* she bought yesterday and discovered *that* it was too small and *that* she would have to return *that* dress to *that* shop on the high street.' Rewrite if something like this appears on the page or computer screen.

That/which

Knowing when to use these two words causes a fair bit of confusion, sometimes angst, but more often insouciance. However, they are not interchangeable, and contrary to popular belief 'which' is not just an upmarket version of 'that'. Using the wrong one could give a different meaning from the one intended, so it's worth noting the distinction.

Grammatically speaking, 'that' goes with *restrictive relative clauses* and 'which' goes with *non-restrictive relative clauses.* 'This soap opera, which I used to watch every day, has gone downhill.' 'This is the soap opera that I used to watch.' 'That' can be omitted quite happily and makes no difference to the sense: 'This is the soap opera I used to watch.' If the 'which' clause is omitted, while still making sense, the sentence will be missing some of the info: 'This soap opera has gone downhill.' The bracketing commas are a clue to the non-restriction.

> Her books, which we publish, are rubbish.

This means all her books are rubbish and we publish them, unfortunately.

> Her books that we publish are rubbish.

This means that we publish her rubbish books, but someone else publishes her good stuff.

Despite what the computer may insist with its bossy wiggly green line, a comma is not always necessary before 'which', so don't use that as a guide. For example, 'She was in no doubt which was the right word to use' or 'Swimming is a sport which is suitable for all ages' or, as Lady Macbeth says, 'That which hath made them drunk hath made me bold'.

In the following sentences, is the missing word 'that' or 'which'?

1 The train — we were on was delayed because of a leaf on the line.

2 The computer, — I was using to write my magnum opus, crashed and I lost everything — I hadn't saved.

3 The company — she'd built from scratch went into receivership.

4 Our play, — opens tomorrow, is under-rehearsed.

5 Is this a dagger — I see before me, the handle toward my hand?

6 The car, — is due for its first MOT, has never been out of the garage.

7 The dress — she wore for the event was a bit too tight.

8 The salmon en croute, — was rather an overambitious dish for him, was inedible.

9 My homework — was eaten by the dog was A* material – honest!

10 The wedding list, — the couple had at Harrods, was beyond the budget of most of their guests.

Titles – upper or lower case?

When writing the title of a book, film, TV programme, etc., start only the main words with upper-case letters. Articles (the, a, an), unless they are at the beginning of a title, should be lower case, as should prepositions and conjunctions. *A Tale of Two Cities, Sense and Sensibility, North by Northwest, Top of the Pops, Book at Bedtime*, etc. (not *A Tale Of Two Cities, Sense And Sensibility, North By Northwest, Top Of The Pops, Book At Bedtime*).

If a hyphenated word is part of a title or heading, each main word should start upper case. *Nineteen Eighty-Four, Winnie-the-Pooh, A Dark-Adapted Eye, Grammar for Grown-Ups*, Chapter Thirty-One. (Not *Nineteen Eighty-four, Grammar for Grown-ups*, Chapter Thirty-one, etc.)

12 a.m. / 12 p.m.

There is no such time – it's either 12 noon, or 12 midnight.

Unique

In theory, 'unique' means 'one of a kind', 'not like anything
else' – 'she has a unique style' (meaning 'her style is a one-off').
Consequently there is a school (isn't there always?) that insists it
cannot be modified by an adverb. But there are occasions when a
modifier such as 'quite' or 'almost' or 'really' fits the context. 'Philip's
piano-playing is quite unique' works because the writer is being
ironic (Philip is tone-deaf). 'Almost uniquely in her family, Flora is
always punctual' fits because once in a while her brother Felix makes
an effort and manages to turn up on time. 'This is a really unique
offer I'm making, so don't turn down my movie' expresses the
director's desperation more obviously than the unmodified 'unique'
– especially as it was the fifth time he'd used it that day.

Don't overuse these constructs, though, and it's probably
preferable to avoid them in writing; 'very unique', 'most unique',
'rather unique' are always no-nos – and more examples of
'Irritating expressions' (see above).

And another don't: 'an unique' – the article is always 'a'.

Use to / used to

'Used to' is the common construction – 'I used to read only
biographies and memoirs', 'I used to go to the gym at lunchtime' –
except in negatives and questions with the auxiliary verb 'do'.
So, 'I didn't use to read fiction' rather than 'I didn't used to read
fiction'; 'Didn't you use to go to my school?' rather than 'Didn't
you used to go to my school?'

Verbing nouns

Many nouns can quite happily become verbs – just look in the
dictionary – but there is a limit, particularly in government-, office-

and business-speak when they can become hyperbolic, meaningless waffle (and don't in fact save any time if that's the intention behind the 'inventiveness'). We can probably all happily live without these: 'gifting' ('giving' is a much nicer gesture), 'summited' ('reaching the summit' sounds like a more genuine achievement), 'calendarize', 'diarize', 'Japanize', 'signaturize' (probably all of American origin, hence the '-ize' endings, but even if they're not, these words come across as rather self-important and disingenuous), 'deplane', 'detrain', 'ideate', 'keynoting', 'medalled' (enough, before we're tempted to inventorize some more).

The same goes for nouning verbs, nouning adjectives, verbing adjectives, adjectiving nouns, and making things up on a whim.

Who pushed whom?

'Whom' is clinging desperately to the lifeboat, and there are those for whom its death could not come soon enough – chiefly because they don't quite know when to use it, or they think it's pompous and old-fashioned (and they are sometimes right about the latter). But it's worth rescuing, because, like 'that' and 'which', there is a distinction between the words, and it's not that difficult to grasp. 'Who' is the subject of the verb; 'whom' is the object of the verb. Try the phrase using different pronouns: if 'he', 'she' or 'they' fits, then use 'who'; if 'him', 'her' or 'them' fits, then use 'whom'.

> '*Who* told you that I was having an affair?' ('My lips are sealed – Oh, OK, *Mandy* told me.')

> '*Who* wants to be a millionaire?' ('*We* do.')

> 'This is the man with *whom* I'm having a secret affair.' ('I'm having an affair with *him*', not 'he').

> 'Ilsa is the person with *whom* I'm writing this book.' ('I'm writing it with *her*', not 'she').

If in doubt, or wary of sounding pompous, one way to avoid using 'whom' is to move the preposition in the sentence. 'To whom does this book belong?' does sound a bit staid, so say 'Who does this book belong to?' And 'About whom is this book?' becomes 'Who is this book about?' (See 'Prepositions at the end of a sentence' above – *they are fine*.)

In the following sentences, is the missing word 'who' or 'whom'?

1 Anyone — knows the answer, stick your hand up.

2 Lorraine, with — I was supposed to go on holiday, has cried off.

3 — banged on my door?

4 With — did you go to the cinema? We're all dying to know.

5 The guy — told the lies was sacked.

6 To — should I send this document for approval?

7 — do you have to suck up to here to get promotion?

8 She is the star without — this movie would not exist, so give her the biggest trailer.

9 — let the cats out?

10 To — it may concern: why oh why oh why have the standards of grammar gone down in your paper?

So, you see, the bell has not quite tolled for 'whom' yet . . .

5 | To America and Beyond

The Americans are identical to the British in all
respects except, of course, language.

Oscar Wilde

Every American child should grow up knowing
a second language, preferably English.

Mignon McLaughlin, *The Neurotic's Notebook*

So, here's the American chapter that's already been mentioned
numerous times in terms of punctuation and spelling.

While English speakers from the US and the UK can of
course be understood in each other's countries, there are
substantial differences in our punctuation, spelling, idioms and
pronunciation. This chapter covers primarily US English, but with
a nod to other parts of the English-speaking world – Australia,
New Zealand, South Africa and Canada.

American punctuation and spelling is an odd mix of
traditional English and simplicity. For example, Oxford commas
and -ize endings were common in the UK over a hundred years
ago, but are not now. However, in the US they are standard. Yet
the practice of always putting commas and full stops within the
closing quote mark is a development – and a rather strange one
at that – all their own. (Maybe to avoid getting themselves tied
in knots the way some Brits do – see Chapter 2.) Similarly, in
the US some word spellings and pronunciations go for the more

unambiguous approach: 'Berkeley', 'clerk', 'derby', 'lieutenant' are spoken as written.

Punctuation

Full stop

Called a 'period' in the US, its primary use is exactly the same as ours. But there are a few key differences. Whereas in the UK we do not use points after contractions, in the US the practice is often to retain them – in the rather old-fashioned British way. So it's Mr., Mrs., Ms., Dr., St., etc., rather than Mr, Mrs, Ms, Dr, St, etc. Similarly there is a tendency in the US to use points in acronyms and initialisms on the grounds that they are abbreviations, so it's U.S., U.K., N.A.T.O., F.B.I., Washington, D.C., though we think it's over-punctuating, messy and confusing, and obviously some US publications feel the same as they don't put them in.

Comma

While this is not an across-the-board practice, on the whole the US style is to opt for the serial, or series or Oxford, comma, on the grounds that it avoids any ambiguity. So: 'The fruit bowl contains apples, bananas and a pineapple' in the UK, but 'The fruit bowl contains apples, bananas, and a pineapple' in the US; i.e. all lists include a comma before the 'and' and final item, unlike the UK practice, which uses that final comma only when there is a genuine possibility of confusion.

Convert the following punctuation marks (and one spelling) into UK English. (NB some might stay the same . . .)

1 Mrs. Smith arrived late for her appointment with Dr. Foster as she got caught in a shower of rain.

2 I'll have the Caesar salad, but hold the anchovies, the croutons, and the Parmesan.

3 Johnny Cash and June Carter, Sonny and Cher, and Ike and Tina Turner: three examples of why not to sing with your husband.

4 Hank Kennedy, Sr., and Hank Kennedy, Jr., were both wanted by the C.I.A.

5 There's a Woody Allen season showing at the movie theater – we could see *Hannah and Her Sisters*, *Crimes and Misdemeanors*, and *Husbands and Wives* next week.

Question mark and exclamation mark

Usage is the same – US practice follows UK practice in not italicising the punctuation mark if the final word is italicised – despite what might be seen in some American publications. 'Are you really thinking of wearing *that?*' 'Yes, I *am!*' are wrong.

Colon

Again, the usage is the same – but, also again, there are a couple of minor variations. It is US style to put a colon between hours and minutes – '9:15' – whereas the UK style is to use a point – '9.15'. After salutations in business letters, a colon is used in the US rather than the UK comma, so 'Dear Ms. Lewinsky:' would be US style, but 'Dear Ms Lewinsky,' would be UK practice. In the US sometimes an introductory colon is followed by a capital letter rather than lower case, and always when what follows the colon could be considered a full sentence – 'This is the task I'm going to give you: Put out the garbage in the yard.'

Semicolon, apostrophe, brackets, solidus

No differences in usage, except that brackets are called parentheses more often than in the UK.

Hyphen

The principle is the same in both 'languages', but the practice can be quite varied. Many hyphenated British words become one in the States – 'back-pedal/backpedal', 'grown-up/grownup', 'half-hearted/halfhearted', 'north-west/northwest', 'pre-eminent/preeminent', 'pre-teen/preteen', 'rear-view mirror/rearview mirror', 'sub-machine gun/submachine gun'.

Dash

Again, the principle is the same when the dash is being used in the 'comma' sense, but the actual mark is an 'em' dash rather than an 'en' dash, so '—' rather than '–'. In addition, there are usually no spaces either side of the dash, unlike the UK practice, so it looks like—this rather than like – this. However, the Americans have one use for the en dash, and that's when it's a replacing dash (for 'to' or 'and'), such as in dates and sports scores, 'Bill Clinton, 1993–2001', 'the Yankees beat the Cardinals 12–2' (the same as UK usage). But for some bizarre (bizarre because the sense is 'and') reason they prefer hyphens to replacing dashes for constructions like 'Mason-Dixon Line' (UK would be 'Mason–Dixon Line') and 'American-Mexican border: Do not cross illegally or you'll get shot' (again, UK would be 'American–Mexican border'). Even more bizarrely, they use a dash, where we would use a hyphen, in a compound word if one of those words is a proper noun, such as 'Pulitzer Prize–winning author', 'World War II–era novel' ('Pulitzer Prize-winning author', 'World War II-era novel' in the UK).

Quotation marks

This is the major one, and there are two key differences. First, in UK English, as seen in Chapter 2, single quotation marks are used primarily, whereas US English always uses double. (And then double within single for UK English and vice versa for US.) For example:

> 'I could feel myself panicking big time as I tried to talk her roond, "I just don't relate to him like I do you." Ken what she sais?'
>> 'Nup. What?'
>> '"It's *how* you're relating that's the issue." And she wouldnae discuss it further.'
>
> Irvine Welsh, *Skagboys*

> She looks up. "Henry, who's your favorite Beatle?"
>> "John. Of course."
>> "Why 'of course'?"
>> "Well, Ringo is okay but kind of a sad sack, you know? And George is a little too New Age for my taste."
>
> Audrey Niffenegger, *The Time Traveler's Wife*

The second difference is that full stops and commas, whether or not they are part of the highlighted word or words, always go inside the closing quotation mark.

This would be UK English:

> Amy's hit record, 'Rehab', topped the charts when she died.

> The Mark Twain quote is 'The report of my death was an exaggeration', and not 'Reports of my death have been greatly exaggerated'.

> 'Scare quotes', as quotation marks are sometimes called, are always double in the US.

> The word Wendy used was 'confusing'.

This would be US English:

> Amy's hit record, "Rehab," topped the charts when she died.

> The Mark Twain quote is "The report of my death was an exaggeration," and not "Reports of my death have been greatly exaggerated."

> "Scare quotes," as quotation marks are sometimes called, are always double in the US.

> The word Wendy used was "confusing."

This would be both UK and US English (although US would be double quotation marks, of course):

> 'I'm going skiing on Thursday,' said Molly.

> Wendy's word for punctuation was 'Confusing!'

As for other punctuation marks: colons and semicolons follow the UK system, and go inside the closing quote mark if they are part of the quoted text, and outside if they apply to the whole piece. Question marks and exclamation marks also follow the UK system.

"What time did we invite them for dinner?" said Billy-Bob.

"Who said anything about 'dinner'?" said Lindy-Lou. "I thought it was just a drink."

"You'd better getting cooking then!"

"See that room there? It's called a 'kitchen'! You fix dinner for once!"

Convert the following punctuation marks into UK English.

1 "After great pain, a formal feeling comes," "Because I could not stop for death," and "I heard a fly buzz when I died," are three well-known poems by Emily Dickinson.

2 "Those are rather groovy pants you're wearing, man," said Austin. "'Groovy'? Who says 'groovy' these days?" said Calvin.

3 "Beware of the dog!" said the sign on the forbidding gate.

4 "*Moulin Rouge!* was the best movie we saw in 2001, don't you think?" said George. "I'm not sure I would use the word 'best,'" said Tom.

5 Elvis's first hit was probably "That's All Right."

Ellipses

Usage is the same, but there is one stylistic difference. In UK English, the ellipsis is always three spaced points whether it is followed by a continuing sentence or a new one. In US English, however, the full stop is included if the ellipsis follows a complete sentence, or precedes a new one.

> There was only one catch and that was Catch-22, which specified that a concern for one's own safety in the face of dangers that were real and immediate was the process of a rational mind. Orr was crazy and could be grounded. . . . Orr would be crazy

to fly more missions and sane if he didn't, but if he was sane,
he had to fly them. If he flew them, he was crazy and didn't have
to; but if he didn't want to, he was sane and had to. Yossarian
was moved very deeply . . . and let out a respectful whistle.

Joseph Heller, *Catch-22*

Those four dots do not equal a four-spaced ellipsis – the ellipsis
is only ever three dots – the additional one in the *Catch-22* extract
is a full stop, not part of the ellipsis.

*In the following, convert the US punctuation marks into UK
punctuation marks.*

1 So what does she really "know"? Does she know how *much*?
   If she does—even if she knows half— we're in big trouble,
   guys. One of us might have to have "words."

2 You convinced him he was part of the deprived generation—
   you corrupted him. And now, as a consequence, Mr. and Mrs.
   Stransky are dead. That make you feel good?

3 According to his mom, the kid came in "about a quarter of
   five." So when he saw our guy it was—what? 4:30? 4:35?

4 You understand the situation now . . . you must understand
   it. . . .

5 How about reading a fairy story? "Cinderella," perhaps, or
   "Little Red Riding Hood."

6 "You're flying to Nebraska, yeah? Now I remember. He couldn't
   tell me why, though; just said it was 'very important.'"

7 "Have some egg-white omelette," Carla-Jo told them. "There's
   heaps left over, because Leslye-Jo and Pammy-Jo wouldn't touch
   it earlier. I shouldn't have told them what it was. 'Egg-white
   omelette!' Pammy-Jo said. 'What's the point of that?'"

8 This was what he had been working toward all the way through high school; he was at last going to college, Berkeley, to study the things that most interested him: astrophysics, track and field, baseball, soccer, and girls.

9 Thelma removed her glasses and looked at Fred. Something clicked in her head she couldn't put her finger on. . . . It was the word "jeepers!" and she knew that Daphne had a fight on her hands.

10 As the limos drew up to the red carpet, people, catching glimpses of the passengers, shouted, "It's Meryl!" or "It's Nicole!" Photographers, reporters, and security gathered around each door as the celeb was gently deposited on the sidewalk.

Other English-speaking countries

On the whole, Australia, Canada, New Zealand and South Africa follow the UK punctuation system, rather than the US. The first three might favour double quotation marks over single, but then so do some UK institutions.

Spelling

-ize / -ise / -yze / -yse

Although the UK spelling of words such as 'idealise', 'recognise' and 'realise' can occasionally be seen as 'idealize', 'recognize' and 'realize' – as in the *Oxford English Dictionary* and texts from one or two British publishing houses – the US spelling is always -ize. The Brits tend to follow the French spelling; the Americans (and *OED*) follow the original Greek derivation (perhaps they have an aversion to the French). However, 'analyze', 'paralyze', etc., won't be seen in a UK publication, as -yze is only ever US.

-or / -our

Words such as 'behaviour', 'colour', 'demeanour', 'favour', 'favourite', 'flavour', 'harbour', 'honour', 'humour', 'labour', 'misdemeanour', 'neighbour', 'rigour', 'rumour', 'savour', 'vigour', etc., become 'behavior', 'color', 'demeanor', 'favor', 'favorite', 'flavor', 'harbor', 'honor', 'humor', 'labor', 'misdemeanor', 'neighbor', 'rigor', 'rumor', 'savor', 'vigor', etc., in the US. These types of words have a Latin or French derivation and the stress is on the first syllable. Words with the stress on the second or third syllable – 'paramour', 'troubadour', 'velour' – are spelt (or in the US more usually 'spelled') the same in both the UK and US.

As with everything, there are variations on a theme. Some UK words lose the 'u' when in their extended forms – words such as 'coloration', 'honorary' 'humorous', 'rigorous', 'vigorous'. And a word like 'glamour' – which, believe it or not, has a Scottish derivation – stays 'glamour' in both US and UK spellings. Conversely, it's always 'squalor', 'tremor' and 'rigor mortis' in both.

-er / -re

Again, UK style follows the Greek, Latin and French derivations, but the US style takes a more pragmatic approach based on pronunciation. So it's 'calibre', 'centre', 'fibre', 'kilometre', 'lacklustre', 'litre', 'louvre', 'lustre', 'manoeuvre', 'meagre', 'metre', 'mitre', 'sabre', 'sepulchre', 'sombre', 'spectre', 'theatre', etc., in the UK, but in the US it's 'caliber', 'center', 'fiber', 'kilometer', 'lackluster', 'liter', 'louver', 'luster', 'maneuver' (double pragmatism here), 'meager', 'meter', 'miter', 'saber', 'sepulcher', 'somber', 'specter', 'theater', etc. However, if one of these words is part of a proper noun, stick to the original spelling, so 'World Trade Center', not 'World Trade Centre' (even though the *Observer* newspaper seems to use the latter for some reason, and it's not always consistent: at the time of the tenth anniversary of 9/11, the main section used 'Centre', the magazine, 'Center'), 'Lincoln Center Theater', not 'Lincoln Centre Theatre', and 'Public Theater', not 'Public Theatre', *but* 'Shubert Theatre', not 'Shubert Theater', and 'Centreville, Virginia', not 'Centerville, Virginia'. Likewise, it's 'Pearl Harbor', not 'Pearl Harbour' (a BBC website referred to the 'World Trade Center' and 'Pearl Harbour' on the same page).

-se / -ce

In a few instances, Americans use the same spelling whether the word is a noun or a verb – for example, 'license' and 'practice' are both the noun and verb. In the UK, the noun is 'licence' and the verb 'license', the noun 'practice' and the verb 'practise' (as seen in Chapter 3, pp. 89 and 91). It's 'defense', 'offense' and 'pretense' rather than the British 'defence', 'offence' and 'pretence', but otherwise they follow the same rules.

-og / -ogue

UK spelling is always '-ogue', and US follows the same, with a few exceptions, such as 'analog' and 'catalog'. US spelling prevails even in the UK with computer terminology, however, so it's always your computer 'program' and hard 'disk' which have been corrupted or lost in the ether.

e- / ae- and oe-

Once more, the spellings spring from Greek and Latin, spellings which the Americans have probably ditched either because the British spelling was wrong etymologically or for simplification (and the British are now following in some instances – see below). For example, words such as 'aeon', 'aetiology', 'anaemia', 'anaesthetist', 'diarrhoea', 'faeces', 'Graeco-', 'gynaecology', 'haematology', 'haemorrhage', 'Judaeo-', 'leukaemia', 'manoeuvre', 'oedema', 'oesophagus', 'oestrogen', 'orthopaedic', 'paediatrician', 'paedophile', 'Palaeolithic', 'palaeontology', 'septicaemia', etc., become 'eon', 'etiology', 'anemia', 'anesthetist', 'diarrhea', 'feces', 'Greco-', 'gynecology', 'hematology', 'hemorrhage', 'Judeo-', 'leukemia', 'maneuver', 'edema', 'esophagus', 'estrogen', 'orthopedic', 'pediatrician', 'pedophile', 'Paleolithic', 'paleontology', 'septicemia', etc., in the US (though in fact an 'anesthesiologist' will put you under in the States rather than an 'anesthetist').

The instances where the UK style now tends to follow the US is for words such as 'encyclopedia', 'ether', 'fetal', 'fetid', 'medieval', 'primeval'. Conversely, the US generally sticks to the UK spelling of 'aesthetics' – possibly for aesthetic reasons . . .

single and double l

In UK spelling, the final 'l' is often doubled when the word is extended – like 'jewel' and 'jeweller', 'marvel' and 'marvellous', 'travel' and 'traveller'. In US spelling, that one 'l' remains on its ownsome – so 'jeweler', 'marvelous' and 'traveler'. Here are a few more: 'cancelled / canceled', 'counsellor / counselor', 'cruellest / cruelest', 'dialling / dialing', 'dishevelled / disheveled', 'enamelled / enameled', 'flannelled / flanneled', 'gruelling / grueling', 'jewellery / jewelry', 'labelling / labeling', 'leveller / leveler', 'libellous / libelous', 'medallist / medalist', 'modelling / modeling', 'panellist / panelist', 'pedalling / pedaling', 'pummelling / pummeling', 'quarreller / quarreler', 'refuelling / refueling', 'signaller / signaler', 'squirrelling / squirreling', 'stencilled / stenciled', 'swivelled / swiveled', 'tranquillity / tranquility', 'tunnelling / tunneling', 'unravelled' / unraveled', 'unrivalled / unrivaled', 'weaselling / weaseling', 'woollen / woolen'.

On the other hand, it is US style to keep the double 'l' when it's already there, as with 'install', whereas UK style is to drop it –

'instalment/installment', 'skilful/skillful', 'wilful/willful'.
And there's the odd word where the US practice is to add an
'l' – like 'appal/appall', 'enrol/enroll', 'instil/instill'. Though in
years to come the UK practice might be the same as the US –
150-odd years ago, Dickens was writing about 'recal'.

no 'e'

UK spelling keeps the 'e' after the 'g' in abridgement,
acknowledgement, judgement (except in legal contexts) –
US spelling doesn't, so 'abridgment', 'acknowledgment',
'judgment'; likewise, UK spelling often keeps the 'e' with
'able' suffixes, as in 'likeable', 'liveable', 'sizeable', 'unshakeable',
rather than the US 'likable', 'livable', 'sizable', 'unshakable',
though both go for 'unbelievable' and 'unmistakable'.

-ward/-wards

In UK English, we tend towards adding an 's' to those '-wards'
prepositions – 'afterwards', 'backwards', 'downwards', 'forwards',
'northwards', 'southwards', 'towards', 'upwards' – while the
Americans tend to leave off the 's' – 'afterward', 'backward',
'downward', 'forward', 'northward', 'southward', 'toward',
'upward' – 'He headed straight toward the diner.'

Round and around . . .

The UK and US usage of these two little words is slightly different
– and often where a Brit would use 'round', an American would
use 'around', and vice versa. In UK English, 'round' is more precise,
'around' more vague (see Chapter 4, p.133); the opposite is the case
in US English. 'She's driving me round the bend', 'That shop is
somewhere around here' (more UK); 'The store around the corner',

'He ran around and around and around, and then threw up'
(more US).

Miscellaneous US/UK spellings

aging / ageing

anymore / any more

annex (noun) / annexe

artifact / artefact

ax / axe

check / cheque

chili / chilli

coz / cos

cozy / cosy

curb / kerb (and curb)

donut / doughnut

draft / draught (and draft)

fulfill / fulfil

furor / furore

gray / grey

inquire / enquire (and inquire)

licorice / liquorice

mold / mould

molt / moult

mom / mum

mustache / moustache

pajamas / pyjamas

phony / phoney

plow / plough

sequined / sequinned

smolder / smoulder

story / storey (and story)

sulfur / sulphur

tire / tyre (and tire)

whodunit / whodunnit

Vocabulary

Of course some of these terms below are used on both sides of the
pond, but the Americans predominantly use the words on the left,
and the Brits use those on the right.

airplane / aeroplane, plane

aluminum / aluminium

alternate / alternate *but* also alternative

anesthesiologist / anaesthetist

apartment / flat

apartment building / block of flats
arugula (same as rucola) / rocket, roquette
ass / arse
attorney / barrister-type lawyer

baby carriage / pram
baby shower / (no translation – but unfortunately
    it's arrived on these shores)
bachelor party / stag night
bachelorette party / hen night
backyard *or* yard / garden
Band-Aid / plaster
bangs / fringe
barrette / hairclip
bathing suit / swimming costume
bathrobe *or* robe / dressing gown
bathroom / bathroom *or* toilet
bathtub *or* tub / bath
bell pepper / pepper
biscuit / scone-type thing
biweekly / fortnightly
blacktop / tarmac
blinkers (same as turn signals) / indicators
boardwalk *or* esplanade if it's a fancy one / promenade
bobby pins / hairpins
bodega / corner shop – particularly in New York
bookstore / bookshop
boondocks *or* boonies / back of beyond, the sticks
braids / plaits
broil / grill
bug / insect
burglarize / burgle . . .
butt / bum

campground / camping site

candy / sweet

cane / walking stick

casket / coffin

cell phone / mobile phone

centennial / centenary

check / bill *or* tick (as in 'tick this box' – Americans would 'check this box')

checkers / draughts

cheers / thanks

chips / crisps

chop meat / minced meat

cilantro / coriander

cleats / football boots

closet / wardrobe

clothespin / clothes peg

cockamamie / ridiculous

comforter / duvet

condominium *or* condo / owner-occupied flat

conniption / tantrum

convenience store / corner shop

cookie / biscuit

cookie-cutter (adjective) / mass-produced – pejorative term

cookie jar / biscuit tin

cookout / barbecue

cop / policeman

cot / camp bed, fold-up bed

cotton candy / candyfloss

countertop *or* counter / worktop

counterclockwise / anti-clockwise

crib / cot

crosswalk / pedestrian crossing

cup / approx. half a pound or half a pint

cupcake / fairy cake

curse / swear

dago tee / sleeveless T-shirt

den / family room

detail a car / valet a car, as in clean it thoroughly (to valet
  a car in the US would be to have it parked for you)

diaper / nappy

dirt / earth

dollhouse / doll's house

dork / nerd

dove / dived

drapes / curtains

dresser / chest of drawers

drugstore (sells more than a pharmacy – see below) /
  high-street chemist

dump / tip

dumpster / skip

edgewise / edgeways

eggplant / aubergine

eggs over easy / double-sided fried egg

eggs sunny side up / one-sided fried egg

egg-white omelette / taste-free omelette

elementary school (same as grade school) / primary school

elevator / lift

entryway / entrance

ER / A&E

eraser / rubber

expiration date / expiry date

fall / autumn

fanny pack / bumbag

faucet / tap

felon / criminal

fender bender / minor car accident

figure / think

figure out / work something out

filet / fillet

finish line / finishing line

fire truck / fire engine

first floor / ground floor

fit / fitted, as in past tense of fit

flameout / complete failure

flashlight / torch

flat / flat tyre

flight attendant / air steward(ess)

flophouse / dosshouse

flutist / flautist

four-way stop / crossroads with equal status but no traffic
    lights (sounds like a crash waiting to happen)

foyer / hall in house or flat

freeway / motorway

French fries *or* fries / chips

front yard / front garden

frosting / icing

garage sale (same as stoop sale and yard sale) / car boot sale

garbage / rubbish (literally), nonsense

garbageman (same as sanitation engineer and trash collector)
    / dustman

gas *or* gasoline / petrol

grade / mark *or* school year

grader / former (as in first-grader / first-former)

grade school (same as elementary school) / primary school

graduate school *or* grad school / place for postgraduate studies

greeting card / greetings card

grocery store / food shop (sadly, usually Sainsbury's Local
 or Tesco Express these days)
ground / minced (as in 'ground' or 'minced meat')

hayseed (same as rube) / country bumpkin
heavy cream / double cream
heist / robbery
high school / upper secondary school
highway / A-road, motorway
hobo / vagrant
hodgepodge / hotchpotch
home free / home and dry
home fries / sliced fried potatoes
hood / car bonnet *or* the neighbourhood
hooker / prostitute
hooky / truant
horseback riding / horse riding
hose / stockings
housing project / council estate

intermission / interval
intersection / crossroads

janitor / caretaker
Jell-O / jelly
jelly / jam
john / toilet
jump rope / skipping rope
junior high / lower secondary school
junkman / man who sells junk
junkyard / scrapyard

kitty-corner / diagonally opposite
knit / knitted, as in past tense of knit

ladybug / ladybird
laundromat / launderette
lawn chair / garden chair
La-Z-Boy / reclining armchair
leash / lead
limousine liberal / champagne socialist
line / queue
liquor store / off-licence
lobby / hall, foyer
lot / waste ground
lox / smoked salmon

mailbox / letter box
mailman / postman
major / study (as in 'I'm majoring in psychology')
making out / snogging
mall / shopping centre
math / maths
messengered / couriered
movie / film (though Americans might go to a 'film' if it's an
    art-house, indy, European one)
movie theater / cinema (though Americans would 'go to the
    movies' more often than they would 'go to the movie
    theater')

nail polish / nail varnish (and a woman in the US polishes her
    nails, she doesn't paint them)
necking / snogging
nightstand / bedside table
nightstick / truncheon
911 / 999

oatmeal / porridge

O.B.G.Y.N. *or* OB/GYN *or* obie-gynie / gynaecologist
off-ramp / slip road
oftentimes (still common in the US, though obsolete
   in the UK) / often
orient / orientate
orientation / induction

pacifier / dummy
pants / trousers
panties / knickers
pantyhose / tights
paper towel / kitchen towel
parking lot / car park
penitentiary / prison
pharmacy (more specifically for drugs than a drugstore –
   see above) / chemist
pitcher / jug
plastic wrap (same as Saran wrap) / cling film
pocketbook / purse, handbag
Popsicle / ice lolly
potluck supper / bring a dish to a party
power outage / power cut
preschool / nursery school
pry / prise
pumps / low-heeled ladies' shoes
purse / handbag
putter / potter (as in 'about')

quite / very, *not* rather

railroad / railway
raise / pay rise
real estate / property

real estate agent *or* realtor / estate agent
refrigerator / fridge
rental car / hire car
restroom / toilet
résumé / CV
roommate / room-mate *or* flatmate *or* housemate
rotary (same as traffic circle) / roundabout
rowboat / rowing boat
row house / terrace house
rubber / johnny
rube (same as hayseed) / country bumpkin
rummage sale / jumble sale
run / ladder (in your stockings or tights)
run interference / intervene on someone's behalf
rucola (same as arugula) / rocket, roquette
RV (recreational vehicle) / camper van

sailboat / sailing boat
sanitary napkin / sanitary towel
sanitation engineer (same as garbageman and trash
    collector) / dustman
Saran wrap (same as plastic wrap) / cling film
scallion / spring onion
school / college, university
schoolyard / playground
Scotch tape / Sellotape
sedan / saloon (car)
Seeing Eye dog / guide dog
semester / term
shopping cart / shopping trolley
sick / ill
sidewalk / pavement
skillet / frying pan

sled / sledge
smokejumper / parachuting firefighter
sneakers / trainers
snicker / snigger
soccer / football
soda / fizzy drink
soy / soya
specialty / speciality
spigot / outside tap
spike heel / stiletto
spit / spat, as in past tense of spit
sports / sport (you do 'sports' in US schools, not 'sport')
sport coat *or* sports coat / sports jacket
sprung / sprang
station wagon / estate car
stick shift / gearstick
stoop / front steps of a house or apartment building
stoop sale (same as garage sale and yard sale) / car boot sale
substitute teacher / supply teacher
subway / Underground
summa cum laude / first-class degree ('magna cum laude'
        is probably a 2:1, 'cum laude' a 2:2)
suspenders / braces
swap meet / flea market, gathering to barter or trade items
sweats / tracksuit

takeout *or* to go / takeaway
tarp / tarpaulin
temple / synagogue
thrift store / charity shop
thumbtacks / drawing pins
tic-tac-toe / noughts and crosses
tony / fashionable

totaled / completely wrecked
track and field / athletics
traffic circle (same as rotary) / roundabout
traffic signal / traffic light
trailer park / caravan site
trailer trash / chav
training wheels / stabilisers
train station / station
tramp / slapper, tramp
trash / rubbish
trash can / rubbish bin
trash collector (same as garbageman and sanitation
    engineer) / dustman
truck / lorry
trunk / boot (of car)
turn signals (same as blinkers) / indicators
turtleneck / polo neck
tuxedo / dinner jacket

underpants / pants
undershirt / vest
undershorts / pants

vacation / holiday
vanity *or* vanity table / dressing table
vanity plate / personalised number plate
vest / waistcoat
Veterans Day / Remembrance Day
vise / vice

walking stick / stick insect
walk-up / building with stairs only, no lift (or elevator)
wallet / purse, wallet
want ads / classified ads

way station / stopping place on a journey
whiskey / whisky
white-out / Tipp-Ex
wifebeater / sleeveless T-shirt
windshield / windscreen

yard sale (same as garage sale and stoop sale) / car boot sale

zee / zed (last letter of the alphabet)
zip code / postcode
zipper / zip
zucchini / courgette

Idiom and phrases

across from / opposite (as in 'She sat across from me
    in math class')
across the street / over the road
and all / and everything (as in 'If I found out she's met
    someone else, it would shatter me, even though
    we're divorced and all')

can I get a skinny soy mocha decaf? / I'd like a cup
    of coffee please

fill a prescription / get a prescription (refill a prescription /
    get a repeat prescription)
from the get-go / from the beginning

gotten / got

headed / heading (as in 'They were headed in the
    wrong direction')

hit on someone / try to pick someone up
hit someone up for something / ask someone for something

in / at (Americans learn 'in school', Brits learn 'at school')
in heat / on heat
in the hospital / in hospital
is all / that's all (as in 'I'm feeling a bit tired, is all')

lay of the land / lie of the land
look-see / quick look

meet with someone / meet someone

monkey wrench into the works / spanner in the works
off of / off (as in 'Could you get that off of the shelf for me?' –
    fine in the US, no-no in the UK)
on a kick / being temporarily enthusiastic about something
    (as in 'I'm on a health kick at the moment')

packing heat / carrying a gun
pissed *and* pissed at / pissed off (as in 'She's really pissed with
    you, so don't expect her to call'), *not* drunk
pop the trunk / open the boot

quiet / quieten

ride / lift, journey (as in 'Can I get a ride to school?')
right away / straight away

speak with someone / speak to someone (the US sounds
    more friendly)
straight ahead / straight on

through / to, until (as in 'I'm working Wednesday through Sunday', 'I'm on vacation from July 4 through July 6')

Slight abbreviation in sentence constructions

come visit me / come *and* visit me

go find a friend to play with / go *and* find a friend to play with

go open the window / go *and* open the window

he's always getting in trouble / he's always getting in*to* trouble

let's meet Friday / let's meet *on* Friday

pouring down rain / pouring down *with* rain

she's written her to say she's coming / she's written *to* her to say she's coming (though both could just say 'she's written to say she's coming')

Dates and times

Americans put the month before the day – as in 'July 4, 2012' or 7/4/12 (though its 'Fourth of July' for some reason). This is why 11 September is referred to as '9/11' rather than '11/9'.

US time terminology is mostly the same as the UK's, but they do sometimes want to meet up at 'a quarter of eight', meaning 'a quarter to eight', and always at 'eight thirty', never 'half eight'.

Numbers and weight

Americans often continue in the hundreds while we would have switched to thousands when referring to large numbers. So 'the rental on the apartment is thirty-seven hundred dollars a month' as opposed to 'three thousand seven hundred dollars', and the president lives at 'sixteen hundred Pennsylvania Avenue', not 'one thousand six hundred Pennsylvania Avenue' (as a Brit might say).

Likewise, Americans weigh three hundred pounds (well, not all of them) as opposed to twenty stone.

Atlantic drift

While many of the above terms and phrases are probably familiar to our ears, some are creeping out of our mouths, with US words and idioms becoming increasingly common. A few years ago, 'knock me up at eight in the morning' would have meant 'Wake me up at eight in the morning'; now it's more likely to mean 'Get me pregnant at eight in the morning'.

In the following extracts, convert the US punctuation, spelling and terminology into standard UK usage.

> One weekend soon after that, on one of the first chilly days of fall, I was out gathering scrap lumber in a vacant lot near the river. Our apartment house was very old and badly kept, but we had a fireplace that "worked." I chose only boards that could be split and broken down to fireplace size, and when I had enough to last a few days I pitched them over the high wire fence that surrounded the lot. From a distance that fence might have looked difficult to scale, but there were enough sagging places in it to make easy footholds. I went up and over it, and had just dropped to the street when I saw Dan Rosenthal walking toward me.
>
> "Well," he said. "You looked pretty good there, coming over the fence. You looked very nimble."
>
> That was a pleasure. I remember being pleased too that he'd found me wearing an old Army field jacket and blue jeans. He was dressed in a suit and tie and a light, new-looking top-coat.
>
> Richard Yates, *Liars in Love*

Our secretary was standing there with a grocery bag on her hip. "Feeling any better?" she asked me.

"Oh, yes."

"Well, I've brought you some soup," she said. "We all just knew you wouldn't be fixing yourself any lunch."

"Thanks, but I'm not—"

"Feed a cold, starve a fever!" she caroled. She nudged the door wider open with her elbow and stepped inside. "People always wonder which it is," she said. "'Feed a cold and starve a fever,' or 'Starve a cold and feed a fever.' But what they don't realize is, it's an 'If, then' construction. So in that case either one will work, because *if* you feed a cold *then* you'll be starving a fever, which you most certainly do want to do, and if you starve a cold then you'll be feeding a nasty old fever."

Peggy was soft and dimpled—a pink-and-gold person with a cloud of airy blond curls and a fondness for thrift-store outfits involving too many bits of lace. I liked Peggy just fine (we'd gone through grade school together, which may have been what led my father to hire her), but the softness was misleading.

Anne Tyler, *The Beginner's Goodbye*

"I don't understand a thing," Mommy says, "but never mind. Come, put your bag down and go wash your hands and face. Dinner's already on the table." Avishai takes off the knapsack, goes into the bathroom, and washes his face. In the mirror over the sink he sees that he's in his school uniform. When he opens the knapsack in the living room he discovers notebooks and textbooks lined in flowered paper. There's a math book, and a box of colored pencils, and a little metal compass with an eraser shoved on the point. His mother comes over to chide him. "This isn't the time for homework. Come and eat. Hurry up, chop-chop, before all the vitamins escape from the salad." Avishai sits at the table and eats in silence. The food is delicious. He'd been surviving solely on takeout and cheap diners for so many years, he'd honestly forgotten that food could taste this good. "Daddy left you money for your after-school program." Mommy points to a sealed white envelope resting on the little hall table next to the rotary phone. "But I'm warning you, Avi, if you pull the same stunt you did with the model-airplane program, and change your mind after one class, you're better off telling us now, before we pay."

Etgar Keret, "Pudding," *Suddenly, a Knock on the Door*

Other English-speaking countries

Canadians use UK spellings on the whole, apart from going for -ize endings, rather than -ise; likewise, the Australians, although it's the 'Labor Party', not the 'Labour Party' (but otherwise they stick to -our). However, as with American English, the vocabulary and idiom of English-speaking countries around the world does vary enormously. This is often because of local and native effect – South African borrows from Afrikaans, Xhosa and Zulu, New Zealand from Maori, etc. – and from immigrant influences, like in the US. Here are some terms and expressions to avoid confusion and possibly embarrassment.

If a South African says to you, 'I'll see you just now,' don't hang around – they could mean five minutes, or next year.

Don't be alarmed if an Australian guy says he's wearing his 'thongs' to the beach – he means his flip-flops.

If a New Zealand girl wants to give you some 'hokey-pokey', she's not being suggestive – she's offering some rather tasty ice cream.

However, if you're on a diet in Canada, turn down the 'triple-triple' in the cafe – it's a coffee with three creams and three sugars.

Antipodean vocab and idiom

The Antipodeans also cross over with a fair few US terms – their vest and pants, for example, doesn't mean a British person's underwear. But here are some terms used in both Australia and New Zealand which probably aren't that familiar or used in either the UK or US.

> across the ditch – Australia or New Zealand (depending on where you are) / across the pond – United States or United Kingdom
>
> bogan / chav
> boilover / surprise result, particularly in a sporting event
> born in a tent / someone is born in a tent if they never close a door behind them
> bring a plate / bring a dish to a party – not just the plate . . .
> Buckley's chance / no chance whatsoever
> bush / forest (though a bit different from a British forest)
>
> capsicum / pepper
> cark / drop dead *or* conk out
> chook / chicken
> chunder / throw up
> crim / criminal
> crook / unwell (as in 'I'm feeling really crook') *or* criminal
>
> daggy / geeky (but 'dagg' does not mean the same either side of the ditch – see below)
> daks / trousers
> dinkum / true
> ditch / Tasman Sea
> dunny / toilet
> dunny diver / plumber

fossick / rummage

g'day / hello
Glad wrap / cling film
gone to the pack / gone to the dogs
good as gold / fine, OK

hot chips / chips

ice blocks / ice lollies

kitchen bench / kitchen worktop

lollies / sweets

munted / broken, wiped out

no worries / no probs

ocker / stereotypical Australian
out of the box / brand new

packing a sad / sulking
pashing / snogging
pike out / chicken out *or* party-pooper
Pom / Brit

ripper / excellent
rooted / exhausted, shagged (in both senses of the word)

she'll be right / it'll be all right
sickie / bunk off work for the day (often 'pull a sickie')
smoko / coffee break

sook / soppy person
spit the dummy / throw a tantrum
stubbies / work shorts *or* small bottles of beer
stoked / feel chuffed

tin-arse / jammy sod
tin-arsed / lucky, thick-skinned
togs / swimming costume
tough bikkies / tough shit
tucker / food
ute / utility car, with open back

weatherboard house / horizontally slatted wooden house

you little beauty / really happy about someone or something
(e.g. your rugby team has just scored a winning try:
'you little beauty')

Australian vocab and idiom

Banana bender / someone from Queensland
blue / argument
bonzer / good
boofhead / thick
bottle shop / off-licence
bucks' night *or* bucknight / stag night
budgie smugglers / too-tight swimming trunks

chuck a U-ey / do a U-turn
Claytons / poor imitation – often applied to a non-alcoholic
drink (originally a brand name)
cluey / intelligent
cot-case / bonkers *or* bedridden

dagg / geek – someone you laugh at, not someone who
    makes you laugh (see New Zealand sense below)
Drizabone / full-length Barbour-type coat
Durex / Sellotape

eshallot / shallot
esky / cool box

fairy floss / candyfloss
fizzer / bit of a let-down

grommet / inexperienced young surfer or skateboarder

hard case / hard nut *or* legless – and therefore a hard nut
    (so cross the road to avoid)
home and hosed / home and dry

little Aussie battler / working-class hard-grafter

middy and schooner / half pint and pint, though slightly
    smaller measures (perhaps because it would get warm
    before you finished it – beer is *always* cold)

op shop / charity shop

roo bar / bull bar

shallot / spring onion
she's apples / all's well
skite / boast
skivvy / cotton polo neck
sticky beak / nosy parker
stoked / really happy

thongs / flip-flops

tinny / beer can *or* small boat with aluminium hull

Vegemite / equivalent, and provokes a similar reaction,
    to Marmite

wag / to play truant

waxhead / surfer

wog / infection (as well as a non-PC term for anyone not of
    British descent, usually Greeks and Italians)

Woop Woop *or* beyond the black stump / far from civilisation,
    back of beyond (e.g. 'he lives out the back of Woop Woop')

New Zealand vocab and idiom

bach (pronounced 'batch') / beach house (the classic Kiwi bach
    is very small and basic, but these days they can be quite
    luxurious too)

box of fluffies / to feel great

cheerio / sausage *as well as* goodbye

chilly bin / cool box

crib / same as bach, but term used more on the South Island

dagg / someone who makes you laugh (a 'dagg' literally, though,
    is a piece of wool with little bits of shit attached that hangs
    from a sheep's bum) – see also 'rattle your daggs'

dairy / corner shop

flag it / forget it, don't bother

full tit / full tilt

greasies / takeaway

green-fingered bro / dopehead – not a gardener . . .

gurgler / lost (e.g. 'gone down the gurgler', like 'gone down the pan')

hokey-pokey / honeycomb ice cream (yum)

jandles / flip-flops

kai / food
kiwi / bird
Kiwi / New Zealander
kiwi fruit / kiwi fruit – never just 'kiwi'
kumara / sweet potato

pearler / very good
pick up your lip before you trip over it / stop sulking
pottle / little pot (e.g. a pottle of yogurt is a single serving)

rark / tell off (e.g. 'That kid needs a good rarking')
rattle your daggs / get a move on (if a sheep is running –
    see 'dagg' – its daggs will rattle . . .)
rej (pronounced 'reej') / reject

snag / another word for sausage
snarler / yet another word for sausage
Swan Dry or swanny / heavy-duty cotton winter shirt
    (brand name but used generically)

tai ho / slow down, wait
twink / Tipp-Ex

waka / vehicle
wop wop / back of beyond

South African vocab and idiom

babbelas (pronounced 'bubulus') / hangover
bagel / male form of kugel – see below
bakkie / pickup truck
biltong / dried meat
blaps (pronounced 'blups') / mistake (e.g. 'Oops, I made
    a blaps')
boerewors (pronounced 'boor-uh-vurse') / sausage
bok *or* bokkie / sweetheart (used by older person for
    younger one)
braai (pronounced 'bry') / barbecue
brak / mongrel
brar / brother

chana *or* china / mate – the former comes from Zulu, the
    latter from cockney rhyming slang
cherry / sweetheart
chommie / friend
chop / idiot

dagga (pronounced 'da hach' – 'gga' is similar to the 'ch'
    in the Scottish 'loch') / marijuana
dorp / provincial little town
doss / sleep

flaterwater / Tipp-Ex

geyser / boiler
gogga (pronounced 'hoch-hoch' –'gga' is similar to the 'ch'
    in the Scottish 'loch') / insect

hold thumbs for me / keep your fingers crossed
howzit? / how are you? *or* hello

is it? (pronounced 'izit') / really? (as in 'We climbed
　　　Table Mountain today.' 'Is it?' No, this doesn't seem
　　　to make much sense, and in fact only makes sense
　　　to Capetonians)

jol / to have a party, have fun

kak / nonsense, crap
kif / cool
kokie / marker pen
kop / hill
koppie / small hill
kraal / enclosure
krimpie / old person
kugel (pronounced 'kooggle') / rather spoilt, materialistic,
　　　overly made-up young woman, with too much time
　　　on her hands

laat lammetjie (pronounced 'laht lumicky') / youngest child by
　　　quite a distance, the happy accident, literally 'late lamb'
lappie (pronounced 'luppie') / cloth
lekker / nice

matric / A levels
mealie / maize, corn on the cob

naartjie (pronounced 'nar-chi') / all orange-coloured citrus
　　　fruits – apart from the orange . . .
nowell (pronounced 'no well') / fine
now-now / not now, but soon

pap (pronounced 'pup') / porridge
put foot / get a move on

robot / traffic light

rooibos (pronounced 'roy-boss') / red bush, as in 'tea'

rooinek (pronounced 'roy-neck') / redneck (slightly derogative
  term for the Englishman who gets burnt in the sun)

sarmie / sandwich ('sarnie' with an 'm')

see you just now / see you later

shame / a sympathetic interjection – 'that's a pity', *not*
  'that's a disgrace' (e.g. 'Shame, he's got a cold'); also
  used like 'sweet' (e.g. 'Ah, shame, what a cute baby!')

shot / thanks

sis / yuk

sjambok (pronounced 'sham-bok') / whip

skollie / thief or bad person

slap chips (pronounced 'slup chips') / soggy chips – as usually
  soaked in vinegar

slops / flip-flops

sosatie / kebab

stoep / veranda

stompie / short person

tekkies (pronounced 'tackies') / trainers

tsotsi (pronounced 'totzi') / gangster

tune / giving lip

voetsek (pronounced 'foot sack') / bugger off

vrying (pronounced 'fraying') / snogging

vuvuzela / very annoying blowy thing

Canadian vocab and idiom

As with punctuation and spelling, the Canadians seem to follow a
mix of US and UK terms and idiom – apart from some rather odd-

sounding food combinations (chips covered with cheese covered with gravy, anyone?). But they do have a few words of their own:

beaver tail / fried dough

Canuck / Canadian

double-double / coffee with two shots of cream and two
    sugars (triple-triple / coffee with three shots of cream
    and three sugars)

loonie / one dollar (toonie / two dollars)

mickey / small bottle of booze

parkade / multi-storey car park
pogey / employment insurance (similar to the dole
    but you have to have been employed to get it)
pop / soda

runners / trainers

toque (rhymes with 'sook' rather than 'soak') / woolly
    hat with pompom

However, the Canadians would *probably* like it to be known that it's two-way traffic – many words could just as easily have come from them, not the Americans. And they would *most definitely* like it to be known that although they share a common language, they are nothing like their next-door neighbours as people (values, outlooks on things, attitudes, behaviour . . .), and the majority of Canadians will be incredibly insulted and offended if you ask them where they are from in the States.

6 | Reading and Writing

A synonym is a word you use when you
can't spell the word you first thought of.

Burt Bacharach

Euphemisms are unpleasant truths
wearing diplomatic cologne.

Quentin Crisp

If the previous chapters focus on the English language and its
various tricky paths, Chapter 6 delves more into literary terms
and linguistics – terms defining particular areas of our language
and speech, terms that crop up now and again and sound quite
intriguing as well as puzzling.

Abridged

This is a condensed form of a book, film or play, which should
retain the sense but not the volume of the original. There are
numerous reasons for doing this: to cut out the boring or naughty
or traumatic bits for schoolchildren; because a 900-page novel
can seem rather daunting; to suit people who don't have the time
or inclination to read the full twelve-volume work; to fit into
the available time slot in the radio or TV schedule. The first two
reasons are not so common nowadays, but the latter two certainly
are – most obviously seen (or heard) in the frequent practice of
releasing an abridged version of an audiobook.

Acrostic

The most familiar acrostic is a crossword. In a more literary vein, it is a poem where the first letter of each line forms a word when it is read from top to bottom, often to conceal a message to a lover or sponsor, or simply for some fun when the author is bored and sitting there twirling his quill. Here is 'An Acrostic' to Elizabeth by Edgar Allan Poe.

Elizabeth it is in vain you say
'Love not' – thou sayest it in so sweet a way:
In vain those words from thee or L.E.L.
Zantippe's talents had enforced so well:
Ah! if that language from thy heart arise,
Breathe it less gently forth – and veil thine eyes.
Endymion, recollect, when Luna tried
To cure his love – was cured of all beside –
His follie – pride – and passion – for he died.

Aga saga / chick lit / lad lit / confessional column / misery memoir / romcom / zomromcom

These are genres of fiction that have appeared in recent years, their subjects as they say on the tin. The Aga saga invariably focuses on a middle-aged, middle-class, Middle England woman meeting some crisis; chick lit centres on a young, single, working woman and her love life; lad lit – much the same from the male angle but with more emphasis on booze and sport; confessional column and misery memoir – 'poor me'; romcom = romantic comedy; zomromcom = romantic comedy with zombies!

Allegory

This means a story that can be understood in more than one way. Often, the leading character or characters are representing a universal idea or event. Allegory can be traced back to classical mythology and the Bible, and is also seen in medieval morality plays, Restoration comedy, Victorian cautionary tales, and contemporary caricature, parody, even ridicule. Allegory overlaps with **metaphor**, **parable** and **satire** (see below). The Song of Solomon, Swift's *Gulliver's Travels* and Belloc's 'Matilda' are all examples of an allegory.

Alliteration

Deriving from the Latin '*alliteratio*', meaning 'added letter', alliteration means the repetition of the initial letter in a line of text for effect. With poetry in particular it can give more resonance and has the added bonus of making the line easier to remember.

> I caught this morning morning's minion, king-
> dom of daylight's dauphin, dapple-dawn-drawn Falcon, in his riding
> Of the rolling level underneath him steady air, and striding
> High there, how he rung upon the rein of a wimpling wing
> In his ecstasy! then off, off forth on a swing.
> As a skate's heel sweeps smooth on a bow-bend: the hurl and gliding
> Rebuffed the big wind. My heart in hiding
> Stirred for a bird, – the achieve of, the mastery of the thing!
>
> Brute beauty and valour and act, oh, air, pride, plume, here
> Buckle! AND the fire that breaks from thee then, a billion
> Times told lovelier, more dangerous, O my chevalier!
> No wonder of it: shéer plód makes plough down sillion
> Shine, and blue-bleak embers, ah my dear,
> Fall, gall themselves, and gash gold-vermilion.

Gerard Manley Hopkins, 'The Windhover'

Listen. It is night in the chill, squat chapel, hymning in bonnet
and brooch and bombazine black, butterfly choker and bootlace
bow, coughing like nannygoats, suckling mintoes, fortywinking
hallelujah; night in the four-ale, quiet as a domino; in Ocky
Milkman's lofts like a mouse with gloves; in Dai Bread's bakery
flying like black flour.

Dylan Thomas, *Under Milk Wood*

It is one of the oldest of poetic devices. When taken to extremes
it produces tongue-twisters: 'If Peter Piper picked a peck of pickled
pepper, where's the peck of pickled pepper Peter Piper picked?',
'She sells seashells by the seashore', 'Betty bit a bit of butter, but
it was a bitter bite: but a bit of better butter Betty never bit', etc.

Allusion

An allusion in a text is an incidental comment on something –
such as a familiar phrase, a well-known event – which the author
presumes the reader will understand without explanation. It's
a hint, conveying a big idea in a small space without having to
spell out the historical or traditional reference; a sort of literary
in-joke, though not necessarily aiming for a laugh. The title of
Radio 4's *This Sceptred Isle* alludes to John of Gaunt's speech in
Shakespeare's *Richard II*, which in turn alludes to the state of
England. James Joyce's *Ulysses* alludes to Homer's *Odyssey*; Haruki
Murakami's *What I Think About When I Think About Running* alludes
to Raymond Chandler's *What I Think About When I Think About
Love*. Outside the literary field, there's the band Franz Ferdinand,
who take their name from the man whose assassination kicked
off the First World War, and Joy Division – the band's name a
reference to the prostitution section of a Nazi concentration camp
in Ka-Tzetnik's *House of Dolls* (and Martin Amis also alludes to this
title with his own *House of Meetings*).

What do the following allude to?

1 John Mortimer's *Summer's Lease*

2 John Steinbeck's *Of Mice and Men*

3 annus horribilis

4 B52s

5 F. Scott Fitzgerald's *Tender is the Night*

6 Noël Coward's *Blithe Spirit*

7 Thomas Hardy's *Far From the Madding Crowd*

8 Evelyn Waugh's *A Handful of Dust*

9 salt of the earth

10 Ernest Hemingway's *For Whom the Bell Tolls*

Anagram

Anagram is derived from the Greek *'ana'* and *'gramma'*, meaning 'back' and 'letter'. It is a word or phrase, which, using the same letters in a different order, forms another word or phrase.

An anagram of Dickens is 'snicked'; of Austen, 'unseat'; of Keats, 'steak' or 'skate'; of Blake, 'bleak'. Hours of fun for some people, particularly for crossword lovers.

Anti-hero/ine

This is the leading character in a work, who lacks the qualities associated with the **hero/ine** (see below) – and is often more interesting and realistic because of that lack. Unlike his intrepid, valiant counterpart, he is invariably flawed – in some cases fatally. Oedipus and Clytemnestra are early examples of the anti-hero/ine, and here are a few more through the ages: Shylock, Richard III, Faust, Don Juan, Carmen, Becky Sharp, Humbert Humbert in

Lolita, Jean Brodie, Tom Ripley, Mother Courage, Jimmy Porter
(in fact, most leading male characters from the pen of John
Osborne), Keith Talent in *London Fields*, Renton in *Trainspotting*,
Rigsby in *Rising Damp*, Blackadder, Homer Simpson.

Antonomasia

This is a figure of speech which substitutes a title or epithet or
sobriquet for the real name – the Bard (Shakespeare), the Sun
King (Louis XIV), the Maid of Orleans (Joan of Arc), the Iron Lady
(Margaret Thatcher), the Beast of Bolsover (Dennis Skinner), the
Big Yin (Billy Connolly), the Special One (José Mourinho). It can
also be an oblique reference to someone's character – a Scrooge,
a Lothario, a Jezebel, a Judas, a Pollyanna.

Antonym

Deriving from the Greek words '*anti*', meaning 'against', and
'*onoma*', meaning 'word' or 'name', an antonym is a word which
is the opposite in meaning to another. For example, 'love/hate',
'bitter/sweet', 'tall/short', 'alive/dead', 'anorexic/obese',
'optimist/pessimist', 'sober/drunk', etc. The opposite of antonym
is **synonym** (see below).

Archaism

An archaism is something old-fashioned or obsolete – a word,
or a way of writing and spelling. They are words which are today
considered archaic, but were at one time in common use; now
they may only be found in old texts, some legal documents and
the odd dialect. For example: 'betwixt', 'blackguard', 'blessèd', 'ere',
'fie!', 'forsake', 'forsooth', 'heretofore', 'morn', 'o'er', 'oftentimes',
'thee', 'theretofore', 'thou', ''twas', 'wherefore', 'wheretofore',

'whomsoever', 'zounds!'. A few spellings: 'connexion', 'gaol', 'inflexion', 'mediaeval'. Writers might use an archaic term or spelling for a particular effect.

Assonance

When vowel sounds are repeated, creating a rhyme within a line, or lines, of verse (and occasionally prose), this is assonance, as in Tennyson's 'On either side the river lie' or Sondheim's 'It's an herb that's superb for disturbances at sea' (the Americans pronounce 'herb' as 'erb'). A couple more examples:

> How a lush-kept plush-capped sloe
> Will, mouthed to flesh-burst
> Gush! – flush the man, the being with it, sour or sweet,
> Brim, in a flash, full!
>
> Gerard Manley Hopkins, 'The Wreck of the Deutschland'

> And the silken sad uncertain rustling of each purple curtain
> Thrilled me – filled me with fantastic terrors never felt before . . .
>
> Edgar Allan Poe, 'The Raven'

Assonance differs from regular rhyme, because a rhyme is usually a matching of words at the end of verse lines, those words a combination of vowels and consonants – and pretty obvious:

> Blest be the man that spares these stones,
> And curst be he that moves my bones.
>
> Shakespeare's epitaph

Autobiography / biography / hagiography

A biography is an account of someone's life. An autobiography is an account of someone's life written (or ghostwritten) by that someone, and therefore is likely to be less impartial than a biography. (Naturally, an autobiography can't cover the whole life, unless the writer is finishing it off on his deathbed.) A hagiography is a biography which eulogises its subject and forgets about objective criticism.

Bildungsroman

This is a novel that follows the leading character through his or her formative years, from childhood to adulthood, usually through tough times. It is a German word (*Bildung* – education, *Roman* – novel) and Goethe was an early exponent. English-language examples are *Great Expectations, Jane Eyre, Maurice, To Kill a Mockingbird, The Catcher in the Rye, Midnight's Children, A Widow for One Year, Any Human Heart, The Sense of an Ending*, Harry Potter – all seven volumes of him . . .

Elegy

Derived from the Greek work *'elegos'*, meaning 'lament', an elegy is usually a mournful poem for the dead – a friend, or a public figure. Examples are Percy Bysshe Shelley's *Adonais* (written for his friend John Keats), Alfred, Lord Tennyson's *In Memoriam A. H. H.* (for his friend Arthur Henry Hallam), Walt Whitman's 'O Captain! My Captain!' and 'When Lilacs Last in the Dooryard Bloom'd' (both for Abraham Lincoln), W. H. Auden's 'In Memory of W. B. Yeats' (self-explanatory). It can also be a piece of prose, such as Roy Strong's *Visions of England* and Roger Scruton's *England: An Elegy*; a poem for a lost way of life, such as Thomas Gray's *Elegy Written in a Country Churchyard* and Oliver Goldsmith's *Deserted Village*; or a musical work, with or without voice, such as Edward Elgar's orchestral *Elegy for Strings* and Hans Werner Henze's opera *Elegy for Young Lovers*.

Encomium

This is derived from the Greek *enkomion*, meaning 'eulogy', which in turn encompasses the Greek words for 'within' and 'revel'. An encomium is similar to an **elegy** (see above), in that it is a piece of writing in praise of a person or event or thing, but the person doesn't need to be dead. It can also be considerably more cheerful – encomiums (or encomia) were written to celebrate winners at the original Olympic Games. Abraham Lincoln and William Golding both wrote encomiums to writing. Gorgias wrote an 'Encomium to Helen', and a more recent example is Oprah Winfrey's to Rosa Parks.

Epic

Derived from the Greek *'epikos'*, meaning 'word' or 'song', an epic is one of the oldest forms of narrative (viz. 'In the beginning . . .'), and at its simplest it is what storytelling is all about.

An epic is usually a long poem or novel on a grand scale. Often it tells of great deeds carried out by a legendary figure, concerning, for example, huge battles fought or sea journeys undertaken to save the citizens of beleaguered cities and towns. They are stories of superheroes, like today's Batman, Spider-Man and Superman. Some of the first epics were Homer's *Iliad* and *Odyssey* and, closer to home (and a bit later), *Beowulf*. More recent epics are generally very long novels like Tolstoy's, or operas like Wagner's, or those many sequelled and prequelled films – *Star Wars*, *Alien(s)*, Indiana Jones, Harry Potter.

Epilogue

From the Greek word *'epilogos'*, meaning 'additional speech',
an epilogue comes at the very end of a work (novel, play, TV
drama or documentary, etc.) and is meant to tie things up neatly.
It usually gives an account of what has gone before and might
give an indication of what has happened to the characters since.
In some of Shakespeare's plays (*All's Well That Ends Well*, *As You
Like It*, *Henry V*, *The Tempest*), the epilogue asks the audience's
forgiveness for any infelicities and to applaud anyway.

> The king's a beggar now the play is done.
> All is well ended if this suit be won,
> That you express content, which we will pay
> With strife to please you, day exceeding day.
> Ours be your patience then, and yours our parts,
> Your gentle hands lend us, and take our hearts.

> *All's Well That Ends Well*

Epistolary

Like the word 'epistle', which it resembles, 'epistolary' is concerned
with the writing of letters, and an 'epistolary novel' refers to one
which is made up, wholly or in part, of letters. Samuel Richardson
in the eighteenth century used this form for his novels *Pamela* and
Clarissa, as did Mary Shelley in *Frankenstein* and Bram Stoker in
Dracula. More recent epistolary novels include *The Color Purple*
by Alice Walker and *We Need to Talk About Kevin* by Lionel Shriver.

Eponymous

In the literary world, this is the word used when the main character
gives his or her name to the title ('eponymous' is another word for

'titular'). Many works by Shakespeare (actually, everything bar the comedies really) and Dickens are eponymous – *Hamlet, Macbeth, Coriolanus, Titus Andronicus, Romeo and Juliet* and *Troilus and Cressida*; *David Copperfield, Nicholas Nickleby, Oliver Twist* and *Barnaby Rudge*. Later and more contemporary examples are *The Adventures of Huckleberry Finn, Emil and the Detectives, Charlie and the Chocolate Factory, Zuckerman Bound, The Sheep-Pig, Oscar and Lucinda, Bridget Jones's Diary, Lionel Asbo*. Eponymous doesn't always have to be the actual name; it can also be the character's job or title or description – *The Jew of Malta, Two Gentlemen of Verona, The Alchemist, The Vicar of Wakefield, The Famous Five, My Naughty Little Sister, The French Lieutenant's Woman, War Horse*. Eponymous can also be applied to things or places named after a real person – for example, a restaurant or dish or drink, such as Gaby's, Jamie's, Joe Allen and Locanda Locatelli; peach Melba, tarte Tatin, pavlova and garibaldi biscuit (hardly a 'dish', but you get the point); the Bellini, Garibaldi and Montgomery cocktails, and the Shirley Temple mocktail.

Euphemism

Another word of Greek origin, euphemism comes from *'euphemismos'*, meaning 'using auspicious words'. It is a more neutral, soft word or phrase used in place of a stronger one, to avoid offence or hurt. Employed well, euphemisms are useful tools of diplomats, the legal profession and encouraging teachers. Employed badly, which they often are, they are the mealy-mouthed epithets of politicians and businessmen, used to stretch the truth or cover up some catastrophe.

Monty Python's 'Dead Parrot' sketch is full of well-known euphemisms for death (along with some not so known): 'gone to meet his Maker', 'shuffled off this mortal coil' (an allusion to *Hamlet*), 'pushing up the daisies', 'kicked the bucket'. Other common euphemisms are 'we're going to have to let you go' ('you're sacked), 'your child's a very lively member of the classroom' ('impossible'), and the rather more dangerous 'collateral damage' ('killing of civilians in war') and 'friendly fire' ('killing of allies').

What are the following euphemisms for?

1 I need to spend a penny.

2 He went swimming in his birthday suit.

3 The theatre is dark.

4 She's between jobs at the moment.

5 It fell off the back of a lorry.

6 'Oi, mind the family jewels,' said Dave.

7 She's got a problem downstairs.

8 He's got a problem with his plumbing.

9 That's an interesting interpretation . . .

10 Would you like to come in for coffee?

Expurgated / unexpurgated

Anything which might be considered unsuitable for publication – usually obscenities or anything libellous – has been removed from a text that is expurgated. The word comes from the Latin *'expurgare'*, meaning 'to clean diligently', and is a form of censorship. If 'expurgated' means bits of text have been removed, then, not surprisingly, 'unexpurgated' means they haven't. An 'unexpurgated' text is entire and follows the original.

Fable

Fables (from the Latin *'fabula'*, meaning 'story') are another very old form of storytelling. Fables illustrate a moral tale, invariably involving animals and plants, rather than people. The most famous fables were written by Aesop in the sixth century BC – such as *The Tortoise and the Hare*, *The Boy Who Cried Wolf*, and *The Crow and the Pitcher* in which a thirsty crow cleverly manages to reach the water in a barrel by filling it with stones. Other famous fabulists are Chaucer (*The Parliament of Fowls*), La Fontaine (adapted Aesop's fables), Rudyard Kipling (*Just So Stories*) and George Orwell (*Animal Farm*).

Figure of speech

A figure of speech, or figurative language, should not be taken literally. The term covers **antonomasia, hyperbole, metaphor, metonymy, onomatopoeia, simile, synecdoche** and **trope** (see entries above and below).

Ghostwriter

A ghostwriter is a person who writes a book in the name of someone else, most typically an autobiography. The ghost's identity is usually kept secret and isn't credited anywhere obvious in the text, but it is common knowledge that Naomi Campbell's and Katie Price's 'novels' were not written by them, although the ideas were theirs (and the writers are, in fact, acknowledged somewhere), and that Wayne Rooney's autobiography was written by Hunter Davies. It goes without saying that the ghostwriter is paid considerably less than the celeb cover author.

Gothic novel

Coinciding with the revival of medieval Gothic architecture in the late eighteenth and early nineteenth centuries, the Gothic novel is typified by horror and suspense, and often features castles and abbeys, and other remote, gloomy spots. Horace Walpole's *The Castle of Otranto*, published in 1764, is recognised as the first Gothic novel, and its second edition was even subtitled 'A Gothic Story'. There are usually elements of doomed romance in these works, and characters such as villainous aristocrats, imperilled heroines, evil monks and a host of ghosts lurking in the murky background. *Frankenstein* and *Dracula* are obvious examples of a genre that has continued to be explored and exploited since its early days. Other novels with Gothic traits are *Northanger Abbey* (although this was Austen in spoof mode, sending up the style), *The Bride of Lammermoor, Jane Eyre, Wuthering Heights, The Woman in White, The Strange Case of Dr Jekyll and Mr Hyde, The Picture of Dorian Gray, The Turn of the Screw, The Hound of the Baskervilles, Rebecca, Gormenghast, Carrie* and *Interview with the Vampire*.

Grand Guignol

Taken from the name of a puppet character and from the Grand Guignol theatre in Paris, this is a type of **melodrama** (see below), but a particularly grisly and sensational one. Grand Guignol 'entertainment' comes mainly from depictions of murder, rape, torture – epitomised more recently with macabre horror films and dramas, such as *Sweeney Todd, Theatre of Blood* and the Hammer Horror oeuvre.

Haiku

This is a verse form using just seventeen syllables – divided into three lines of five, seven, five. Developed in the seventeenth century in Japan chiefly by Matsuo Basho, it has been widely used in Western literature since the nineteenth. Such diverse poets as Ezra Pound, Amy Lowell, Jack Kerouac, W. H. Auden, Seamus Heaney and Wendy Cope have written haikus.

> November evening;
> The moon is up, rooks settle
> The pubs are open.
>
> Wendy Cope

Hero/ine

The hero or heroine is the main protagonist in a novel (or play, or film, etc.). The leading character doesn't necessarily possess the 'traditional' heroic traits – courage, nobility, determination, dashing looks – but he will have a basic goodness, and the reader will sympathise with and be rooting for him. Among many examples are Elizabeth Bennet, Jane Eyre, Nicholas Nickleby, Yuri Zhivago, Captain Corelli, Bridget Jones, Charlie Bucket and Tracy Beaker. Flawed heroes have that basic goodness, but it can all go horribly wrong, due to a 'flaw' (no shit, Sherlock) in their personality and outside, malign, influences – Hamlet, Macbeth, Lear, Othello, Inspector Morse, Sarah Lund. **Anti-heroes** (see above) lack the qualities typically associated with heroes.

Hyperbole

Pronounced 'hy-per-bo-lee', this means exaggeration, something to be taken with a pinch of salt. It is deliberate and used for effect.

Shakespeare and Dickens – that old double act – are *forever* going in for hyperbole.

> She told me . . . that I was duller than a great thaw, huddling
> jest upon jest with such impossible conveyance upon me that I
> stood like a man at a mark, with a whole army shooting at me.
> She speaks poniards, and every word stabs. If her breath were as
> terrible as her terminations, there were no living near her, she
> would infect to the North Star. I would not marry her, though
> she were endowed with all that Adam had left him before he
> transgressed. She would have made Hercules have turned spit,
> yea, and have cleft his club to make the fire too.

Much Ado About Nothing

> Why, man, he doth bestride the narrow world
> Like a Colossus, and we petty men
> Walk under his huge legs and peep about
> To find ourselves dishonourable graves.

Julius Caesar

> It was the best of times, it was the worst of times, it was the
> age of wisdom, it was the age of foolishness, it was the epoch
> of belief, it was the epoch of incredulity, it was the season of
> Light, it was the season of Darkness, it was the spring of hope,
> it was the winter of despair, we had everything before us, we
> had nothing before us, we were all going direct to Heaven,
> we were all going direct the other way.

A Tale of Two Cities

> I'd better go into the house, and die and be a riddance.

David Copperfield

Some not so literary but familiar hyperbolic phrases: 'I've told you a million times, don't exaggerate', 'I'm freezing to death here – put the heating on', 'I was so embarrassed, I wanted the earth to swallow me up', 'This is the worst comedy programme ever written', 'I've been on-hold for hours' (not always hyperbole . . .). And any 'Best of' lists and most award ceremonies are hyperbolic.

Idiom

Idiom is a term referring to syntax, phrases or speech patterns that are particular to one place or language, and cannot be literally translated. Such as 'raining cats and dogs', 'chattering classes', 'cheap as chips', 'elephant in the room', 'thick as two short planks', 'piece of piss', 'happy as a pig in shit', 'casting couch', 'a glass half full', 'what the dickens?', 'pull the wool over his eyes', 'warm the cockles of your heart', 'shoot the breeze', 'throw the baby out with the bathwater', 'happy-clappy', 'clutching at straws'.

In a more general sense, it means a dialect, a way of speaking, typical to that place – though that place could be an entire country, or just a village. From America: 'Can I get a ride in your station wagon to the diner?'; from Australia/New Zealand: 'Fair dinkum'; from South Africa: 'Is it?' (For more, see Chapter 5.) Numerous ones from Scotland: 'bidie-in' for 'common-law spouse', 'dreich' for 'grey drizzly [Scottish] weather', 'scunnered' for 'fed up', 'sittie-ootie' for 'balcony' (you could be on your wee sittie-ootie with your scunnered bidie-in if it's not too dreich), 'ye ken?' for 'you know?', and specifically Edinburgh: 'Weedgie' for 'Glaswegian' and 'how', meaning 'why', as in 'How do you want to know that for?'; a few from Wales: 'that's hanging, that is' for 'that's hideous', 'that's lush, that is' for 'that's lovely', 'I'll do it after now' for 'I'll do it later', 'I could sleep on a chicken's lip' for 'I'm knackered', and 'tidy!' for 'cool!'; 'hutch up' for 'shuffle up', 'snicket' for 'alley' (northern English), 'she's a reet mardy bum' for 'she's a sulky so-and-so'

(Sheffield English), 'shift' for 'snog', 'catch yourself on' for 'behave yourself' or 'wise up' (Irish); and a few terms of address from around the country: 'chuck' (north England), 'pet' (north-east England), 'my lover' (West Country), 'hen' (Scotland), 'cariad' (Wales).

This is also why there are certain foreign (usually French) phrases in our English language: because they are untranslatable – such as 'je ne sais quoi', 'joie de vivre', 'plus ça change', 'raison d'être', 'tour de force'.

Idyll

In literary terms, an idyll (sometimes spelt 'idyl') is a little poem, or part of a poem or piece of prose, in praise of the idealised rural life. It is derived from the Greek *'eidullion'*, meaning 'little picture' or 'little form'. Examples are Theocritus' *Idylls*, Tennyson's *Idylls of the King* (though the use of the word 'idyll' is somewhat of a misnomer, as it is a series of poems mourning the passing of King Arthur, written soon after the death of Prince Albert, Browning's *Dramatic Idyls*, J. M. Barrie's *Auld Licht Idylls* and Les Murray's 'The Idyll Wheel'.

In more general, everyday terms, it refers to something picturesque, happy, 'idyllic' – the chocolate-box country cottage, with thatched roof and roses round the door. It is similar to a **pastoral** (see below).

Imagery

Imagery is a fairly broad term that encompasses numerous other terms, such as figurative, metaphor, simile. It describes images – objects or ideas – in evocative, rich and expressive language, and can appeal to any of the senses, not just sight. Imagery crops up all the time in literature – 'But, soft! what light through yonder window breaks? / It is the east, and Juliet is the sun' – and also in art and music.

Irony

With irony, what is said and what is meant are not the same thing, and often are the opposite of each other. Irony is similar to sarcasm but a bit more subtle. It is used for comic and emphatic effect – most obviously in satire. It is also used for dramatic effect – when the audience knows something the character does not. *Twelfth Night, A Midsummer Night's Dream, Much Ado About Nothing* all use irony for dramatic, though humorous, effect; *Othello, Romeo and Juliet, Hamlet* all use irony for dramatic, but tragic, effect. Outside Shakespeare, there is often humorous irony in the works of Austen, Twain and Ayckbourn; and tragic irony in the works of Sophocles, Eliot and Hardy.

Jeu d'esprit

A French phrase, literally meaning 'game of the mind', *jeu d'esprit* is often used to describe a quick-witted remark, a pithy comment, an epigram, though it can extend to a whole work. *Jeux d'esprit* (note the plural) crop up in Chaucer:

> And what is bettre than wisedoom? Womman. And what is
> bettre than a good womman? Nothyng.

Shakespeare (as always):

> Beatrice: I wonder that you will still be talking, Signior
> Benedick: nobody marks you.
> Benedick: What, my dear Lady Disdain! Are you yet living?

Wilde:

> To lose one parent, Mr Worthing, may be regarded as a
> misfortune; to lose both looks like carelessness.

Today they crop up on TV and radio panel shows (*Mock the Week,*
Would I Lie to You?, I'm Sorry I Haven't a Clue) and occasionally on
Twitter and in the House of Commons.

Lacuna

A lacuna is a gap, or, for literary purposes, a missing portion
in a text.

Leitmotif

A German phrase, meaning 'leading motif', leitmotif (sometimes
spelt 'leitmotiv') is a repeated phrase or image used for effect, and
can apply to one piece of work or a body of work. Originally coined
by a music critic describing recurrent themes in Wagner's operas,
it soon spread to other art forms, including literature and theatre.
Proust and Tolkien – both of whom wrote rather long tomes –
frequently employ leitmotif (memory and rings respectively).

Ligature

A ligature in general terms ties or links something together –
especially bones or arteries. The meaning is very similar in the
written or printed word: when two letters are joined together,
this is a ligature, such as the 'oe' in '*trompe l'œil*' and the 'ae' in
'*Encyclopædia Britannica*'. Although a reader might still come
across ligatures, they will only be in ye olde bookes. For writing
and printing these days, its use is pretty much obsolete.

Limerick

A verse form of five lines, with a rhyming scheme a, a, b, b, a,
limericks first appeared in the early nineteenth century and were

made popular by the nonsense verse of Edward Lear – Lear and limerick are almost synonymous. The name comes from the line 'Will you come up to Limerick?' which was the chorus to nonsense verses sung at lively gatherings. Limericks are invariably humorous – and often filthy – and are still a popular verse form today.

There was a young lady whose eyes,
Were unique as to colour and size.
When she opened them wide
People all turned aside
And started away in surprise.

Lear

There was a young girl from Rabat,
Who had triplets, Nat, Pat and Tat;
It was fun in the breeding,
But hell in the feeding,
When she found she had no tit for Tat.

Terry Walsh

The limerick fan from Australia
Regarded his work as a failure:
His verses were fine
Until the fourth line
. . .

Maurie Houseman

Longueur

A French word, meaning 'length', longueur is applied to a tedious passage or section in a book, film, piece of music, etc. That unbelievably boring passage in ******** (take your pick), any film labelled 'The Director's Cut', much of the recitative in opera . . .

Magic (or magical) realism

This is a term used to describe a type of fiction, in which strange and surreal events occur in an otherwise realistic work. The episodes of magic realism take their themes from fables, fairy tales, dreams, even horror and Gothic. Magic realism crops up frequently in Latin American literature, such as in the works of Isabel Allende, Jorge Luis Borges, Paulo Coelho and Gabriel García Márquez. Elsewhere, there's Angela Carter, Günter Grass, Haruki Murakami, Audrey Niffenegger and Salman Rushdie. The following is an example of magic realism.

> 'Hello there,' the old man called out.
> The large, elderly black tomcat raised its head a fraction and wearily returned the greeting in a low voice.
> 'A very nice spell of weather we're having.'
> 'Um,' the cat said.
> 'Not a cloud in the sky.'
> '. . . for the time being.'
> 'Is the weather going to take a turn for the worse, then?'
> 'It feels like it'll cloud up towards evening.' The black cat slowly stretched out a leg, then narrowed its eyes and gave the old man another good long look.
> With a big grin on his face, the man stared right back. The cat hesitated for a time, then plunged ahead and spoke. 'Hmm . . . so you're able to speak.'
> 'That's right,' the old man said bashfully. To show his respect, he took off his threadbare cotton walking hat. 'Not that I can converse with every cat I meet, but if things go well I can. As right now.'

> *Kafka on the Shore*, Haruki Murakami

Magnum opus

This is a term used to describe an author's best or most important work – deriving from the Latin *'magnum'*, meaning 'great', and *'opus'*, meaning 'work'.

Malapropism

The term comes from Mrs Malaprop – a character in Sheridan's *The Rivals* who uses inappropriate, though similar-sounding, words, while trying to seem learned – 'Promise to forget this fellow – to illiterate him, I say, quite from your memory.' (Should be 'obliterate' of course.) 'He is the very pineapple of politeness.' (Should be 'pinnacle'.) 'Sure, if I reprehend any thing in this world it is the use of my oracular tongue, and a nice derangement of epitaphs!' (Four in one sentence – 'apprehend', 'vernacular', 'arrangement', 'epithets'.) A couple of more recent malapropisms: 'Republicans understand the importance of bondage between a mother and child' (Dan Quayle), 'We cannot let terrorists and rogue nations hold this nation hostile or hold our allies hostile' (G. W. Bush), 'It will take time to restore chaos and order' (Bush again), 'They've misunderestimated me' (and again) – in fact, Bush has delivered so many malapropisms, he's earned his own noun: Bushism.

Melodrama

A sensational, exaggerated drama popular in the nineteenth century, it was originally interspersed with songs – the term comes from the Greek *'melos'*, meaning 'music', and from the French *'drame'*, meaning 'drama' – although these were gradually ditched. The plays take their audiences on an emotional roller coaster, and despite the goodies coming close to the very brink of doom, they are saved in the nick of time, as there is always a happy ending in a melodrama.

Metaphor

A metaphor is a figure of speech. It is a word or phrase used to link two unrelated things together, suggesting a commonality, though not a literal one. A metaphor is used to make an image more vivid, and therefore a frequently used device in literature.

> But, look, the morn in russet mantle clad
> Walks o'er the dew of yon high eastern hill.

Horatio's metaphor here is the morning being clad in a mantle and walking, a metaphor because the morning clearly isn't literally going for a hike in its red waterproofs.

An **extended metaphor** is taking that image and running away with it, as it were, so the image is repeated in a piece of text. In 'To His Coy Mistress', Marvell uses an extended metaphor:

> Let us roll all our strength and all
> Our sweetness up into one ball,
> And tear our pleasures with rough strife
> Through the iron gates of life:
> Thus, though we cannot make our sun
> Stand still, yet we will make him run.

In *Macbeth* (well, probably most of his plays), Shakespeare uses several extended metaphors:

> Life's but a walking shadow, a poor player
> That struts and frets his hour upon the stage,
> And then is heard no more. It is a tale
> Told by an idiot, full of sound and fury,
> Signifying nothing.

A **dead metaphor** is one that people use without a second thought, because it is part of everyday speech. The metaphor has lost its original image (and originality) because it has been overworked, and therefore could be considered a cliché. 'To *add insult to injury*, everyone's *heard on the grapevine* that your career's *gone down the pan*.' (That's *killed three/four birds with one stone*.)

Mixed metaphors occur when two or more metaphors combine but conflict with each other – giving unintentional amusement to others (sports commentary providing a rich source). Such as: 'I can see the carrot at the end of the tunnel', 'We can still hang our heads high', 'He's not the sharpest marble in the drawer', 'She was having sleepless kittens', 'It isn't rocket surgery'. . .

In the following, which metaphors are being mixed?

1 Don't brand us all with the same brush.

2 We were up a tree without a paddle.

3 I've been burning the midnight oil at both ends.

4 She could read him like an open can of worms.

5 Let's burn that bridge when we come to it.

6 The cat's on the other foot now.

7 He took to it like a fish out of water.

8 She couldn't see the woods for the end of the tunnel.

9 If you do that, you'll be putting a spanner in the coffin.

10 He hit the nail on the dot.

Metonymy

Derived from the Greek word '*metonumia*', meaning 'change of name', this is a figure of speech used when one word is substituted for another with which it is closely associated. So, 'the Crown' instead of the monarch or monarchy; 'the press' instead of journalism; 'the House', members of the House of Commons or House of Lords; 'Westminster' and 'Washington', the UK and US governments respectively; 'Downing Street' and 'the Oval Office', the UK and US leaders' offices; 'the City' and 'Wall Street', the UK and US financial districts; 'Scotland Yard', Metropolitan Police; 'Hollywood', American film industry; 'Broadway', New York theatre; 'the West End', London theatre; 'the cloth', clerical profession; 'suits', businessmen; 'muscle', doormen; '4 × 4', four-wheel drives.

Metonymy also crops up in poetry and prose. In 'Give every man thine ear' and 'Friends, Romans, countrymen, lend me your ears', Shakespeare is using 'ears' rather than 'listen'.

Metre

Metre is the rhythm of a line of poetry. It is formed by putting groups of syllables together – long and short ones, stressed and unstressed. Iambic pentameter, which is the best-known rhythm, uses five (hence 'penta') pairs (hence 'iambic') of syllables: a short (unstressed) word or syllable, followed by a long (stressed) one. It is the metre Shakespeare uses most.

If <u>mu</u>sic <u>be</u> the <u>food</u> of <u>love</u>, play <u>on</u>.

To <u>sleep</u>: per<u>chance</u> to <u>dream</u>: ay, <u>there</u>'s the <u>rub</u>.

A <u>horse</u>! A <u>horse</u>! My <u>king</u>dom <u>for</u> a <u>horse</u>!

Mise en scène

This is a term for the set or scenery of a stage or film production – from the French for 'put on stage'.

Monologue / soliloquy

A monologue can be a whole play performed by one actor or it can be a very long speech delivered to the audience and other actors onstage. A soliloquy is a speech given by an actor alone onstage, or as an aside, in which his character reveals his innermost thoughts to the audience. Hamlet, Macbeth and Othello have numerous soliloquies; Samuel Beckett, Alan Bennett and Brian Friel are masters of the monologue. In non-theatrical circumstances, a monologue bores the pants off people – it comes very close to 'monotonous' in the dictionary.

Muse

Generally, a muse is a woman who gives inspiration to an artist. The term comes from the nine Muses in Greek mythology. They were the daughters of Zeus and each was responsible for one of the arts (though that extended to history and astronomy), including epic poetry, lyric poetry, comedy, tragedy and choral dancing (whatever that was). Muses have inspired all the art forms since then. Boccaccio had Maria, Dante had Beatrice, and the Pre Raphaelites had numerous muses – often sharing them – most notably Lizzie Siddall, Jane Morris and Effie Gray. Today, the concept of a muse has been expanded, and might simply mean an idea. Here are a few lines evoking muses – and for some of them that inspiration is clearly not working.

> Biting my truant pen, beating myself for spite
> 'Fool,' said my muse; 'look in thy heart, and write.'

> Sidney, *Astrophel and Stella*

Then, rising with Aurora's night,
The Muse invoked, sit down to write;
Blot out, correct, insert, refine,
Enlarge, diminish, interline . . .

Swift, 'On Poetry'

O for a muse of fire, that would ascend
The brightest heaven of invention.

Shakespeare, *Henry V*

Yes, thus the Muses sing of happy swains,
Because the Muses never knew their pains.

Crabbe, *The Village*

The man worthy of praise the Muse forbids to die.

Horace, *Odes*, Book 4

Mythology

This is a set of myths, or tales, usually from a religious (Christian, Hindu, Jewish) or cultural (Greek, Roman) tradition. Although they are stories, there will be an element of instruction in there, a moral message for the listener (originally) or reader. The stories are invariably linked, with characters often appearing, or being referred to, in more than one. Those characters are generally gods and goddesses (such as Zeus and Hera), heroes and heroines (Jason and Penelope), monsters and strange creatures (the Cyclops and the centaur). Myths and legends are frequently lumped together, but there is a slight difference between them, legends having some historical, albeit tenuous, basis. Myths, especially the Greek ones, have been borrowed by writers through the ages (Chaucer,

Keats, Joyce, etc.), a practice that continues today (Atwood, Byatt, Winterson, etc.).

Narrative

At its simplest, narrative is storytelling, the narrated part of a story rather than the dialogue. It is an account of a story given by the 'narrator'. The plot (or order of narrative) and the technique used will dictate its success, or otherwise. Technique, or method, encompasses prose and verse, can be in the first person, third person or occasionally second person (which works fine in poems and short stories, but is slightly irritating with a novel, and usually the author forgets his idea halfway through or decides it was a bad one to begin with). There are countless examples, since almost everything ever written contains some narrative. Verse narratives include Homer's *Iliad* and *Odyssey*, Anon's *Beowulf*, Chaucer's *Canterbury Tales*, Malory's *Morte d'Arthur*, Milton's *Paradise Lost*, Coleridge's *The Rime of the Ancient Mariner*, Keats's *Endymion*, Byron's *Don Juan*, Ted Hughes's *Meet My Folks!* and *Birthday Letters*. Examples of first-person narratives in prose are Dickens's *Great Expectations*, Miles Franklin's *My Brilliant Career* and Téa Obrecht's *The Tiger's Wife*; third-person narratives are Austen's *Emma*, F. Scott Fitzgerald's *Tender is the Night* and Howard Jacobson's *The Finkler Question*; second-person narratives include Chuck Palahniuk's short story 'Foot Work' from *Haunted*, Jennifer Egan's 'Out of Body' chapter in *A Visit from the Goon Squad* and parts of A. L. Kennedy's *Day*. An example of narrative in drama is a chorus, often a major component of ancient Greek plays and as used in *Henry V* and *Romeo and Juliet*. Narrators are sometimes used to drive a plot along if explanation is needed and can't be provided through dialogue, such as in *Under Milk Wood*, *Joseph and his Amazing Technicolor Dreamcoat* and *Blood Brothers*.

Naturalism

Naturalism is an extension of **realism** (see below), showing characters as hopeless against things beyond their control, such as the environment and their position in life. It originated in nineteenth-century France with Zola, who attached a 'scientific' theory to his ideas, no doubt influenced by contemporary developments in science, including the publication of Darwin's *Origin of Species*. Naturalism depicts an uncompromisingly and brutal true-to-life approach to art.

Nemesis

Nemesis was the goddess of retribution (her name deriving from the Greek *'nemein'* for 'dispense'), who dished out punishment to the mortals for wrongdoings and insolence. Nowadays, it has two meanings: either that agent of punishment causing someone's downfall, or an enemy who stands in the way of another. Sherlock Holmes's nemesis is Professor Moriarty; Batman's nemesis (or one of them, anyway) is the Joker; Claudius is Hamlet's nemesis, but, equally, it could be the other way round.

Neologism

Derived from the Greek *'neo'*, meaning 'new', and *'logos'* meaning 'word', this is the term used for a new word (there's a surprise) or phrase coined, or an idea taken up, which soon becomes part of a language. Neologisms come from all kinds of sources, but here are some literary ones: 'Kafkaesque', 'Brechtian', 'Orwellian', 'Pinteresque' are all adjectival neologisms taken from authors' names, as are 'Rabelaisian', 'sadistic' and 'Machiavellian'; 'Lothario', 'Scrooge', 'quixotic', 'malapropism' and 'braggadocio' are neologisms derived from characters' names (and their traits).

'Big Brother' and 'catch-22' are neologisms invented by Orwell and Heller; numerous examples have come from Lewis Carroll ('Cheshire cat', 'jabberwocky', 'snark') and Swift ('Lilliputian', 'yahoo'), likewise Tolkien ('hobbit'), Joyce ('quark'), Rowling ('quidditch') and, it goes without saying, Shakespeare ('critic', 'lacklustre', 'puke').

Recent neologisms in the English language are: 'blog', 'email', 'ebook', 'texting', 'googling', 'dongle', 'online', 'offline', 'search engine' (any of that computer jargon); 'yuppie', 'dinky', 'Nimby', 'landline', 'ringtone', 'metrosexual', 'baby boomer', 'asbo', 'twoc', 'chav', 'global warming', 'clinically obese' (literally becoming more widespread).

Nom de plume

A French word literally meaning 'name of feather', but really meaning a pen (or 'quill') name, a nom de plume is a made-up name used by a writer instead of his or her real name. Examples include George Eliot (real name Mary Ann, later Marian, Evans), Lewis Carroll (Charles Lutwidge Dodgson), George Orwell (Eric Blair), John le Carré (David Cornwell) and Barbara Vine (Ruth Rendell). Charlotte, Emily and Anne Brontë published under the names Currer, Ellis and Acton Bell originally, to keep their identities secret and their sex ambiguous, but now of course the novels are published under their own names. (See also **pseudonym** below.)

Novella

In length, this is a text halfway between a short story and a novel – though usually costing the same price as a novel if the publisher can get away with it.

Oeuvre

A French word meaning 'work', this is the term used for a body of work by an artist – an author, composer, painter, etc. Shakespeare's oeuvre includes 37 plays and 154 sonnets; Beethoven's oeuvre includes symphonies, concertos, chamber pieces, sonatas, songs, one opera, etc., etc.

Onomatopoeia

Derived from the Greek words *'onoma'*, meaning 'name' or 'word', and *'poios'*, meaning 'making', onomatopoeia is the name given to words that mimic the sound they're referring to. 'Boo', 'crack', 'thwack', 'whack', 'squelch', 'hiss', 'fizz', 'sizzle', 'cuckoo', 'zzzz' are examples, as are the numerous words given to the sounds animals make ('baa', 'miaow', 'moo', 'quack', 'woof'). It is also a **figure of speech** (see above), and often used in poetry, when it might not be taken quite so literally, but more through association, or used to create atmosphere or deliver a pun.

> I steal by lawns and grassy plots,
> I slide by hazel covers;
> I move the sweet forget-me-nots
> That grow for happy lovers.
>
> I slip, I slide, I gloom, I glance,
> Among my skimming swallows;
> I make the netted sunbeam dance
> Against my sandy shallows.
>
> Tennyson, 'The Brook'

The grey sea and the long black land;
And the yellow half-moon large and low;
And the startled little waves that leap
In fiery ringlets from their sleep,
As I gain the cove with pushing prow,
And quench its speed i' the slushy sand.

Then a mile of warm sea-scented beach;
Three fields to cross till a farm appears;
A tap at the pane, the quick sharp scratch
And blue spurt of a lighted match,
And a voice less loud, thro' its joys and fears,
Than the two hearts beating each to each!

Browning, 'Meeting at Night'

Palindrome

A palindrome is a word or number which is exactly the same
backwards, and is a delight to come across for nerdy, wordy people.
A few examples: 'civic', 'deed', 'kook', 'level', 'madam', 'marram',
'minim', 'noon', 'nun', 'pip pip', 'poop', 'radar', 'rotor', 'tenet', 'terret',
'wow', 'yay'. Some names: Ada, Anna, Bob, Eve, Hannah, Lil, Otto,
and Abba, Aviva, Omo and Xanax. And some dates: 11.11.11, 06.6.60,
19.3.91, 6.5.56, 7.9.97. And even a sentence: 'Madam, I'm Adam.' The
word 'palindrome' comes from the Greek, *'palindromos'*, meaning
'running back again'. A pity they couldn't come up with a word that
is a palindrome itself – wouldn't that be more fun? – something like
'palilap' or 'emordidrome' . . .

Panegyric

Pronounced 'pan-a-jirr-ik', the term is derived from the Greek words '*pan*', meaning 'all', and '*aguris*', meaning 'assembly'. It is a speech or text in lavish praise of someone or something, and quite similar to **encomium** (see above).

Parable

A parable is a simple story used to illustrate a moral or lesson, with an underlying universal truth. More straightforward than an **allegory** (see above) parables are most associated with Jesus and the gospels – such as the stories of the Good Samaritan and the Prodigal Son – and modern parables often take these biblical tales as a starting point.

Pastiche

A pastiche imitates the style of another work. The term can be used to describe an inferior piece – the writer has copied someone else, and not very successfully – or it can describe a humorous, deliberate tribute to another's work. It is not intended to insult or mock – unlike satire and parody. John Fowles's *French Lieutenant's Woman* and Sarah Waters's *Fingersmith* are pastiches of Victorian melodrama. *The Real Inspector Hound* is a pastiche of the stage thriller; *Young Frankenstein* is a pastiche of *Frankenstein*; *Acorn Antiques* is a pastiche (just about) of *Crossroads* and other dodgy soaps; *The Artist* is a pastiche of silent movies.

Pastoral

A pastoral is a genre of writing – verse and plays usually – portraying an idealised form of country life, most commonly featuring shepherds and shepherdesses (and sheep). *As You Like It* and *The Winter's Tale* feature pastoral scenes; Milton and Shelley wrote pastoral poetry. Similar in form to the **idyll** (see above), the pastoral's idealism was later superseded by more real images of country life – such as in the poems of Crabbe and Wordsworth.

Portmanteau

Derived from the French words *'porter'*, meaning 'carry', and *'manteau'*, meaning 'cloak', a portmanteau word combines two words to make a new one. It refers to the suitcase of the same name, which consists of two halves, and was first used in this more literary sense by Lewis Carroll, who came up with several of his own – such as 'slithy' (from 'lithe' and 'slimy') and 'chortle' (from 'chuckle' and 'snort'). Other examples of portmanteau words are: 'Brangelina' (Brad and Angelina), 'brunch' (breakfast/lunch), 'camcorder' (camera/recorder), 'chillax' (chill out/relax) 'chugger' (charity/mugger), 'Chunnel' (Channel/tunnel), 'docusoap' (documentary/soap opera), 'emoticon' (emotion/icon), 'infomercial' (information/commercial), 'Jedward' (John and Edward), 'motel' (motor/hotel), 'Slanket' (sleeve/blanket – and yes, as hideous as it sounds) 'smog' (smoke/fog), 'Spam' (spiced/ham), 'tweenager' (between/teenager). Portmanteau is a branch of **neologism** (see above).

Prologue

Derived from the Greek word *'prologos'*, meaning 'before saying', the prologue comes before the main action of a work. It sets the scene of a novel or play. Shakespeare uses prologues in *Romeo and Juliet* and *Henry V*, for example, and, as with his epilogues, he asks forgiveness from the audience for any mistakes the players may make.

Two households, both alike in dignity,
In fair Verona, where we lay our scene,
From ancient grudge break to new mutiny,
Where civil blood makes civil hands unclean.
From forth the fatal loins of these two foes
A pair of star-crossed lovers take their life,
Whose misadventured piteous overthrows,
Doth with their death bury their parents' strife.
The fearful passage of their death-marked love,
And the continuance of their parents' rage,
Which, but their children's end nought could remove,
Is now the two hours' traffic of our stage:
The which if you with patient ears attend,
What here shall miss, our toil shall strive to mend.

Romeo and Juliet

(This prologue is also a **sonnet** – see below.)

Prosody

Derived from the Greek '*prosoidia*', meaning 'sung to music', prosody is the analysis of the patterns and rhythms of sound in poetry, or the inflections and emphases in a language.

Pseudonym

A made-up name, derived from the Greek '*pseudes*', meaning 'false', and '*onoma*', meaning 'name' or 'word', it is another term for **nom de plume** (see above). The latter is usually only associated with writers, while a pseudonym covers a wider range of fields – actors, singers, people who wish to remain anonymous or assume another identity, etc.

Purple prose

A derogatory term for overwritten prose – usually over-adjectival, over-detailed, elaborate, tortuous, flowery, pretentious, showy and OTT (like this definition).

Realism

Realism as an artistic and literary movement came to prominence in the nineteenth century, and its main characteristic is the representation of people or things as they really are. Realism rejects romanticism, idealisation and flights of fancy, depicting instead the problems and complexities of life for ordinary folk in ordinary situations. It is quite a broad term, however, and one person's realism is not always the same as another's. While some might consider Zola, Hardy and D.H. Lawrence to be realist writers, others might claim more justification for Flaubert, (George) Eliot and Wharton. Kitchen-sink drama of the 1950s and 60s is a later form of realism – notably in the plays of John Osborne, Shelagh Delaney and Arnold Wesker. Realism is often preceded by the adjective 'gritty' . . .

Rhetoric

Rhetoric is effective or persuasive speech – originally mainly associated with public speaking or oratory. It was almost considered an art form – the art of speaking – in the classical world. Today, however, rhetoric is often considered to lack integrity and sincerity – particularly political rhetoric, with those spin doctors hovering rather too closely in the background.

Roman à clef

A French term, literally 'a novel with a key', a *roman à clef* is a work about real people whose identities are concealed with invented names, but the reader should be able to see through the disguise – there will be hints, 'keys'. Jérôme and Jean Tharaud's *Dingley, l'illustre écrivain*, Somerset Maugham's *The Moon and Sixpence*, Sylvia Plath's *The Bell Jar*, Nora Ephron's *Heartburn*, Lauren Weisberger's *The Devil Wears Prada*, Robert Harris's *The Ghost* are a few examples.

Satire

Satire uses ridicule, humour, exaggeration, sarcasm, irony, invective or parody to illustrate the stupidity or failing of an institution or person, especially in the political arena. Satire has been around since the Romans, when it was written in verse – the name is derived from the Latin *'satira'*, meaning 'poetic medley'. In Britain, the golden age of satire was during the late seventeenth and eighteenth centuries, with Dryden, Defoe, Swift, Gay, Pope and Hogarth. It fell out of favour a bit in the nineteenth century – perhaps stemming from Queen Victoria, who wasn't renowned for her sense of humour. It re-emerged in the twentieth century with such writers as Belloc, Orwell, Waugh, (Kingsley) Amis, and with the writers and performers in *Beyond the Fringe*, *That Was The Week That Was* and the Establishment Club. More recent examples of satire include *Private Eye*, *Oh What a Lovely War*, *Dr Strangelove*, *Spitting Image*, *Monty Python's Life of Brian*, *I'm Sorry I Haven't a Clue*, *The News Quiz*, *Have I Got News for You*, *The Simpsons*, *Saturday Night Live*, *The Thick of It*, and numerous characters created by Chris Morris and Sacha Baron Cohen.

Semantics

From the Greek word *'semantikos'*, meaning 'significant' (*'sema'* means 'sign'), semantics is the branch of linguistics concerned with the meaning of words, the study of words, and why we choose one word rather than another.

Simile

A figure of speech, a simile is the same as a **metaphor** (see above), but always includes either 'like' or 'as' in the analogy. 'The sleeping and the dead are but as pictures', 'O my Luve's like a red, red rose', 'That makes me feel as sick as a parrot', 'She sticks out like a sore thumb in the chorus line'.

Sonnet

One of the best-known forms of verse, *sonetti* (or sonnets) first appeared in fourteenth-century Italy, and by the sixteenth century had become popular in Britain. Originally love poems, they later took on such subjects as religion, special events, commemoration, rural life, city life, even politics. The traditional English sonnet consists of fourteen lines, divided into three quatrains (four lines) and one couplet (two lines). The metre is invariably iambic pentameter (see **metre** above), and the rhyming scheme is: a, b, a, b, c, d, c, d, e, f, e, f, g, g. Shakespeare wrote 154 sonnets, and number 18 is probably his most famous.

> Shall I compare thee to a summer's day?
> Thou art more lovely and more temperate.
> Rough winds do shake the darling buds of May,
> And summer's lease hath all too short a date.
> Sometime too hot the eye of heaven shines,
> And often is his gold complexion dimmed,

And every fair from fair sometime declines,
By chance or nature's changing course untrimmed:
But thy eternal summer shall not fade
Nor lose possession of that fair thou ow'st,
Nor shall death brag thou wand'rest in his shade,
When in eternal lines to time thou grow'st.
So long as men can breathe or eyes can see,
So long lives this and this gives life to thee.

Spoonerism

A term used when a speaker accidentally transposes two initial consonants or sounds, usually to humorous effect. It takes its name from the Reverend William Archibald Spooner (1844–1930) of New College, Oxford, who frequently muddled his consonants (or cuddled his monsonants) such as his toast to 'the queer old Dean'. In 2001, the ever-reliable George Bush came out with 'If the terriers and bariffs are torn down, this economy will grow'. A more recent slip-up was the Radio 4 *Today* presenter James Naughtie mangling the name of Jeremy Hunt, the Culture Secretary (though he never got as far as 'Hulture' – too overcome with hysteria by then). It certainly woke up the listeners that morning. (And went viral on YouTube.) Sometimes spoonerisms are deliberate – like the tongue twister 'pheasant plucker' and the women's theatre group Cunning Stunts – but not all are rude – 'mean as custard' and 'bad salad' are rather sweet.

Sturm und Drang

A German phrase meaning 'storm' and 'stress', the term comes from the title of a play, which then gave its name to a literary movement in late-eighteenth-century Germany – capturing the **zeitgeist** (see below) of the moment. It was anti-rationalism, anti-neoclassicism and anti-French, and Herder, Goethe and Schiller were among its exponents. Its main theme was emotional turbulence – so if a work today is described as having something of the *Sturm und Drang* about it, that's what it means.

Symbolism

Derived from Latin and Greek words denoting recognition, or a token, symbolism is the use of symbols to represent something else, an idea or a quality. The term can overlap with **imagery** (see above) but is usually more tangible. Symbols are everywhere – encompassing religion, politics, allegiance, sport, nature. In literature and art, stock symbols are used for standard themes, and so it is almost a code.

In medieval and Renaissance art, for instance, saints and angels are depicted with certain symbols so that they can be identified – St Peter has a beard and key, the Angel Gabriel has a shield or trumpet, the Virgin Mary wears a particular blue; a skull suggests mortality, a lute represents love, a dove peace, a crow adultery. A few centuries on, the Pre-Raphaelites, as the name suggests, echo the themes of medieval painters, and add their own, as does Blake. While many writers and painters use symbolism to some extent, there are those who are particularly associated with it – indeed, there was a whole symbolist movement in nineteenth-century Europe, beginning in France with such writers as Mallarmé, Rimbaud and Verlaine. Ibsen, Maeterlinck and Strindberg are dramatists associated with symbolism; T. S. Eliot, Ezra Pound and W. B. Yeats are poets influenced by the movement.

Synecdoche

Pronounced 'sin-ek-ducky', the term is derived from the Greek words *'sun'*, meaning 'together', and *'ekdokhe'* meaning 'taking up', and it is a figure of speech, a branch of **metonymy** (see above). It takes a part of something and uses it to represent the whole – so 'wheels' for 'car', 'ABC' for 'alphabet', 'bums on seats' for 'members of the audience', 'the blonde' for 'the girl with blonde hair', 'Number Ten' for 'Ten Downing Street'. Synecdoche and metonymy are similar, but the difference is that 'part' – metonymy, on the whole, covers a wider reference, but there is often an overlap.

Synonym

Synonym comes from the Greek words *'sun'*, meaning 'together', and *'onoma'* meaning 'name'. It denotes a word or phrase that means the same or nearly the same as another word or phrase. For example, 'phrase', 'term', 'expression' are synonymous; 'akin', 'same', 'identical', 'alike', 'synonymous' are, well, synonymous. These words can be found in a thesaurus, wordfinder, wordbook, synonym dictionary . . . The opposite of synonym is **antonym** (see above).

Syntax

Syntax is derived from the Greek words *'sun'*, meaning 'together', and *'tassein'*, meaning 'arrange'. It is a term that describes the order of words and phrases used to construct a sentence. What constitutes a good sentence, or good syntax, is governed by certain rules. What constitutes a good writer is what he or she does with that sentence.

Tragicomedy

A tragicomedy is, believe it or not, a play that combines tragedy and comedy. It has been a popular genre since the Middle Ages, flourishing in Elizabethan and Jacobean theatre, and staying the course because it is true to life. What constitutes a tragicomedy is not clear-cut; what might be considered a tragedy may have moments of comedy, and vice versa. In Shakespeare's tragedies there's a bit of comic relief – *Hamlet*'s gravedigger, *Macbeth*'s Porter (although today's audiences might not get all the 'jokes' any more); likewise, most of his 'comedies' have elements of tragedy – *Twelfth Night*, *Measure for Measure*, *The Winter's Tale*, even *Much Ado About Nothing*. The term could cover virtually all drama – apart from farce and weepie, but, among others, the plays of Chekhov, Beckett, Pinter and Ayckbourn seem to strike the right balance and represent tragicomedy in the real sense of the word. Soap operas – the best, anyway – could also be described as tragicomedies.

Trope

From the Greek '*tropos*', meaning 'turn', trope is a figurative use of a word or expression – in other words, a figure of speech. It therefore encompasses other figures of speech – such as **metaphor, metonymy, simile, synecdoche** (see above).

Urtext

'*Ur-*' means 'original' in German, so urtext means the original, or first version, of a text. Later versions are sometimes compared to it, and the urtext is not necessarily the best – the comparisons will clinch it. There are endless debates over urtexts, with advocates claiming those are the superior ones, particularly where Shakespeare is concerned. But there are often good reasons why a later version is better – the fact that an author goes through numerous drafts before publishing being one.

Vernacular

From the Latin *'vernaculus'*, meaning 'domestic' or 'native', the vernacular is the language, the dialect, of the people, in other words everyday or colloquial speech. In a more literary sense, it is a term used to differentiate it from a formal style of writing. For example, both Dickens and Hardy use the vernacular for dialogue, particularly to highlight the differences between the lower-class characters – the Crunchers in *A Tale of Two Cities*, Wackford Squeers in *Nicholas Nickleby*, John Durbeyfield in *Tess of the d'Urbervilles*, Jude Fawley in *Jude the Obscure* – and the higher-class ones. Other vernacular writers are D. H. Lawrence, Anthony Burgess and Irvine Welsh. Vernacular poets include William Langland, old Geoff Chaucer, Robert Burns and William Barnes.

Zeitgeist

First coined in the nineteenth century, zeitgeist – from the German *'zeit'*, meaning 'time', and *'geist'*, meaning 'spirit' – denotes capturing the mood of a particular time. If someone is said to have 'really captured the zeitgeist' in his novel, he has caught the 'spirit of the age'.

This final exercise is a round-up of Chapter 6.

1 What term describes these titles and names?

Daniel Deronda, Ivanhoe, The Go-Between, Little Women, Omelette Arnold Bennett, Tom Collins

2 These titles are examples of what?

Milton's *Paradise Lost*, Huxley's *Brave New World*, Proust's *Remembrance of Things Past*, Pullman's *His Dark Materials*, Boney M's 'By the Rivers of Babylon'

3 The following are examples of what?

'tickle the ivories', 'tread the boards', 'burn rubber', 'England'

4 What (and who) are the King and the Duke?

5 What is the name given to the following types of verse?

How have I hurt you?
You look at me with pale eyes,
But these are my tears.

An old silent pond . . .
A frog jumps into the pond,
Splash! Silence again.

6 What term describes the following?

'Fleet Street', 'the Firm', 'the Square Mile', 'the Smoke', 'the Windy City'

7 These lines contain what?

Gallop apace, you fiery-footed steeds,
Towards Phoebus' lodging: such a wagoner
As Phaëthon would whip you to the west,
And bring in cloudy night immediately.

The breezes blew, the white foam flew,
  The furrow followed free;
We were the first that ever burst
  Into that silent sea.

8 The following phrases are large doses of what?

'the entire nation held its breath at the penalty shoot-out', 'the world's most distinguished writer', 'the sexiest man alive', 'the greatest show on earth', 'the funniest film ever made'

9 What term describes these words?

'alack', 'alas', 'gadzooks', 'nay', 'oft', 'pox'

10 These lines contain examples of what?

His lids are like the lilac-flower
And soft as a moth, his breath.

11 The following are examples of what?

'blog', 'boxercise', 'bromance', 'docudrama', 'gastropub', 'mockney', 'moobs', 'moped', 'paratrooper', 'stagflation'

12 These lines contain examples of what?

I'm a riddle in nine syllables,
An elephant, a ponderous house,
A melon strolling on two tendrils.

13 These two lines are examples of what?

on a proud round cloud in a white high night

So, we'll go no more a-roving

14 What term describes the following words?

'blogger', 'Generation X', 'McJob', 'prequel', 'replicant', 'textspeak'

15 The following are examples of what?

'kayak', 'redder', 'repaper', '21.11.12'

16 Apart from being used in an advert, 'snap', 'crackle' and 'pop' are examples of what?

17 What term links the following writers?

Boz, Hergé, Saki, George Sand and Mark Twain

18 The following are examples of what?

'He was a man of great statue', 'This is unparalyzed in the state's history'

19 The following books feature examples of what?

Nights at the Circus, The House of the Spirits, Midnight's Children, The Time Traveler's Wife, The Tiger's Wife

20 The following are what?

'T. S. Eliot', 'litotes' and 'toilets'.

'Seven Bar Jokes' by Eric K. Auld

1 A comma splice walks into a bar, it has a drink and then leaves.

2 A dangling modifier walks into a bar. After finishing a drink, the bartender asks it to leave.

3 A question mark walks into a bar?

4 Two quotation marks 'walk into' a bar.

5 A present participle and an infinitive walk into a bar, drinking to drink.

6 The bar was walked into by the passive voice.

7 Three intransitive verbs walk into a bar. They sit. They drink. They leave.

These should be comprehensible after reading this book . . .

Answers

1: Basic Grammar

Here are 20 nouns. Are they proper, common, abstract or collective?

1 bully – common

2 telling-off – abstract

3 York – proper

4 gaggle – collective

5 Rose – proper

6 rose – common

7 Bill Clinton – proper

8 bill – common

9 happiness – abstract

10 apple – common

11 flock – collective

12 tolerance – abstract

13 Kew Gardens – proper

14 crowd – collective

15 weariness – abstract

16 Stonehenge – proper

17 litter – common *and* collective

18 teapot – common

19 luck – abstract

20 murmuration – collective

Here are 30 nouns in the singular. Give the plural of each one.

1 loaf – loaves	16 mouse – mice
2 apple – apples	17 house – houses
3 proof – proofs	18 tomato – tomatoes
4 goose – geese	19 half – halves
5 swine – swine	20 volcano – volcanoes *or* volcanos
6 scissors – scissors	21 whisky – whiskies
7 trousers – trousers	22 turkey – turkeys
8 mother-in-law – mothers-in-law	23 rhinoceros – rhinoceros *or* rhinoceroses
9 beach – beaches	24 sponge – sponges
10 bully – bullies	25 moose – moose
11 copy – copies	26 pulley – pulleys
12 crisis – crises	27 whiskey – whiskeys
13 calf – calves	28 storey – storeys
14 cock-up – cock-ups	29 chicken – chicken
15 species – species	30 story – stories

Here are 5 sentences. Are the verbs being used transitively or intransitively?

1 Penny threw the tedious book away. (transitive)

2 Caesar came, he saw, he conquered. (all intransitive)

3 Felicity fainted. (intransitive)

4 Zack ran a marathon. (transitive)

5 Al beat Michael in the badminton match. (transitive)

*Look at the infinitives of the following verbs (i.e. their basic forms –
'to come', 'to see', 'to conquer') and decide whether they are regular
or irregular.*

1 to feel (irregular)

2 to think (irregular)

3 to linger (regular)

4 to go (irregular)

5 to swim (irregular)

6 to levitate (regular)

7 to warble (regular)

8 to kill (regular)

9 to describe (regular)

10 to shut (irregular)

11 to make (irregular)

12 to lend (irregular)

13 to be (irregular)

14 to agree (regular)

15 to treat (regular)

16 to seek (irregular)

17 to drink (irregular)

18 to fish (regular)

19 to paint (regular)

20 to buy (irregular)

*In the following sentences, indicate which are the principal verbs,
and which the auxiliary.*

1 British troops have been put on standby. (auxiliary, auxiliary,
principal)

2 I should be told about these things. (auxiliary, auxiliary,
principal)

3 Will there be cake for tea? (auxiliary, principal)

4 The earthquake could have triggered a tsunami. (auxiliary,
auxiliary, principal)

5 There might be a heatwave this summer. (auxiliary, principal)

Here are 20 sentences. Which tense is being used in each?

1 You will have been renovating the house for ten years come spring. (future perfect continuous)

2 They are playing a dirty game. (present continuous)

3 She had eaten all my favourite biscuits. (past perfect)

4 We will be hiring a car at the weekend. (future continuous)

5 How tense am I? (present)

6 Reader, I married him. (past)

7 He will have finished his exams next week. (future perfect)

8 She has been churning out the same drivel for years. (present perfect continuous)

9 I'll be back. (future)

10 They had been working on the project for six months. (past perfect continuous)

11 The cat was eating the goldfish. (past continuous)

12 We have always wondered what her name is. (present perfect)

13 The train had stopped yet again. (past perfect)

14 She will have been cooking at the same place for twenty years. (future perfect continuous)

15 The goldfish will be fondly remembered. (future)

16 She will have been in this soap for thirty years next month. (future perfect)

17 He lost the match yet again. (past)

18 That's blown our cover. (present perfect)

19 They had been hoping for a quick sale. (past perfect continuous)

20 I love you. (present)

Here are 10 examples of adjectives. Decide whether they are attributive, predicative or postpositive.

1 the cool drink (attributive)

2 time immemorial (postpositive)

3 the evidence was inconclusive (predicative)

4 a busy road (attributive)

5 that meal was delicious (predicative)

6 a running gag (attributive)

7 a lazy boy (attributive)

8 the situation is bleak (predicative)

9 mission impossible (postpositive)

10 the milk was sour (predicative)

Here are 10 sentences. Decide which type of adjective each is using – demonstrative, possessive, numerical or interrogative.

1 Four people boarded the bus. (numerical)

2 Which train are you catching? (interrogative)

3 His flies are undone. (possessive)

4 This book is doomed. (demonstrative)

5 What film are we going to see? (interrogative)

6 The first taxi is yours. (numerical)

7 Those cakes are stale. (demonstrative)

8 Their home is for sale. (demonstrative *and* possessive)

9 Our plan won't work. (possessive)

10 My idea was rubbish. (possessive)

Here are 10 sentences. Decide whether the adverb in each is one of time, place, manner or degree.

1 The crowd cheered <u>enthusiastically</u>. (manner)

2 Jack was <u>so</u> exhausted. (degree)

3 The teacher spoke <u>too quickly</u>. (degree *and* manner)

4 The train will be leaving <u>soon</u>. (time)

5 We're going to move <u>abroad</u>. (place)

6 Come <u>inside</u>. (place)

7 They walked <u>through</u> the garden. (place)

8 She knocked <u>loudly</u> on the door. (manner)

9 They finished <u>at the same time</u>. (time)

10 They were <u>totally</u> unsuitable. (degree)

Here are 20 sentences using pronouns. Identify the type underlined.

1 Is this <u>yours</u>? (possessive)

2 <u>He</u> loved his new trousers. (personal)

3 The pony <u>whose</u> rider was too heavy was fed up. (relative)

4 <u>Her</u> husband was late. (personal)

5 The plumber <u>who</u> did the bathroom was excellent. (relative)

6 <u>Which</u> one shall we go for? (interrogative)

7 That's <u>my</u> house. (possessive)

8 It's down to the two of <u>us</u>. (personal)

9 To <u>whom</u> does this belong? (relative)

10 The missing diamonds were <u>hers</u>. (possessive)

11 <u>That</u> was rubbish. (demonstrative)

12 She kept the best praline for <u>herself</u>. (reflexive)

13 They followed <u>one another</u> down the stairs. (reciprocal)

14 Don't believe <u>everything</u> you read. (indefinite)

15 <u>Whose</u> line is it anyway? (interrogative)

16 The deadline was fast approaching <u>them</u>. (personal)

17 The co-stars loathed <u>each other</u>. (reciprocal)

18 <u>Nobody</u> said a word. (indefinite)

19 He made <u>himself</u> at home. (reflexive)

20 <u>These</u> are to die for. (demonstrative)

In the following extract, pick out all the definite and indefinite articles.

> <u>The</u> dining-room was inconveniently crowded. There was <u>a</u> KC
> and his wife, <u>a</u> Government official and his wife, Mrs Strickland's
> sister and her husband, Colonel MacAndrew, and <u>the</u> wife of <u>a</u>
> Member of Parliament. It was because <u>the</u> Member of Parliament
> found that he could not leave <u>the</u> House that I had been invited.
> <u>The</u> respectability of <u>the</u> party was portentous. <u>The</u> women were
> too nice to be well dressed, and too sure of their position to be
> amusing. The men were solid. There was about all of them <u>an</u> air
> of well-satisfied prosperity.
>
> W. Somerset Maugham, *The Moon and Sixpence*

In the extract below, pick out all the prepositions.

> A vulture flapped and shifted <u>on</u> the iron roof and Wilson looked
> <u>at</u> Scobie. He looked <u>without</u> interest <u>in</u> obedience <u>to</u> a stranger's
> direction, and it seemed <u>to</u> him that no particular interest attached
> <u>to</u> the squat grey-haired man walking alone <u>up</u> Bond Street. He
> couldn't tell that this was one of those occasions a man never
> forgets: a small cicatrice had been made <u>on</u> the memory, a wound
> that would ache whenever certain things combined – the taste

of gin <u>at</u> midday, the smell of flowers <u>under</u> a balcony, the clang of corrugated iron, an ugly bird flopping <u>from</u> perch <u>to</u> perch.

Graham Greene, *The Heart of the Matter*

In the extract below, pick out all the conjunctions.

<u>When</u> I found so astonishing a power placed within my hands, I hesitated a long time concerning the manner in which I should employ it. <u>Although</u> I possessed the capacity of bestowing animation, <u>yet</u> to prepare a frame for reception of it, with all its intricacies of fibres, muscles, <u>and</u> veins, still remained a work of inconceivable difficulty <u>and</u> labour.

Mary Shelley, *Frankenstein*

Supply an interjection for each of the following.

1 The ball whacked Bob on the head. '_____!' said Bob.
2 The curtain came down on the opera. '_____!' yelled the audience.
3 '_____ – I hope that wasn't your favourite vase.'
4 '_____, are you really wearing that this evening?'
5 Marmite? _____

Take your pick, really, from the list of interjections given on p. 35, or a post-watershed equivalent.

In the extract below, pick out an example of each of the nine types of words that make up the English language.

<u>The</u> [article] policeman looked at me for a while without speaking. Then he <u>said</u> [verb], 'I am arresting you for assaulting a police officer.'

This made me [pronoun] feel a lot calmer because it is what policemen [noun] say on television and in films.

Then he said, 'I strongly [adverb] advise you to get into the back of the police car because if you try any of that monkey-business again, you little shit, I will seriously lose my rag. Is that understood?'

I walked over to the police car which was parked just outside [preposition] the gate. He opened the back door and I got inside. He climbed into the driver's seat and made a call on his radio to the policewoman who was still inside the house. He said, 'The little [adjective] bugger just had a pop at me, Kate. Can you hang on with Mrs S while I drop him off at the station? I'll get Tony to swing by and [conjunction] pick you up.'

And she said, 'Sure. I'll catch you later.'

The policeman said, 'Okey-doke [interjection],' and we drove off.

Mark Haddon, *The Curious Incident of the Dog in the Night-time*

An example of each of the nine types is underlined above, but there are of course many other examples in the extract.

2: Punctuation

In the following passage of five sentences, put in the full stops and capitals.

Dolly slammed the door behind her in a fit of temper. Then she realised that was rather a stupid thing to do. Her keys were on the hall table. It was pouring outside and she had no coat. But Dolly was damned if she was going to humiliate herself by ringing the doorbell.

Are the following examples contractions or abbreviations? And what are they contracting or abbreviating?

1 dept (contraction – department)

2 Revd (contraction – Reverend)

3 Fr (contraction – Father)

4 Dec. (abbreviation – December)

5 Wed. (abbreviation – Wednesday)

6 ibid. (abbreviation – *ibidem*)

7 e.g. (abbreviation – *exempli gratia* or for example)

8 Rt Hon. (contraction / abbreviation – Right Honourable)

9 i.e. (abbreviation – *id est* or that is)

10 St (contraction – Saint or Street)

11 abbrev. (abbreviation – abbreviation)

12 Ave (contraction – Avenue)

13 gall. (abbreviation – gallon)

14 Dr. (abbreviation – Drive)

15 Dr (contraction – Doctor)

16 fwd (contraction – forward)

17 Jr (contraction – Junior)

18 sc. (abbreviation – scene)

19 edn (contraction – edition)

20 no. (abbreviation – number)

Here are 10 sentences. Insert commas where appropriate, and for bonus points name the type of comma.

1 Types of commas include listing, joining, replacing, separating, bracketing and direct speech. (listing)

2 Penny and Kathy wrote the book, though Sally took the credit. (joining)

3 Despite being up against an unseeded competitor, Andy still managed to lose. (separating)

4 Everyone in the play, apart from Lady Macbeth, was really good. (bracketing)

5 'I ate too much cake,' she said, 'so I feel a bit sick.' (direct speech)

6 Charlie likes the chocolate ice cream, and Veronica, the vanilla. (replacing)

7 Olivia, in her orange, pink and red outfit, had no taste. (bracketing and listing)

8 The ratings had gone down, so the show was cancelled. (joining)

9 Scarlett has an allergy to wheat, nuts, dairy, eggs and shellfish. Or so her mother says. (listing)

10 As Tilly turned the corner, she realised she was completely lost. (separating)

Put a colon in each of the following sentences.

1 I have two people to thank for this award: Brad and George.

2 There is only one solution to a dull party: alcohol.

3 And Rhett declared: 'Frankly, my dear, I don't give a damn!'

4 The houses at Hogwarts are: Gryffindor, Ravenclaw, Hufflepuff and Slytherin.

5 Here's an idea: let's have lunch.

Replace some of the commas with semicolons in the following sentences.

1 Books by Ian McEwan include *First Love, Last Rites*; *On Chesil Beach*; *Atonement*; *Solar*.

2 The lovers go upstage behind the tree; meanwhile, the jealous husband enters downstage left, with a gun . . .

3 Sarah was an *Archers* addict; Lionel, however, would turn the radio off at the first note of the theme tune.

4 The cast includes Romeo, Leonardo DiCaprio; Juliet, Claire Danes; the Nurse, Miriam Margolyes; and Friar Laurence, Pete Postlethwaite.

5 The spaghetti western trilogy consists of *A Fistful of Dollars*; *For a Few Dollars More*; *The Good, the Bad and the Ugly*.

Put the apostrophe in the correct place in the following.

1	the girl's dress	6	wits' end
2	the dog's bollocks	7	donkey's years
3	Vicky's violin	8	Women's Institute
4	the children's party	9	season's greeting
5	the cat's whiskers	10	Mother's Day

Put quotation marks in the following sentences.

1 The disc she decided she would run to save from the sea was 'I Will Survive'.

2 Babs said, 'There's a short-story competition in the *Guardian*. I think I might enter "Dolly in Denial".'

3 I'll have to resend the document, as Fred 'claimed' he never received my email with the info.

4 Shouldn't it be 'for whom the bell tolls', not 'for who the bell tolls'?

5 It could be argued that 'there is just too much to take in on quote marks. However, it will sink in eventually.'

6 'I don't think I can make it in to work today,' Colin croaked, 'I've got really bad flu.'

7 Colin had 'really bad flu', though actually it was a bit of a sore throat.

8 This is perhaps the most famous opening line of a Shakespeare play: 'Now is the winter of our discontent'.

9 William said, 'Let's call it a day.'

10 'Do you think you could stop playing with your mobile phone? We're trying to watch the play,' Wendy whispered to the boy next to her. She was told to 'eff off'.

Insert hyphens, if necessary, in the following sentences.

1 The examples given in the grammar book were rather old-fashioned.

2 The gauge's pointer showed the racing driver had to leave the track for a fill-up.

3 Dave's dog trampled all over Dolly's dahlias in the flower bed.

4 For an optimist the glass is always half full.

5 Captain Bligh was a tall-ships' captain.

6 The pre-Roman artefacts went unnoticed by the kids in the museum owned by my ex-husband, because they were really boring.

7 The war lasted for six days, so it became known as the Six Day War.

8 The TV series *Upstairs Downstairs* depicts above- and below-stairs life in one house in Edwardian England.

9 The badly organised event was a cock-up from the outset.

10 The waiter had to re-serve the potatoes because the first batch was stone cold.

Here are unpunctuated extracts from three published novels. Insert punctuation and capital letters as appropriate. (See if your choices match the authors' . . .)

George has just gulped nearly a quarter of his Scotch, to drown out a spasm which started when he talked about Jim and the animals. Now he feels the alcohol coming back on him with a rush. It is exhilarating, but it is coming much too fast.

'You don't realise how many kids my age just dream about the kind of set-up you've got here. I mean, what more can you want? I mean, you don't have to take orders from anybody. You can do any crazy thing that comes into your head.'

'And that's your idea of the perfect life?'

'Sure it is!'

'Honestly?'

'What's the matter, Sir? Don't you believe me?'

'What I don't quite understand is, if you're so keen on living alone – how does Lois fit in?'

'Lois? What's she got to do with it?'

'Now, look, Kenny – I don't mean to be nosey – but, rightly or wrongly, I got the idea that you and she might be, well, considering – '

'Getting married? No. That's out.'

'Oh – ?'

'She says she won't marry a Caucasian. She says she can't take people in this country seriously. She doesn't feel anything we do here *means* anything. She wants to go back to Japan and teach.'

A Single Man, Christopher Isherwood

I was staring at the ends of her hair against the rock, an inch or two from my eyes, and trying to bring myself to the point of confession. But it seemed like treading on a flower because one can't be bothered to step aside. I pushed up, but she held me by the shoulders, so that I had to stare down at her. I sustained her look, its honesty, for a moment, then I turned and sat with my back to her.

'What's wrong?'

'Nothing. I just wondered what malicious god made a nice kid like you see anything in a shit like me.'

'That reminds me. A crossword clue. I saw it months ago. Ready?' I nodded,* '"She's all mixed up, but the better part of Nicholas"… six letters.'

I worked it out, smiled at her. 'Did the clue end in a full-stop or a question-mark?'

'It ended in my crying. As usual.'

And the bird above us sang in the silence.

The Magus, John Fowles

* A full stop is probably the better option here, but Fowles, for some reason, chose a comma.

Gerber whistles. 'Lotta stuff in here … *"drug use … cache of semi-automatic weapons … inappropriate behaviour with children"*?'

'See, that's what I'm thinking, if we –'

'Not much for us here really though, Gerry. On the gun stuff? A dozen or so semi-automatic pistols, an assault weapon or two, some hunting rifles. Christ, half the basements and rec rooms in Texas are better armed than that. The guy's hardly fucking Rambo.'

'Yeah, but they're not his. It's unlawful possession.'

'Technically, yeah, but – '

'I know what you're saying, boss, but listen, the FBI have been keeping a loose eye on this guy. He's made a bunch of public pronouncements in favour of legalising marijuana, talked openly about using it, and if you look here on the aerial shots –' Cauldwell leaned across the table and pointed with his pen – 'they've indicated what might be a possible marijuana patch. Now, none of this interests the Feds too much, but they do want to take a look at the child-abuse claims. So, I was thinking –'

'A multi-agency effort?'

'You got it.'

The Second Coming, John Niven

3: Spelling

In the following sentences, select the correct spelling.

1 Stuart was on the beers last night, and came in to work this morning completely wasted.

2 The heroine in the story died of a heroin overdose.

3 The seamen were hoping for a good haul of plaice and sole, but the weather was foul and they returned with naught caught.

4 The nun had been standing at the altar all morning, singing hymns and praying, and was now feeling faint as well as rather bored.

5 The author had finished the final draft, but before she could put it in the drawer, a draught blew the whole story away.

6 The council was in the final phase of building the new dam, which hopefully would not leak like the last one.

7 The principal tenor and bass were exercising their vocal cords, practising for the premiere of the revue.

8 The seeded player ceded play.

9 The current was against them in the rough sea as the thunder and lightning continued apace, so they brought the ship in to berth.

10 It was pouring with rain, and the reigning Queen reined in her hoarse horse, but in vain, as she was thrown to the floor.

In the following sentences, underline the stressed syllable in each italicised word for the correct meaning.

1 The _re_fuse collector re_fused_ to take away the rubbish as the paper and plastics weren't in _sep_arate bags.

2 The portions in the restaurant were so mi_nute_ [equal stress] that the main course lasted less than a _min_ute.

3 The _buf_fet was barely worth a _sec_ond glance.

4 The e_lab_orate front _en_trance was a _con_trast to the more _mod_erate servants' door round the back, which was far less en_tranc_ing.

5 The _reb_els de_sert_ed and set up a _sep_arate party.

6 The winner ob_ject_ed to a _re_count, even though there was very little to _sep_arate him from the others.

7 The _in_valid found to her distress that her parking per_mit_ had expired, and was in_val_id.

8 With _con_summate skill, he _con_summated the marriage.

9 She, however, didn't think it was quite so con_sum_mate, and went for their en_tranc_ing _Pol_ish builder instead.

10 The builder felt a bit like a sex _ob_ject, though, and rather re_sent_ed being used in this way.

In the following sentences, fill in the blanks.

1 Let's find an alternative explanation, to ensure there's no confusion.

2 The only way to stop her continual requests was to accept an invitation to one of Maureen's dull parties.

3 Alison's advice was ignored as usual; her role as confidante is obviously superfluous.

4 She was loath* to ask the gourmet for supper as she was an unconfident cook.

5 Despite the musicians being out of sync with the conductor, the last movement of the symphony was climactic.

6 My imminent operation is to be performed by an eminent surgeon.

7 The morale of the Olympian was low as he was the Briton who mucked up the 400 metres relay.

8 The vicious thug was thrown head first into the vat of viscous oil.

9 The soup scalded the gourmand because he was too greedy to let it cool.

10 As he was on death row, he knew that his internment would end with his interment.

*Trick question – loath stays the same, i.e. it is not loathe.

In the following sentences, fill in the correct prefix or suffix.

1 A scientist works in a laboratory.

2 You didn't have to join the scheme – membership was voluntary.

3 The trains were intermittent due to the wrong weather yet again.

4 The fish had no use for the bicycles – the machines were completely redundant.

5 Maria had the tuna melt as usual. The waitress said, 'You're so predictable.'

6 Wayne could feel the wind in his hair – his new car was a convertible.

7 The sergeant was despondent when the defendant was found not guilty.

8 George was feeling irritable because the weeds in his garden were proving indestructible.

9 The courtroom was silent after the barrister's formidable summing-up, and the tension was palpable.

10 Luckily the portions in the cafe were pretty mean, as the chef's cooking was generally indigestible.

In the following extracts, correct the spelling mistakes and confusions.

Her experience had been of a kind to teach her, rightly or wrongly, that the doubtful honour of a brief transit through a sorry world hardly called for effusiveness, even when the path was suddenly irradiated at some half-way point by daybeams rich as hers. But her strong sense that neither she nor any human being deserved less than was given, did not blind her to the fact that there were others receiving less who had deserved much more. And in being forced to class herself among the unfortunate she did not cease to wonder at the persistence of the unforeseen, when the one to whom such unbroken tranquillity had been accorded in the adult stage was she whose youth had seemed to teach that happiness was but the occasional episode in a general drama of pain.

Thomas Hardy, *The Mayor of Casterbridge*

Ironically, it was Begbie who was the key. Ripping off your mates was the highest offence in his book, and he would demand the severest penalty. Renton had used Begbie, used him to burn his boats completely and utterly. It was Begbie who ensured he could never return. He had done what he wanted to do. He could now never go back to Leith, to Edinburgh, even to Scotland, ever again. There, he could not be anything other than he was. Now, free from them all for good, he could be what he wanted to be. He'd stand or fall alone. This thought both terrified and excited him as he contemplated life in Amsterdam.

Irvine Welsh, *Trainspotting*

As the saint was borne away, the people, in an agony of suspense, scrutinised the patients in order to see if there had been any change. Someone spotted Socrates and pointed. He was shaking his shoulders like an athlete about to throw a javelin, and he was staring with amazement at his hands, moving his fingers in order one by one. He looked up suddenly, saw that everyone was watching him, and waved shyly. An unnatural howl went up from the crowd, and Socrates' mother fell to her knees, kissing her son's hands. She stood up, threw up her arms to the wide sky, and called, 'Praise to the saint, praise to the saint,' so that in no time at all the whole assembly was hysterical with exhilarated awe. Dr Iannis pulled Pelagia away from the impending crush, and wiped the sweat from his face and the tears from his eyes. He was trembling in every part of his body, and so, he saw, was Pelagia. 'A purely psychological phenomenon,' he muttered to himself, and was struck suddenly by the sensation of being an ingrate. The bell of the church began to peal out wildly as nuns and priests decorously fought each other for a tug of the wire.

Louis de Bernières, *Captain Corelli's Mandolin*

4: Beyond the Basics

In the following sentences, should 'although' or 'though' be used?

1 Even <u>though</u> Daisy was one of the smallest girls in her class, she could run very fast and won the 400-metre race.

2 <u>Although</u> James would rather be watching the telly, he hadn't finished his homework.

3 Her books are unreadable, <u>although</u> *or* <u>though</u> that doesn't stop the gullible public buying them.

4 Michael claimed he was far too busy to see his relatives; he could still find the time to play solitaire on the computer, <u>though</u>.

5 Ben wanted to leave his job, <u>although</u> *or* <u>though</u> he decided it was better to wait until he'd got his bonus.

6 Fred bought a coat for his wife, <u>although</u> *or* <u>though</u> the shop said he could bring it back if she didn't like it.

7 William started to make a Christmas list, <u>although</u> *or* <u>though</u> it was only January.

8 <u>Although</u> he suffered from acrophobia, Archie braved it up the Eiffel Tower.

9 If I were you, <u>though</u>, I wouldn't do that.

10 It looks as <u>though</u> it's going to snow again.

In the following sentences, should 'around' or 'round' be used?

1 <u>Round</u> and <u>round</u> the garden like a teddy bear . . .

2 There isn't enough food to go <u>round</u>.

3 <u>Around</u> the windows the roses were in full bloom.

4 She slipped her arm <u>around</u> *or* <u>round</u> his waist, and smirked at his ex-girlfriend.

5 What's a girl supposed to do to get a drink <u>around</u> here?

6 David is hanging <u>around</u> with the wrong people.

7 Go <u>round</u> the <u>round</u>about, take the second exit, then first left, and the optician's is <u>around</u> there, I think.

8 The tradesmen's entrance is <u>round</u> the back.

9 We're meeting <u>around</u> eight o'clock.

10 There were red faces all <u>round</u> when the wrong version of Jonathan Franzen's *Freedom* was published.

In the following sentences, put in the correct verb or pronoun.

1 The government <u>are</u> ruining the country and they will be voted out at the next election.

2 Random House always treats <u>its</u> authors well.

3 The choir <u>were</u> out of sync with the orchestra and so they got a bollocking from the conductor after the performance.

4 The football team performed so badly that even their fans booed <u>them</u> off.

5 The flight of swallows <u>was</u> feeling a bit cold, so it decided it was time to head south.

6 The cast were gloomy when <u>their</u> play closed early.

7 That family <u>has</u> had enough of this intrusion into its privacy.

8 The flock of sheep were making so much noise <u>they</u> frightened the dog away.

9 The army <u>was</u> fed up with having its budget cut yet again.

10 England has improved <u>its</u> performance since the last Test match.

In the following sentences, should 'fewer' or 'less' be used?

1 There were <u>fewer</u> disruptive children in the class so the teacher was <u>less</u> distracted.

2 The rugby team scored <u>fewer</u> tries than they did last season.

3 The author sold <u>fewer</u> books than he thought he would, as there was <u>less</u> of a crowd than expected at the literary festival.

4 <u>Less</u> is more . . .

5 Standing in the queue for five items or <u>fewer</u>, Carmen was <u>less</u> than pleased to see the man in front had six items in his basket.

6 The door was <u>less</u> than ten metres away, so Don decided to make a quick exit.

7 It will take about three hours or <u>less</u> to get there.

8 There are <u>fewer</u> police on the streets these days.

9 You'll consume <u>fewer</u> calories if you eat <u>less</u> food.

10 <u>Less</u> than a year after they married, the couple split up.

In the following sentences, should 'I' or 'me' be used?

1 Since the dishwasher packed up, it seems to be <u>me</u> doing the dishes every night.

2 Are you and <u>I</u> going to get a new dishwasher?

3 Who was the last person to be picked for the team? <u>I</u> was.

4 The last person to be picked for the team was <u>me</u>.

5 Who is doing this exercise – you or <u>me</u>?

6 <u>I</u> love you – will you marry <u>me</u>?

7 It wasn't <u>me</u> who messed up our marriage.

8 For an early-morning swim, Minne and I broke the ice on the pond.

9 Who's going to Barbados on holiday? My husband and me!

10 My grandmother really loathed my brother and me.

In the following sentences, fill in the correct form and tense of 'lie' or 'lay'.

1 We lay under the blanket, because we were hiding from Rupert.

2 Don't lie on that side of the bed.

3 The books had lain unread on the bedside table for months.

4 Why do they always have to lay concrete at six o'clock in the morning?

5 The presents were laid under the Christmas tree.

6 Lying on her back during a massage always sent her to sleep.

7 Lizzie was exhausted after laying carpet for ten hours and went for a lie-down.

8 She had lain for too long in the sun and was burnt to a crisp.

9 Camping is no fun in Wales – have you ever tried laying a fire in the rain?

10 The cat proudly laid the mouse at my feet.

In the following sentences, fill in the correct pronoun.

1 That was a damn good meal, if I say so myself.

2 You yourself admitted it was a mistake to marry him, so don't blame your bridesmaid for spilling the beans.

3 If it were up to me, I'd say no.

4 The children were left to <u>themselves</u> while the teacher went for a fag break.

5 His badly made suit did nothing for <u>him</u>.

6 We only had <u>ourselves</u> to blame.

7 She said she'd made it <u>herself</u>, but I saw the Waitrose packet in the bin.

8 They can do the rest of the clearing-up <u>themselves</u> tomorrow, we've done enough.

9 She <u>herself</u> came to the decision that the job was beyond her.

10 He asked <u>me</u> if I needed a brandy after the shock.

In the following sentences, is the missing word 'from', 'since' or 'when'?

1 He has become a nightmare to deal with <u>since</u> he married the boss.

2 <u>When</u> he stopped fiddling the books, our profits went down.

3 She was on duty <u>from</u> six o'clock.

4 <u>Since</u> the birth of her triplets, she has had no sleep.

5 They didn't speak to each other <u>from</u> that day on.

6 Letter-writing, <u>since</u> the advent of the email, has fallen by the wayside.

7 That child was trouble <u>from</u> the day he was born.

8 The nice teacher who has taught us <u>since</u> September has been sacked.

9 <u>From</u> the moment our eyes met across the library, we were destined to be together.

10 She put on rather a lot of weight <u>when</u> the ice-cream parlour opened next door to the office.

In the following sentences, is the missing word 'that' or 'which'?

1 The train <u>that</u> we were on was delayed because of a leaf on the line.

2 The computer, <u>which</u> I was using to write my magnum opus, crashed and I lost everything <u>that</u> I hadn't saved.

3 The company <u>that</u> she'd built from scratch went into receivership.

4 Our play, <u>which</u> opens tomorrow, is under-rehearsed.

5 Is this a dagger <u>which</u> I see before me, the handle toward my hand? (Actually, Shakespeare might have got this wrong . . .)

6 The car, <u>which</u> is due for its first MOT, has never been out of the garage.

7 The dress <u>that</u> she wore for the event was a bit too tight.

8 The salmon en croute, <u>which</u> was rather an overambitious dish for him, was inedible.

9 My homework <u>that</u> was eaten by the dog was A* material – honest!

10 The wedding list, <u>which</u> the couple had at Harrods, was beyond the budget of most of their guests.

In the following sentences, is the missing word 'who' or 'whom'?

1 Anyone <u>who</u> knows the answer, stick your hand up.

2 Lorraine, with <u>whom</u> I was supposed to go on holiday, has cried off.

3 <u>Who</u> banged on my door?

4 With <u>whom</u> did you go to the cinema? We're all dying to know?

5 The guy <u>who</u> told the lies was sacked.

6 To <u>whom</u> should I send this document for approval?

7 <u>Who</u> do you have to suck up to here to get promotion?

8 She is the star without <u>whom</u> this movie would not exist, so give her the biggest trailer.

9 <u>Who</u> let the cats out?

10 To <u>whom</u> it may concern: why oh why oh why have the standards of grammar gone down in your paper?

5: To America and Beyond

Convert the following punctuation marks (and one spelling) into UK English. (NB some might stay the same . . .)

1 Mrs Smith arrived late for her appointment with Dr Foster as she got caught in a shower of rain.

2 I'll have the Caesar salad, but hold the anchovies, the croutons and the Parmesan.

3 Johnny Cash and June Carter, Sonny and Cher, and Ike and Tina Turner: three examples of why not to sing with your husband. (stays the same)

4 Hank Kennedy Sr, and Hank Kennedy Jr, were both wanted by the CIA.

5 There's a Woody Allen season showing at the movie theatre – we could see *Hannah and her Sisters*, *Crimes and Misdemeanors* and *Husbands and Wives* next week.

Convert the following punctuation marks into UK English.

1 'After great pain, a formal feeling comes', 'Because I could not stop for death' and 'I heard a fly buzz when I died' are three well-known poems by Emily Dickinson.

2 'Those are rather groovy trousers you're wearing, man,' said Austin. '"Groovy"? Who says "groovy" these days?' said Calvin.

3 'Beware of the dog!' said the sign on the forbidding gate.

4 *'Moulin Rouge!* was the best movie we saw in 2001, don't you think?' said George. 'I'm not sure I would use the word "best",' said Tom.

5 Elvis's first hit was probably 'That's All Right'.

In the following, convert the US punctuation marks into UK punctuation marks.

1 So what does she really 'know'? Does she know how *much*? If she does – even if she knows half – we're in big trouble, guys. One of us might have to have 'words'.

2 You convinced him he was part of the deprived generation – you corrupted him. And now, as a consequence, Mr and Mrs Stransky are dead. That make you feel good?

3 According to his mom, the kid came in 'about a quarter of five'. So when he saw our guy it was – what? 4.30? 4.35?

4 You understand the situation now . . . you must understand it . . .

5 How about reading a fairy story? 'Cinderella', perhaps, or 'Little Red Riding Hood'.

6 'You're flying to Nebraska, yeah? Now I remember. He couldn't tell me why, though; just said it was "very important".'

7 'Have some egg-white omelette,' Carla-Jo told them. 'There's heaps left over, because Leslye-Jo and Pammy-Jo wouldn't touch

it earlier. I shouldn't have told them what it was. "Egg-white omelette!" Pammy-Jo said. "What's the point of that?"'

8 This was what he had been working toward all the way through high school; he was at last going to college, Berkeley, to study the things that most interested him: astrophysics, track and field, baseball, soccer and girls.

9 Thelma removed her glasses and looked at Fred. Something clicked in her head she couldn't put her finger on . . . It was the word 'jeepers'! and she knew that Daphne had a fight on her hands.

10 As the limos drew up to the red carpet, people, catching glimpses of the passengers, shouted, 'It's Meryl!' or 'It's Nicole!' Photographers, reporters and security gathered around each door as the celeb was gently deposited on the sidewalk.

In the following extracts, convert the US punctuation, spelling and terminology into standard UK usage.

One weekend soon after that, on one of the first chilly days of autumn, I was out gathering bits of wood in an empty plot of land near the river. Our building was very old and badly kept, but we had a fireplace that 'worked'. I chose only pieces that could be split and broken down to fireplace size, and when I had enough to last a few days I threw them over the high _____* fence that surrounded the waste ground. From a distance that fence might have looked difficult to climb, but there were enough sagging places in it to make easy footholds. I went up and over it, and had just dropped down to the street when I saw Dan Rosenthal walking towards me.

'Well,' he said. 'You looked pretty good there, coming over the fence. You looked very nimble.'

That was a pleasure. I remember being pleased too that he'd found me wearing an old Army field jacket and _____ * jeans. He was dressed in a suit and tie and a light, new-looking overcoat.

Richard Yates, *Liars in Love*

*The 'wire' and 'blue' seem superfluous in UK English.

Our secretary was standing there with a shopping bag on her hip. 'Feeling any better?' she asked me.

'Oh, yes.'

'Well, I've brought you some soup,' she said. 'We all just knew you wouldn't be making yourself any lunch."

'Thanks, but I'm not – '

'Feed a cold, starve a fever!' she carolled. She nudged the door wider open with her elbow and stepped inside. 'People always wonder which it is,' she said. '"Feed a cold and starve a fever", or "Starve a cold and feed a fever". But what they don't realise is, it's an "If, then" construction. So in that case either one will work, because *if* you feed a cold *then* you'll be starving a fever, which you most certainly do want to do, and if you starve a cold then you'll be feeding a nasty old fever.'

Peggy was soft and dimpled – a pink-and-gold person with a cloud of airy blonde curls, and a fondness for charity-shop clothes involving too many bits of lace. I liked Peggy well enough* (we'd gone through primary school together, which may have been what led my father to take her on*), but the softness was misleading.

Anne Tyler, *The Beginner's Goodbye*

*Or variations on a similar theme – there aren't exact translations.

'I don't understand a thing,' Mummy says, 'but never mind. Come, put your bag down and go and wash your hands and face. Dinner's already on the table.' Avishai takes off the knapsack, goes into the bathroom _ and washes his face. In the mirror over the sink he sees that he's in his school uniform. When he opens the knapsack in the living room he discovers notebooks and textbooks lined in flowered paper. There's a maths book, and a box of coloured pencils, and a little metal compass with a rubber shoved on the point. His mother comes over to chide him. 'This isn't the time for homework. Come and eat. Hurry up, chop-chop, before all the vitamins escape from the salad.' Avishai sits at the table and eats in silence. The food is delicious. He'd been surviving solely on takeaways and cheap restaurants for so many years, he'd honestly forgotten that food could taste this good. 'Daddy left you money for your after-school club.' Mummy points to a sealed white envelope resting on the little hall table next to the dial phone. 'But I'm warning you, Avi, if you pull the same stunt you did with the model-aeroplane club, and change your mind after one class, you're better off telling us now, before we pay.'

Etgar Keret, 'Pudding', *Suddenly, a Knock on the Door*

6: Reading and Writing

What do the following allude to?

1 John Mortimer's *Summer's Lease* (Shakespeare, Sonnet 18)

2 John Steinbeck's *Of Mice and Men* (Burns, 'To a Mouse')

3 annus horribilis (phrase made famous by the Queen in 1992, an allusion to Dryden's 'Annus Mirabilis')

4 B52s (band named after a World War II bomber)

5 F. Scott Fitzgerald's *Tender is the Night* (Keats, 'Ode to a Nightingale')

6 Noël Coward's *Blithe Spirit* (Shelley, 'To a Skylark')

7 Thomas Hardy's *Far From the Madding Crowd* (Gray, 'Elegy Written in a Country Churchyard')

8 Evelyn Waugh's *A Handful of Dust* (T. S. Eliot, *The Waste Land*)

9 salt of the earth (Bible, Matthew 5:13)

10 Ernest Hemingway's *For Whom the Bell Tolls* (Donne, *Devotions upon Emergent Occasions*, Meditation 17)

What are the following euphemisms for?

1 I need to spend a penny = need a wee

2 He went swimming in his birthday suit = naked

3 The theatre is dark = closed

4 She's between jobs at the moment = unemployed

5 It fell off the back of a lorry = stolen

6 'Oi, mind the family jewels,' said Dave = genitals

7 She's got a problem downstairs = something gynaecological

8 He's got a problem with his plumbing = something urinary

9 That's an interesting interpretation . . . = utter rubbish

10 Would you like to come in for coffee? = sex

In the following, which metaphors are being mixed?

1 Don't brand us all with the same brush – brand with an iron/ tar with the same brush.

2 We were up a tree without a paddle – barking up the wrong tree/up the creek without a paddle.

3 I've been burning the midnight oil at both ends – burning the midnight oil/burning the candle at both ends.

4 She could read him like an open can of worms – read him like a book/open up a can of worms.

5 Let's burn that bridge when we come to it – burn bridges/cross that bridge when we come to it.

6 The cat's on the other foot now – the cat's out of the bag/the boot's on the other foot.

7 He took to it like a fish out of water – a duck to water/a fish out of water.

8 She couldn't see the woods for the end of the tunnel – couldn't see the woods for the trees/there's light at the end of the tunnel.

9 If you do that, you'll be putting a spanner in the coffin – spanner in the works/nail in the coffin.

10 He hit the nail on the dot – nail on the head/arrived on the dot.

This final exercise is a round-up of Chapter 6.

1 *Daniel Deronda, Ivanhoe, The Go-Between, Little Women,* Omelette Arnold Bennett, Tom Collins are **eponymous** titles/dish/cocktail.

2 Milton's *Paradise Lost* (the fall of Adam and Eve in Genesis), Huxley's *Brave New World* (Shakespeare's *The Tempest*), Proust's *Remembrance of Things Past* (Shakespeare's Sonnet 30), Pullman's *His Dark Materials* (Milton's *Paradise Lost*), Boney M's 'By the Rivers of Babylon' (Psalm 137) are **allusions.**

3 'tickle the ivories' (play the piano), 'tread the boards' (perform in the theatre), 'burn rubber' (drive very fast), 'England' (Great Britain or the United Kingdom – and a quick and easy way to piss off the Scots, Welsh and Northern Irish) are examples of **synecdoche**.

4 These are examples of **antonomasia**: 'the King' for Elvis Presley, 'the Duke' for John Wayne.

5 These are **haikus**.

> How have I hurt you?
> You look at me with pale eyes,
> But these are my tears.

Amy Lowell

> An old silent pond . . .
> A frog jumps into the pond,
> Splash! Silence again.

Matsuo Basho

6 'Fleet Street' (the press), 'the Firm' (the royal family), 'the Square Mile' (the City of London), 'the Smoke' (London) and 'the Windy City' (Chicago) are **metonyms**.

7 These lines contain **alliteration**.

> Gallop apace, you fiery-footed steeds,
> Towards Phoebus' lodging: such a wagoner
> As Phaëthon would whip you to the west,
> And bring in cloudy night immediately.

Shakespeare, *Romeo and Juliet*

> The breezes blew, the white foam flew,
>   The furrow followed free;
> We were the first that ever burst
>   Into that silent sea.

Coleridge, 'The Rime of the Ancient Mariner'

8 The phrases 'the entire nation held its breath at the penalty shoot-out', 'the world's most distinguished writer', 'the sexiest man alive', 'the greatest show on earth' and 'the funniest film ever made' are **hyperbole**.

9 The words 'alack', 'alas', 'gadzooks', 'nay', 'oft', 'pox' are **archaisms**.

10 These lines contain **similes**.

His lids are like the lilac-flower
And soft as a moth, his breath.

Sylvia Plath, *Three Women*

11 The words 'blog' (web/log), 'boxercise' (boxer/exercise), 'bromance' (brother/romance), 'docudrama' (documentary/ drama), 'gastropub' (gastronomy/pub), 'mockney' (mock/ cockney), 'moobs' (man/boobs), 'moped' (motor/pedal), 'paratrooper' (parachute/trooper), 'stagflation' (stagnant/ inflation) are **portmanteau** words.

12 The lines contain **metaphors** (the poem's title is a bit of a giveaway).

I'm a riddle in nine syllables,
An elephant, a ponderous house,
A melon strolling on two tendrils.

Sylvia Plath, 'Metaphors'

13 These lines are examples of **assonance**.

'on a pr__ou__d r__ou__nd cl__ou__d in a wh__i__te h__i__gh n__i__ght'

e. e. cummings, 'if a cheerfulest Elephantangelchild should sit'

'S__o__, we'll g__o__ n__o__ more a-r__o__ving'

Byron, 'So we'll go no more a-roving'

14 The words 'blogger', 'Generation X', 'McJob', 'prequel', 'replicant', 'textspeak' are **neologisms**.

15 The words and date 'kayak', 'redder', 'repaper', '21.11.12' are **palindromes**.

16 The words 'snap', 'crackle' and 'pop' are examples of **onomatopoeia**.

17 Boz, Hergé, Saki, George Sand and Mark Twain are the **noms de plume** of, respectively, Charles Dickens, Georges Prosper Remi, Hector Hugh Munro, Amandine-Aurore Lucille Dupin and Samuel Langhorne Clemens.

18 'He was a man of great statue [stature]' (Thomas Menino, Boston mayor) and 'This is unparalyzed [unparalleled] in the state's history' (Gib Lewis, Texas Speaker of the House) are **malapropisms** (or Bushisms, since the speakers are American).

19 *Nights at the Circus, The House of the Spirits, Midnight's Children, The Time Traveler's Wife, The Tiger's Wife* contain examples of **magic realism**.

20 T. S. Eliot is an **anagram** of 'litotes' and 'toilets'.

Acknowledgements

Thanks to Sue Amaradivakara, Neil Bradford, Roger Bratchell,
Alastair Campbell, Chez Nous of Belsize Park, Julia Connolly,
Ken Cugnoni, Rachel Cugnoni, Hugh Devlin, David Drewienka,
Holly Duggan, George Engle, Briony Everroad, Dan Franklin,
Renata Giacobazzi, Ceinwen Giles, David Gooding, Sheila Irwin,
Anne Jappie, Enid Lacob, Lisa Lacob, Christian Lewis, Cian
McCourt, Frances Macmillan, Steven Messer, Cosmo Murphy,
Katherine Murphy, Kay Peddle, Kirsten Pedersson, Sarah Polden,
Carmel Regan, Simon Rhodes, Enid Skelton-Wallace, John
Skelton-Wallace, Tali Stein, Justine Taylor, Jenny Uglow,
Christopher Wakeling, Irvine Welsh, Patsy Wilkinson, Matt Wolf,
Hilly Zidel; Frys: Lionel, Minne, Michael, Tessa, Zachary and
Daisy; Kirtons: Andrew, James and William.

Particular thanks to Mary Chamberlain, Rosemary Davidson,
Ben Dryer, Yuka Igarashi, Myra Jones, Leslye Jourdan-Whittaker,
Al Senter, Vicki Traino and Ilsa Yardley.

Credits

Extract from *The Moon and Sixpence* by W. Somerset Maugham, published by Vintage Classics. By permission of A. P. Watt Ltd on behalf of the Royal Literary Fund.

Extracts from *The Heart of the Matter* by Graham Greene, published by Vintage Classics; *Under Milk Wood* by Dylan Thomas. By permission of David Higham.

Extracts from *The Curious Incident of the Dog in the Night-time* by Mark Haddon © Mark Haddon 2003, published by Jonathan Cape; *The Magus* by John Fowles © J. R. Fowles Ltd, published by Vintage Classics. By permission of Aitken Alexander Associates.

Extracts from *A Single Man* by Christopher Isherwood, published by Vintage Classics; *Trainspotting* by Irvine Welsh, published by Secker & Warburg; *Skagboys* by Irvine Welsh, published by Jonathan Cape; *Captain Corelli's Mandolin* by Louis de Bernières, published by Secker & Warburg; *The Time Traveler's Wife* by Audrey Niffenegger, published by Jonathan Cape; *Liars in Love* by Richard Yates, published by Vintage Classics; 'Pudding' from *Suddenly, a Knock on the Door* by Etgar Keret, published by Chatto & Windus; *Kafka on the Shore* by Haruki Murakami, published by Harvill Secker; *The Beginner's Goodbye* by Anne Tyler, published by Chatto & Windus. Reprinted by permission of The Random House Group Limited.

Extract from *The Second Coming* by John Niven, published in the UK by William Heinemann © John Niven 2011.

Extract from *Catch-22* by Joseph Heller, reproduced with permission of Curtis Brown Group Ltd, London, on behalf of the Estate of Joseph Heller © Joseph Heller 1961, published by Vintage Classics.

Extract from 'Chrysanthemum Tea' from *Pacific Overtures*, Words and Music by Stephen Sondheim © 1975 (Renewed), 1979 RILTING MUSIC, INC. All Rights Administered by WB MUSIC CORP. All Rights Reserved. Used by Permission. Reprinted by Permission of Hal Leonard Corporation.

Grateful thanks to Faber & Faber Ltd for permission to quote 'Strugnell's Haiku' by Wendy Cope; and to Faber & Faber Ltd and the Estate of Sylvia Plath for permission to quote from 'Metaphors' and *Three Women*.

'Seven Bar Jokes' by Eric K. Auld, originally published on *McSweeney's Internet Tendency*, reproduced by permission of Eric K. Auld.

The publisher has made every effort to trace copyright holders. Any who have not been acknowledged are invited to contact the publisher so that appropriate acknowledgement may be made in future printings.